Understanding Soviet Politics
through Literature

Understanding Soviet Politics through Literature

A book of readings

Martin Crouch

Lecturer in Soviet Political Institutions,
University of Bristol

and

Robert Porter

Lecturer in Russian Studies, University of Bristol

London
GEORGE ALLEN & UNWIN
Boston   Sydney

George Allen & Unwin (Publishers) Ltd,
40 Museum Street, London WC1A 1LU, UK

George Allen & Unwin (Publishers) Ltd,
Park Lane, Hemel Hempstead, Herts HP2 4TE, UK

Allen & Unwin Inc.,
9 Winchester Terrace, Winchester, Mass. 01890, USA

George Allen & Unwin Australia Pty Ltd,
8 Napier Street, North Sydney, NSW 2060, Australia

First published in 1984
Second impression 1985

British Library Cataloguing in Publication Data

   Understanding Soviet politics through literature.
1. Politics in literature—Soviet Union—History
—20th Century
I. Crouch, Martin   II. Porter, Robert, *19—*
891.709'0042   PG3020.5.P/
ISBN 0–04–320155–5
ISBN 0–04–320158–X Pbk

Library of Congress Cataloging in Publication Data

Main entry under title:

   Understanding Soviet politics through literature.
Bibliography: p.
Includes index.
1. Russian literature—20th century—Translations into
English.   2. English literature—Translations from
Russian.   I. Crouch, Martin.   II. Porter, R. C.
(Robert C.)
PG3213.U5   1984   891.7'08'0044   83–21410
ISBN 0–04–320155–5
ISBN 0–04–320158–X (pbk.)

Set in 10 on 11½ point Sabon by Inforum Ltd, Portsmouth
Printed and bound in Great Britain by
Biddles Ltd, Guildford and King's Lynn

Contents

Translator's Note

Unless stated otherwise, the translations are by Robert
Porter in consultation with Martin Crouch. In these
passages we have tried to be consistent in transliteration
without being too pedantic. Wherever specifically 'Soviet'
words appear we offer an English translation and then put
the original in square brackets, sometimes with an
explanation; e.g. 'collective farm [*kolkhoz*]'. Likewise all
our other annotations appear in square brackets.

Preface

This book has come about because of our joint conviction that modern Russian literature is an excellent and sometimes neglected source for understanding contemporary Soviet politics and society; indeed, an especially valuable tool in the Soviet case, given the long and complex relationship between writers and the state. As was the case in the days of Pushkin or Dostoevsky, the authorities today take literature seriously, both as a potentially explosive phenomenon that needs to be controlled and censored and as a vehicle for positively inculcating regime values and attitudes. Politics and literature are thus inextricably intertwined.

This linkage can be seen today in the leading literary publications, such as the weekly *Literary Gazette* [*Literaturnaya gazeta*] and the monthly *New World* [*Novy mir*] which devote their columns to such topics as education, housing, single-parent families, or international affairs in a way that an English-language equivalent, such as *The Times Literary Supplement*, never does. *Novy mir* is in fact subtitled 'a monthly literary–artistic and socio-political journal'.

The indivisibility of literature and politics in the Soviet Union does not mean that today the former is as subordinate to the latter as it was in Stalin's time. The literary 'thaw' of the Khrushchev era produced an exciting and, at times, volatile literature, and the effects of that experience have not gone away since, though controls over literature have been tightened. This has led to a steady emigration of disaffected writers to the West since the mid-1960s. It is now difficult, if not impossible, to label modern Russian writers or to define 'Soviet literature'. Today's stalwart may be tomorrow's dissident; yesterday's firebrand may now be happily accommodated. The distinctions that are often made between 'regime' and 'dissident' writers, too, can neglect the fact that there may be significant overlapping concerns.

This classification problem applies equally to Soviet politics and society since Khrushchev fell from power in 1964. The Brezhnev era was often described as 'the return to normalcy' after the upheavals of previous decades, but there is still much debate about whether the Soviet system is best seen as totalitarian or incipiently pluralist, bureaucratically degenerate or modernising and reformist. Dissidents have been harshly treated, but, on the other hand, there is probably greater freedom of discussion and a greater range of debate on most issues than there has been since the 1920s. The Soviet Union is now a complex modern industrial society and not easily defined. Nowhere is this more evident than in the ambiguity of tone that now pervades much Russian literature.

In the chapters that follow we have sought to bear in mind these points. This anthology is designed to enable students to get beneath the surface of contemporary Soviet politics and society via literature; not necessarily 'good' literature, but works that seem relevant to this purpose. We have drawn our material widely from both official and unofficial writing in an attempt to give range and balance to the issues discussed. Each chapter consists of between one and three extracts from literary works published between 1964 and 1980, for our concern has been to focus on the post-Khrushchev era. This has meant delving back into the Stalinist era, for much post-1964 literature has still been concerned with the past, notably the 1941–5 Great Patriotic War. We have thought it appropriate, too, to include in a chapter on the war some material that helps one understand the very high priority still afforded to the military in Soviet politics. Other chapters examine urbanisation and the housing shortage, the importance of education and career, the role of women, and the national and religious minorities. We also consider the Party and its functions, and problems of the national economy. These are all distinct themes which we present in what we hope is a logical order, but of course none is entirely self-contained, and the reader will certainly discover that cross-references can and should be made. Moreover, the first chapter necessarily deals with abstruse issues, and some students may find it suits them better to approach other chapters first.

Perhaps inevitably, there are omissions and imbalances. We have not directly focused on corruption or the second economy; there is nothing on the media; and the first chapter, on the Russian tradition, has been constructed to emphasise what we consider to be the less familiar side of the argument rather than to produce an exact balance. Equally, the literary merits of our selection are varied, and there are several important modern writers whom we have had to omit, including, for example, Trifonov, Shukshin, Belov, Sinyavsky, Aksyonov and others, not to mention Solzhenitsyn.

Indeed, to some extent it can be argued that all anthologies are unsatisfactory in one way or another, and an assembly of extracts is even more so. The Marxist critic Georg Lukács speaks of a 'totality of objects' in Tolstoy, and it is certainly true that a reading of *Anna Karenina* will tell one a great deal about many different aspects of nineteenth-century Russian society. Bulgakov's *The Master and Margarita*, similarly, tells one much about the 1930s in Russia – about mysterious disappearances, the black market, cowardice, the housing shortage, literary charlatans and arbitrary power. To take just a short extract from any one long work to illustrate a particular point is in one sense to debase the whole text. One might take a passage from *Tess of the d'Urbervilles* and give the impression that Thomas Hardy's sole aim in writing this novel was to describe how to milk a cow. We acknowledge this risk and apologise to our authors if they feel misrepresented.

On the other hand, we believe there are distinct advantages to a reader of this kind. Many of the works from which we have taken extracts are extremely long and often not available in English translation in any case. Both for students of Soviet politics and society and for students of literature the book will, we hope, prove a useful way of acquiring some 'feel' for the subject. Above all, it is a reminder that, beneath an all too often uniform surface, the Soviet Union is a rich and vital society with a serious literary tradition that confronts social, political and moral issues with vigour. It is our hope that this reader will encourage students to probe deeper and read entire works (even if they have to learn Russian to do so!), for in some cases it has been a frustrating task to make mountains into molehills.

Throughout this project we have been helped by many people, not least our wives and children. We should particularly like to thank Helle Dalgaard of the Academic Bookshop, Århus University, for giving freely of her time and expertise, and Galina Ransome of the Russian Department, University of Bristol, for explaining some of the trickier Russian idioms we encountered in our translating. Anne Merriman, Barbara Case and Mary Woods also deserve thanks for typing an often illegible manuscript, and Michael Holdsworth at George Allen & Unwin for help with copyright and other matters. One of the pleasures of a jointly edited book is that each editor can blame the other for the remaining errors.

Martin Crouch
Robert Porter

1
Ideology and the Russian Tradition

In recent years much has been written about the 'erosion of ideology' in the Soviet Union. The clear-cut and often brutal certainties of the early post-revolutionary era have certainly long been submerged beneath a less than heroic daily reality in which cynicism, apathy and disillusion are all too common. But a declining belief in Marxism–Leninism by itself would not make for a nation of nihilists, and this is certainly not the case in the Soviet Union. What do the Soviet people believe in, however, and how far do their beliefs and expectations diverge from those of the regime? How 'Russian' rather than 'Soviet' is the Soviet Union? To such questions there are perhaps no simple answers, but several points can be made and will be examined in this chapter.

First, any decline in belief in the official rhetoric has been more than offset by a resurgence of interest in religious and national identity. This is as striking among Russians as among non-Russians in the Soviet Union (and is examined further in Chapter 8).

Second, Soviet ideology has come to encompass more than just Marxism–Leninism. In practice Soviet history itself, notably the 1917 Revolution, the figure of Lenin as a founding father, and the Victory over Fascism (1941–5), is widely accepted as a positive and unifying force. So, too, is a belief in progress through planned industrialisation, in the welfare state aspects of socialism, and in the Soviet Union as a true superpower. These broader forms of Soviet ideology, which can border on what Aleksandr Solzhenitsyn has called 'National Bolshevism', are not to be underestimated as a legitimising and stabilising force.

Third, there is a continuing Russian political culture and tradition which predates the 1917 Revolution, and permeates both regime and people. It is a political culture that is both authoritarian and teleological: authoritarian in the sense that citizens have obligations not rights (the state is entitled to expect service and obedience from its people); teleological in that there is meant to be some purpose higher than mere survival. As Aleksandr Zinoviev suggests in his satire *The Yawning Heights*: 'Russians do not live in the old-fashioned and commonplace sense of the word, as it is applied to other people in other places . . . [They] do not live, but carry out epoch-making experiments.' Obedience to the state is therefore absolute, not conditional; collective duties take precedence over individual rights, and the outside world poses a constant spiritual and material, as well as military, threat. These aspects of the political tradition are deeply rooted and are difficult to disentangle from regime politics.

Russian political culture is very complex, and the presence of authoritarian aspects does not exclude belief in freedom, democracy, or human rights as understood in Western Europe or North America. If it did, the revolutions of 1905 and 1917 and the modern dissident movement, for example, would all have been very different. The dominant traditions, however, are autocratic and teleological.

Whether this entitles us to regard the Soviet system as therefore essentially legitimate and 'normal' is a matter of great dispute, not least among modern Russian dissidents, who have continued to debate long-standing arguments about how far Russia should be Westernised, to what extent the state has shaped society or vice versa, and, above all, how far the 1917 Revolution was a break with the past or a recognisable continuation of it. Aleksandr Solzhenitsyn, at one end of the spectrum, has argued powerfully in his *Letter to the Soviet Leaders* (London, 1974) that the legacy of 1917 was the destruction of a native tradition and the imposition of an alien, materialist ideology. The result has been a totalitarian regime, imposed upon a downtrodden people and maintained by a deadly combination of force, fear and inertia. In all major respects the Soviet era has been an avoidable national tragedy whose roots lie, not in the Russian tradition, but in Marxism:

> This ideology bears the entire responsibility for all the blood that has been shed . . . For a long time now, everything has rested solely on material calculation and the subjection of the people, and not on any upsurge of ideological enthusiasm . . . This ideology does nothing but sap our strength and bind us. It clogs up the whole life of society – minds, tongues, radio and press, with lies, lies, lies.

The answer, therefore, is to 'cast off this cracked ideology. In ridding ourselves of it, we shall also rid ourselves of the need to fill our life with lies.'

This Manichaean view, familiar enough in many Western writings on the Soviet Union, too, did not go unchallenged. Several of the more articulate dissenters in particular questioned such an analysis. Andrey Sakharov, for example, argued that many of the central characteristics of contemporary Soviet politics were only too clearly rooted in earlier Russian history: 'I don't accept that Russia preserved her well-being up to the twentieth century. I consider the slavish, servile spirit which existed in Russia for centuries . . . to be the greatest misfortune, not an indication of national well-being.' To the extent that Russian national traditions and Soviet regime values are intertwined, the Soviet system is widely accepted as both legitimate and normal; indeed, increasingly so, for, as another writer and critic, Boris Shragin, has put it, 'the ancient landmarks of the past are increasingly visible behind the specifically Soviet features of our present stagnation' (*The Challenge of the Spirit*, New York, 1978).

The two extracts which follow have both been chosen to illustrate and develop this particular argument about ideology and the national tradition. They are by very different writers but both appear to stress, in contrast to Solzhenitsyn, the, as it were, hopeless normality of the Soviet political system and its congruence with Russian national tradition.

The author of the first extract, Aleksandr Zinoviev, was one of the Soviet Union's leading philosophers and the author of many specialist works in the field of logic and philosophy. One of eleven children, of working-class origins, Zinoviev was latterly on the Faculty of Philosophy in the University of Moscow, where he held the Chair of Logic, and was a member of the Finnish Academy of Sciences. In 1976, after being refused permission to travel to Finland to attend an international symposium on logic, Zinoviev circulated in samizdat a recently completed and monumental satire on Soviet life, *The Yawning Heights* ('yawn' as used of openings and abysses); the title itself is a pun on official jargon phrases like 'the gleaming (or radiant) heights of socialism' [*ziyat'*, 'to gape'; *siyat'*, 'to shine']. When this work was published in the West shortly afterwards, Zinoviev was deprived of all his appointments and expelled from the Communist Party. He emigrated to the West in 1978, President Brezhnev signing a decree at the time revoking his Soviet citizenship for 'behaviour damaging to Soviet prestige'.

The Yawning Heights, an almost uncategorisable work, described by one critic as a 4-million-letter expletive aimed at the Soviet leadership, is a seemingly random and chaotic compilation. It includes about a hundred brief conversations, many essays, a dissertation, notes for a book, a report on an experiment with rats, and dialogues and disquisitions on set themes, the whole tied together by a long 'Ballad' which, at certain intervals, provides scatalogical commentary on all the matters touched upon. There is no plot, though things do develop from the days of the Boss (Stalin) when part of the people were in the camps, 'another part was set to guard them and a third were preparing cadres for the other two', to the Time of Perplexity (i.e. the 1970s) and then on (almost) into the future agony of the Age of Prosperity.

There is much sharp political and social commentary in Zinoviev. 'Things happen in Ibansk [i.e. the Soviet Union – a literal translation would be something like 'Fuckland'] for one reason or another, and usually for another.' The bosses are concerned not with the discovery of crime but with creating the impression that crimes will not remain undiscovered if they are committed. Prisons are 'part of the super-structure'. 'We are often asked if God exists,' writes a Party secretary. 'We answer this question affirmatively. Yes. God does not exist.'

There is also a serious and important argument about ideology and politics in *The Yawning Heights* which is further developed in two subsequent works, *The Radiant Future* and *The Yellow House*. In contrast to Solzhenitsyn, for example, it is Zinoviev's central contention that Soviet politics and society, far from having been thrown disastrously off course by the Revolution, are the logical and, in their own terms, successful outcome of the marriage between Marxism and the Russian national tradition. The Soviet Union is therefore, as it were, 'a self-regulating concentration camp'. The extract below focuses on this debate.

THE YAWNING HEIGHTS

Aleksandr Zinoviev

An Argument about Ideology

['Truth-teller' is Solzhenitsyn. The other figures are probably just archetypes, although 'Scientist' may well be Sakharov, 'Dauber' the sculptor Neizvestny. 'Ibanism' is Marxism and 'Soc-Ism' is communism or scientific socialism.]

'Truth-teller's proposal to renounce official ideology is childishly naïve,' said Careerist. 'It's a long time now since the leadership took account of it in its actions. So he's only saying it for appearance's sake.' 'So why not renounce it officially?' asked Scientist, 'if it only makes for trouble.' 'There is no way of renouncing it completely,' said Neurasthenic. 'And it wouldn't make any sense because no one believes in it anyway. And its real role in society is insignificant compared with the one ascribed to it by Truth-teller.' The argument that began stopped only because everyone got tired of talking. 'What do you say about it?' Dauber asked Chatterer. 'Clearly, from the scientific point of view,' said Chatterer, 'Truth-teller's position is absurd. But therein lies its strength. Serious conversations on this subject will have no effect at all. Everything serious is regarded as grey, boring, passive, banal. The suggestion that something is serious makes a large-scale success impossible. And absurdity is in the spirit of the time. Absurdity creates an illusion of breadth and audacity. The more absurd the claim, the stronger the protest expressed. Absurdity is sensational. It is an excellent literary device for producing a mass effect.' 'But what do you think about the essence of the matter?' asked Dauber.

'From one point of view,' said Chatterer, 'ideology plays an enormous role in the life of society. From another point of view it plays none at all. It has an influence on everything, but it can never be pinned down. Because of this we get these contradictory judgements which vary between zero and infinity. This is the origin of the naïve illusion that the leaders of the country can change the official ideology at will, with a noticeable effect on their conduct. The leadership is powerless to change the official ideology of any society at will, even if they wanted to, even if they didn't believe in the ideology. A lack of faith in the truth of an ideology plays no role here, if for no other reason than that it is totally meaningless to talk about the truth of an ideology. But, even if the leaders were able to change the ideology, this would have no effect on the social essence of their power and the nature of their activity. What is important for social mechanisms is the very existence of some ideology, its normal functioning and not its content. The content of an ideology is determined by the concrete historical conditions of the spiritual life of a society. As for the formal mechanism, it is determined by its social nature and structure. If we consider ideology as a science and as a guide for conduct, then it does not need great intelligence to observe its "falsity" and its "sterility". But, if it is an ideology, it is for the very reason that it is neither a science nor a guide to conduct, but a very particular form which serves as a framework for phenomena which are very different from, even at times directly opposed to, its declarations. To say that it is the source of all evil is senseless. It is equally senseless to say that it is a source of good. There are no false ideologies. Nor are there any true ones. Its role in society must be described according to a quite different system of concepts. A society like ours would be unthinkable without some form of ideology. It is an ideological society at its very base.'

Ibanism

Ibanism, which is often for convenience referred to as the Ism, is the theoretical basis of Soc-Ism. So Ibanism is sometimes also called Soc-Ism. Ibanism is the highest, the most fundamental, the most profound, all-embracing, omnipotent, irrefutable doctrine of society, affirmed by the whole of man's past development and confirmed by all man's future development. Such is the unshakeable dogma of Ibanskian [Soviet] society. When Truth-teller said that Ibanism had been imposed by force on the Ibanskian people, and that it stopped them living, he was making a crude error. The Ibanskian people bound themselves voluntarily to Ibanism and can no longer live without it. It is Ibanism which lights its way forward. There is no social problem which with the help of Ibanism cannot be resolved in the most exhaustive and uniquely correct way. Moreover, if anyone tries to resolve these problems without the help of Ibanism, then he is doomed in advance to the gravest errors, to total incomprehension, to monstrous distortion and to other similar crimes. And the least of them presents a crack through which idealism might infiltrate. A nod towards idealism is graver still, while to embrace idealism is a still worse crime. And this headlong plunge into crime only ends when, as a result of the inner logic of the struggle, the sinner openly becomes a lackey of imperialism . . .

Despite its manifest absurdity, or perhaps because of it, Ibanism is an irrefutable truth. When Truth-teller attacked it as the source of all evil, he committed a grave error. Ibanism has never been and could never be the source of all evil, if only for the reason that it is not any ordinary source at all but the prime source. And from the prime source everything proceeds – both evil and good – and consequently nothing at all. For Ibanism itself is derived from everything.

According to the doctrine of Ibanism no one created the world, and indeed it had no birth. It has existed throughout eternity and will go on existing throughout eternity. It develops from the lowest stage to the highest. As an exception, certain parts of the world may skip a few stages of development, provided they have the authorisation of the Ibanskian government, and that Ibansk supplies them with disinterested aid. Starting from the electron, which has inexhaustible depths, the world developed to the highest level attainable – the level of Ibanskian society. From now on the entire future development of the world can go forward only on the basis of Ibansk, through the medium of Ibansk, in line with the development of society in Ibansk. Consciousness is the highest form of our capacity for reflection which lies at the basis of existence. It is nothing more than a reflection of existence. Naturally the highest form of consciousness is the consciousness achieved by Ibanskian society, incarnated in Ibanism and in its wise leadership. Nothing higher than that can exist. This of course does not mean that everything stops there in a state of stagnation. The Ibanskian leadership creatively develops Ibanism on the basis of the experience it has derived from the practice of building the total Ism. The latest speeches of Ibanskian leaders and the latest decrees of government are the pinnacle of human consciousness at the present time. And that holds good until the next speeches and decrees.

Briefly, Truth-teller confused the form and the essence of Ibanism. The essence of Ibanism is very simple. Our society is the most perfect, the most humane, the most free, the best organised, the most . . . the best . . . the most . . . The doctrines of Ibanism are the most intelligent, the most profound, the most . . . the most . . . the most . . . of every doctrine of society in general, and of Ibanskian society in particular. If you stumble upon anything good anywhere you must know that it is much better done in Ibansk. If anywhere you discover something bad, you must know that in Ibansk this does not exist, since in Ibansk, as a matter of principle, nothing bad can exist. If anywhere you hear a wise thought, you must know that there are still wiser thoughts on the subject in the concept of Ibanism. If anywhere you observe an error, you must know that this error does not exist in the doctrines of Ibanism, since Ibanism excludes error as a matter of principle. Such, by definition, are Ibanskian society and its scientific interpretation – Ibanism.

Personalism

'In your circle,' said Journalist, 'I have never heard you discuss the fate of the Ibanskian people, of Ibanskian science, of Ibanskian art. Surely you must be disturbed about these things?' 'The Ibanskian people,' said Chatterer, 'don't need us to worry about them. They are entirely happy with the care shown by their leaders. It's a very long time now since the Ibanskian people were a downtrodden and ignorant mass whom heroic, enlightened intellectuals had to set on the true path. The Ibanskian people are quite well enough educated, well enough read, and they know perfectly well how matters stand. They know what they want to know. And on the whole they have what they want as well. The activity of the leadership corresponds with the interests of the people. At all events, there is no question with us of any conflict, even potential conflict, between the people and their leaders. I would stress that this is not because the leadership represses the people. The leadership does not repress the people. It is because the leadership is of the people, and the people are of the leadership. The people bear full responsibility for the activity of the leadership. The people are the co-partners of their leadership in all its actions, good and bad.'

The state

All the traditional concepts of social science lose their sense when applied to Ibanskian society, said Slanderer. This refers in the first instance to concepts of the state, brotherhood, politics and law. The official point of view on these matters is well known. And I shall not trouble to set it out or enter into polemic with it, since it is a non-scientific phenomenon.

The state is the system of social power in a given society. In Ibanskian society it is a system made up of a vast number of people and organisations. At least a fifth of the adult population is engaged in some part or other of the system of power [i.e. through member-ship of the Party or other mass public organisations]. If the society as a whole is regarded as a social individual, the state is its controlling organ, its will.

The overwhelming majority of the representatives of power are low-paid officials. That is a power of misery or a miserable power. This is very important. Hence comes the inevitable tendency to compensate for low earnings by exploiting one's position in the apparatus. So there is nothing surprising in the fact that many low-paid representatives of authority live considerably better than their highly-paid fellow citizens. So power is materially attractive, even at the lowest levels. The great majority of the representatives of authority have in theory a negligible share of power: whence the tendency to compensate for this by exceeding official powers. Here there are almost unlimited possibilities. Nor is it surprising that the most insignificant officials of the apparatus have an enormous amount of power at their disposal.

It is for this reason among others that the lowest ranks of power bear such a hatred for the scientific–technical intelligentsia of higher rank, a hatred which by way of compensation is directed at the most defenceless and impecunious members of the creative intelligentsia. Hatred for the intelligentsia is a general feature in the ideology of the broad masses in the Ibanskian power structure, if only for the reason that at the lowest levels its members are drawn from the least educated and the least talented strata of society, while the higher échelons consist of people who, in terms of education and ability, have always had to yield place to those of their contemporaries who have become scientists, artists, writers, and so on.

Ibanskian power is both omnipotent and impotent. It is omnipotent in the negative sense that it can do any evil it likes and remain unpunished. It is impotent in the positive sense that any good it may do remains unrewarded. It has a huge destructive force, and a wholly insignificant power of creation. Any economic success the country may have owes nothing to the authorities as such. These successes are, as a rule, seen by the authorities as a necessary evil. The same is even truer of successes in the field of culture. That is in no way a function of authority. The illusion that these things do result from the exercise of power springs from the Ibanskian practice of making decisions about everything, preparing plans for everything, handing out orders about everything, and writing reports on everything. In fact, there is no connection between these activities and any success the country may achieve. They represent merely a formal superposition. The existence of a self-sufficient power here assumes the form of controlling everything – even the weather, even the biological nature of man.

In Ibansk the omnipotent power is impotent to carry out the most trifling reform on a nationwide scale if this reform is required for the better organisation of society, in other words if the reform is positive. It is capable of destroying in a trice entire branches of science and the arts, or of the economy, of putting an end to age-old traditional ways of life, of exterminating entire peoples. But it is quite incapable of defending the tiniest fragment of creative activity against its environment, if the environment wishes to reduce this fragment to dust.

Power of the Ibanskian type is in principle unreliable. It is incapable of fulfilling its promises in a systematic or durable way. This is not because it is made up of frauds and swindlers. Even with the best will in the world, the power is inhibited, by the very conditions of its functioning, from keeping its word. This applies of course primarily to positive intentions and only to a certain extent to negative ones. Why is this? The people who have promised to do something are easily replaced by people who regard that very promise as an error (for the purpose of discrediting the people they replace). As the norms regulating living-standards tend to instability, and as the authorities tend to favour reforms, the situation can so change that earlier promises become either meaningless or forgotten. For instance, Hog [Khrushchev] is replaced. Who will remember that he promised free public transport by a certain year, and a hundred per cent increase in the housing stock [at the 1961 22nd Party Congress]? As a general rule the authorities always have a false image of the state of things in the country, a necessary element of which is an overestimate of the good and an underestimate of the bad. In principle power excludes a scientific view of the society it governs, and consequently bases its intentions on false premises. For instance, Hog was convinced of the success of his maize-growing programme. Had anyone tried to convince him that this enterprise was doomed in advance because of the very social principles in operation, he would have wasted his breath!

The unreliability of the promises made by the authorities becomes a habitual form of government. Deep down, no one trusts the authorities. And the authorities don't trust themselves. And when they make decisions they have this idea *a priori* in their minds, unaware of it though they are. And I repeat that this applies merely to their positive activity. As far as their negative activity is concerned, they only need a signal. It is easier to destroy than to construct.

To all this we must add an almost total irresponsibility so far as the conduct of government business is concerned. Power takes the credit for everything positive, whatever its nature, and so arranges its affairs as to bear no responsibility for setbacks and shortages. To this end there exists within the power structure a collective guarantee system. Here punishments are an exception and not very much to be feared. It is not much of a punishment if a vice-minister is demoted to be a deputy vice-minister. In the worst case scapegoats can be found to take the blame for everything.

The Ibanskian authorities are represented as having been freely elected by the population. This contains both a monumental lie and a profound truth. The falsehood is well known and requires no comment. How can there be any talk of free elections if candidates for elected office are chosen by the authorities, if there is only one candidate, and if those who are elected have only one function – to applaud superior authority and to approve everything they are instructed to? Yet the Ibanskian system of power is the product of the goodwill of the people. It is absurd for the Ibanskian authorities to try to preserve sham elections, by which everyone is thoroughly bored and which provoke only ridicule. They should simply oblige the population to consider the free choice of power from another point of view.

Denunciation

Among the people I know there isn't a single person who hasn't at some time or another been taken as either a secret police agent or an informer, said Chatterer. When Truth-teller's first book was published [*One Day in the Life of Ivan Denisovich*, 1962], it was said, even of him, that he'd written it on the orders of the secret police. To say nothing of Dauber. Ninety per cent of Ibanskian artists are convinced that he's at the very least a secret police colonel. If not, they could never understand why he's stayed at liberty so long. What are the causes of all this? There are many, beginning with the most harmless. For example, let's take the currently fashionable way of discrediting someone, to show oneself in a favourable light. And then there are more serious causes. I'll list the main ones. First there's the ideology which is stuffed into everyone's minds to the effect that every action of the opposition is committed with the knowledge and under the control of the secret police. The secret police know about everything that is happening from the very start, and if something happens that means that it must have been decided in advance. The action has taken place because it has been allowed to happen in the pursuit of a particular aim, and it has been stopped in time from going further than was intended. Otherwise things would be worse.

Secondly, there is the monstrously inflated number of secret police staff and their regular informers. They have representatives in every kind of enterprise. And at least one in ten of the adult population is an informer. And on top of that every citizen regularly carries out the functions of an informer, often without even suspecting it, and at all events without seeing anything wrong in it. For example, respectable citizen A is called in and asked whether he has noticed anything blameworthy about citizen B. Citizen A is indignant and rushes to the defence of B. And in the process he reveals everything he knows about him.

Yet the secret police apparatus and all its grandiose system of information is a typical – perhaps even a super-typical – Ibanskian institution. It selects for its purposes the most sociable individuals who turn in due course into run-of-the-mill scroungers, layabouts, liars and careerists. They function effectively only when the need arises to set a hundred such collaborators on to one defenceless man. In cases like that they perform miracles of idiotic ingenuity and perspicacity. The stupid, the idle and the deceitful are as a rule virtuoso inventors of absurdity. So all the grandiose apparatus of investigation, denunciation and surveillance is still not enough to explain the informomanic psychology of Ibanskian society.

The underlying basis of this phenomenon lies in a general system of mutual denunciation which is rooted in the very foundations of society and which becomes the norm, the customary form of its existence. We are conditioned to this daily phenomenon from our childhood and are not even aware of it. But just try and look at our life from outside. Look at our newspapers, our films, our magazines, our novels, our meetings, our symposia, our assemblies, our conversations, our reports, and so on. What are they all? Nothing but denunciations, denunciations, denunciations: denunciations of ourselves, our neighbours, our colleagues, our superiors, our subordinates. What is referred to as a system of control and accountability is in fact an official system of denunciation as the normal pattern of life in society. Information about the progress of work in hand, about results achieved, and so on, occupies a minute place in all this. Results can be seen without any need for progress reports, conversations, communications, and so on. All this is done not as a matter of control, or of a genuine need to know, but as a purely social phenomenon. It is through all this that every citizen has, as it were, an invisible dossier – and in many cases a real, visible dossier – which can be brought into play at any time. Every individual is held up to the light from all directions in such a way that none of his inner secrets can be hidden. And, indeed, the individual learns not to have any secrets and to avoid acquiring them. And a man without secrets is nothing but a cog in the social machine; a hollow empty object; a naked form who can do nothing but perform a function.

So the apparatus of the secret police is not an anomaly in the life of our society. It is its legitimate creation and expression. If there were no secret police, society would somehow or other perform its functions, maybe in yet more terrible forms. For example, perhaps every apartment house, every institution of any kind, would contain its own secret cell. The secret police are even perhaps a little better than the body which has produced them, in the sense that they are to a certain degree professional. And, even if there were no need to catch spies and enemies of the people, even if we were not ruled by the principle which, in his time, Writer expressed so well:

> The secret enemy of the masses –
> He's never far away
> As the war between the classes
> Sharpens day by day

even then the secret police would have taken the form we know as a true expression of one of the real aspects of the Ibanskian way of life.

And also, in passing, as an expression of the mysterious Ibanskian soul — mysterious, that is, for westerners.

The Brotherhood

You know just as well as I, said Slanderer, the role that the Brotherhood [the Communist Party] plays in the life of Ibanskian society. But nevertheless I shall dwell rather longer on this question than usual, since it is the key to the understanding of all the visible side of Ibanskian life.

It is superfluous and impossible to define what the Brotherhood is. All that we need here is merely a description of this phenomenon and the way it functions, similar to a description of the human nervous system. The Brotherhood is an empirical reality of Ibanskian society with its own structure and function. I merely wish to draw your attention to certain of its characteristics which are of major importance in any analysis of the epoch in which we live.

The Brotherhood in Ibanskian society is the essence, the nucleus of state power, the association of all forms of power into a unified system. It can either be regarded as a social power as such, or as power in its purely social function. And, to understand the Ibanskian concept of state, one must understand the essence of the Brotherhood. Here we must discard our personal sympathies and antipathies and be wholly objective. Otherwise error is inevitable. A slight degree of apologia might even be preferable to tendentious denigration. I believe that the apologists of the role of the Brotherhood come closer to the truth than do its enemies. At all events in Ibansk, the Brotherhood is not only what the demagogues and propagandists make it out to be; it is the only force able to maintain order in society, to contain, up to a point, an unruly eruption of social forces, and to guarantee a certain progress. It is not the most powerful force, it is the only force. And it is impossible to ignore this factor. It would be an unserious approach. I would point out in passing that the mass repressions of the period of the Boss [i.e. the Stalin Purges] took place to some extent because certain forces in the land had succeeded in placing themselves above the Brotherhood and in submitting it to their power.

The Brotherhood consists of people. So, if one wishes to understand it, the first question to consider is that of its membership. It must be accepted as an indisputable fact that membership of the Brotherhood is purely voluntary. It is clear to all why people join the Brotherhood; it is mainly from career and profit motives. But it is, I repeat, voluntary. Many people long to become members of the Brotherhood, but it is a blessing not accorded to all. More of this later. There are cases where people are obliged to join the Brotherhood for work reasons. For example, non-members find it almost impossible to get work in the fields of many humane sciences. But this does not gainsay the voluntary principle. People freely choose these spheres of activity themselves, usually knowing in advance that they will have to seek membership of the Brotherhood. The higher management of all kinds of institutions are usually members of the Brotherhood. They seek to move into management of their own free will, and for this purpose they join the Brotherhood. Anyone who says that he was forced to join the Brotherhood against his will is a hypocrite.

It is possible, and it happens, that once people have joined the Brotherhood they do not believe in its ideals or its moral purity, that they despise the Brotherhood discipline, its demagogy, its assemblies, and so on. There are very many people like this. But this is of no importance since people behave formally as sincere members of the Brotherhood should behave. What matters is actual behaviour. There is nothing immoral in this since there is no way of detecting that a man is merely playing a part, that he is not a sincere supporter of the programme, the ideology, and the demagogy of the Brotherhood. If such cases are detected (and this happens very rarely), the person concerned is expelled and that is the end of that. The hypocrisy which can accompany the act of joining the Brotherhood does not contradict the voluntary principle, but on the contrary confirms it, for in cases like this application for membership can only be based on the calculation and the decision of the individual.

The voluntary nature of Brotherhood membership is the basis of the whole of Ibanskian statehood. It is a task for those who take pleasure in resolving paradoxes to explain how a power system of the most total and unbridled constraint can be built on a completely voluntary basis. The oppression which it exercises is the resultant of the free will of individuals, not any malevolent design of tyrants. The tyrants are just as much pawns in the hands of a power which has been allowed to develop voluntarily, as are their victims. The alleged unlimited power of the tyrants is an illusion produced by a situation where the victims of the power are themselves all-powerful.

The second principle governing membership of the Brotherhood is the principle of selectivity. Membership of the Brotherhood is voluntary, but not all applicants are accepted. The selection takes place according to strictly defined principles. It is this selection process which determines the direction which will be the sum of the will of all the separate individuals who make up this collective power. Once it is established the system of election of people to membership of the Brotherhood is reproduced in a stable form day after day, year after year, with a few minor modifications which reflect the modifications of the general make-up of the population.

It must further be recognised as a fact that it is far from the worst citizens who are selected to be members of the Brotherhood. Take any average Ibanskian institution and consider the composition of its Brotherhood organisation. Of course in view of the enormous size of the Brotherhood many of its members are villains, libertines, drunkards, corrupt, and so on. That is inevitable. But relatively speaking the proportion of criminal and amoral elements detected officially within the Brotherhood is lower than in the non-Brotherhood population. I do not mean by this that only good people are accepted into the Brotherhood. Judgements of this kind would be quite inappropriate. The Brotherhood selects individuals who by the official criteria of Ibanskian society are the best citizens. These individuals must be mentally healthy, have a modicum of political education (in other words, they should read the newspapers and remember what they have read), they should observe everyday moral standards, accept normal standards of discipline at work, be socially active (be a militant), and so on. We use other terms to describe these qualities: careerism, a greed for profit, lack of principle, and so on. But these terms are ambiguous. They have both a sociological and a moralistic meaning. Sociologically speaking, for example, careerism is a normal and healthy phenomenon. In the moral sense it is something rather different. It means making one's career by morally reprehensible means.

In other words, the Brotherhood selects citizens who have clearly defined social characteristics. From a formal point of view they meet all the demands of morality, law and labour. They are not to be despised. As for their so-called real aspect, it has no official existence. So it cannot be unmasked. And no one, apart from a few opponents and doughty fighters for truth, has any interest in unmasking it.

On Social Systems

It is of no consequence for the theory of social systems whether a particular system arose naturally or whether it was artificially invented. Such a distinction is wholly absurd when applied to a society. When people say that the peculiarities of Ibanskian society derive from the fact that it is artificially conceived, they are talking absolute nonsense. Even if a society is constructed on a plan made by a single man, a large number of people are needed to serve either as building materials or as builders. And this leads to the inevitable result that social laws come into play. And those who have taken part in the realisation of the original conception will, sooner or later, begin to live by these laws. They will begin to form groups, to struggle for power and privilege, and so on. When the artificial nature of Iban- skian society is interpreted as an excess of bureaucracy, a system of bans, an ideology imposed by force, and so on, those who so inter- pret it are overlooking a simple and self-evident truth: that all this is not some deviation from the norm of this society, but its legitimate product, its real existence, its true nature.

Aleksandr Zinoviev, *The Yawning Heights* [*Ziyayushchiye vysoty*], trans. G. Clough (London: The Bodley Head, 1978)

The second author, Viktor Sosnora, is a very different writer from Zinoviev. Born in 1936 in Leningrad, he experienced the wartime blockade there. After being evacuated to the Crimea, Sosnora returned to Leningrad and became a metalworker before making a name for himself as a poet in the 1960s. His published poetry has been marked by the use of surrealist fantasy and unusual or arresting imagery, sometimes applied (as in his 'production poems') to every- day industrial labour. Some of this can be seen in his short story '*The Flying Dutchman*,' from which the following extract is taken. This fantasy in prose about the legendary ghost ship is replete with puns and macabre humour, and is set firmly in the 'grotesque' tradition of Russian literature.

It can be interpreted, however, as a discourse on where the Revolu- tion is going, and whether one can escape, stressing the teleological elements in the Russian tradition; that Russia, as Zinoviev has put it, 'is an ideological society at its very base'. It also satirises the muddled Darwinian progressivism that official propaganda has often encouraged, and touches on the fear of anarchy and conse- quent compliance with tyranny that, as Nadezhda Mandelshtam has argued in her memoirs, *Hope Against Hope*, is a prominent feature of Russian, and particularly Soviet, history. 'This fear of chaos is perhaps the most permanent of our feelings.' The popular uprising on Sosnora's *Flying Dutchman*, as so often in Russian history, fails because of internal disagreements about ends and means.

THE FLYING DUTCHMAN

Viktor Sosnora

Captain Gram came up on deck. The captain was wearing a tunic of copper, and clutched a dirk in his red fist. He held the dirk by the blade, the dirk swung back and forth like a pendulum and flashed in the sunlight.

Someone was playing a heart-felt song on the guitar. It was not even a song, just a tune.

'All's well that swings well,' said Captain Gram, looking at the hanged man.

Passenger Daniy was sleeping upside down.

Daniy just could not adapt to the pitching and rolling at all and he had fatally put his pillow the opposite way round.

In terms of shape Daniy resembled two spheres on goose feet: the large sphere was his torso and the small one his head.

They were having a spree in the crew's quarters.

The sailors called the cold stores their quarters because they were always there, that is, 'doing time' there. There in the cold stores was everything a sailor needed for a normal life bereft of ordeals and illusions. The temperature there was way below zero, there was herring and wine in barrels, high-calorie pork produce, sable and fox furs, kangaroo-meat pies, marinated bananas, television and cellos.

It sometimes happened that when the sailors were drunk they froze to death.

Their corpses were promptly thrown into the sea. The corpses thawed out and sank. But the number of sailors always stayed the same, no more, no less.

They were having a spree in the crew's quarters.

Forty sailors with big moustaches and a philosopher, the forty-first man, were having a spree. The philosopher was called Daniy and he was a passenger. He was an old childhood friend of Captain Gram, his comrade-in-arms.

There was only one bottle of brandy for forty men.

The philosopher was drinking the brandy while the sailors lent him their ears. Daniy was discussing happiness.

'Happiness,' Daniy was saying, 'is something we already have, and not a little of it, though not a great deal either. We are sailing to where there is a lot of happiness. We've been sailing for many years now, and, as you all appreciate, we will arrive.'

'Where?' asked Fenelon.

He was the most unequivocal good-for-nothing on the ship, 'The Flying Dutchman': drunkard, womaniser, hooligan, pimp, card-sharp, went around barefoot, swore, was loutish, played the drum, a gangster, read the Bible, wrote letters – all in all, a bad lot.

It was he, Fenelon, whom they had wanted to hang from the yardarm, and no one understood how it turned out that they hanged the well disciplined Bal instead, a sailor who did not drink and usually did not do anything at all except support the captain and Daniy.

Bal supported the captain and Daniy under the armpits when they got drunk.

They had already put the rope around Fenelon's neck when that pansy Piros brought up a keg of brandy and they all got drunk and the hanged man turned out to be the remarkable, industrious sailor Bal.

Many people grieved afterwards.

But everyone had a thought for himself too.

'We've been sailing for many years now, and, as you all appreciate, we will arrive,' said Daniy

'Where?' asked Fenelon.

'I've just explained to you in detail: at happiness.'

'Thank you,' said Fenelon with a bow. 'We're sailing and all the other ships keep running away from us. All the ships, the entire fleet, are afraid of "The Flying Dutchman".'

'No, we're sailing forward and everyone is putting his hopes on us.'

'They're all putting their hopes on our sinking so they'll have nothing to be afraid of.'

The sailors were eating sprats, white ones, like vermicelli, and pieces of chocolate, big pieces, like bits of peat. There were forty sailors and all forty had moustaches. Specks of sunlight flew through the porthole and flew round the crew's quarters.

Everyone was in a sunny mood.

Daniy demolished the bottle of brandy.

'Try not to get drunk,' said Daniy, pointing to the empty bottle.

'We'll try,' promised the sailors.

An international artist of the realist school had drawn a naked woman on the label – a star of the screen. Her costume consisted of three feathers: two on her nipples and one, also a bird feather, a bit lower. Fenelon heeded Daniy's syllogisms and examined the empty bottle and its label with blue melancholy.

'What's a mammoth?' asked Daniy.

'A mammoth is a useful fossil,' said Fenelon.

'There was the Archeazoic era,' said Daniy. 'The temperature was high and so was the pressure of a column of air. The living albumen occurred at this stage. This initiated the first living organisms, the simplest ones.'

'What did the albumen come from, then?' asked Fenelon.

'That's no concern of yours,' replied Daniy. 'You may be bright, but this is science. Thousands and thousands of years went by. Then came the Proterozoic era. The most highly organised animals at that time were the trilobites. The last remaining representative of this race is here in front of us.' Daniy pointed at Fenelon. 'Stop looking at that naked woman, you trilobite.'

'Let him look, we sailors want to improve our minds!' said the sailors.

'The Proterozoic era lasted about 600 million years. But in terms of our history that's nothing at all, a laughably small figure, just like the Paleazoic era, the Mesozoic era and all their notorious periods. We're interested in the last, the Cainozoic era. This is the era that really concerns us. This was the time when the pterodactyls and pterosauri flew south. The pareiasauria and theriodontia inostran-cevia crawled away. The ichthyosauri and cephalopodic molluscs swam off. The reptiles – diplodoci, the tyrannosauri-rex and the machairodi – ran away. So they all died out, because although they were in warm territory they were still in foreign lands. Then, out of the blue, came the Neanderthals. For millions of years they roamed all over the earth after the Heidelburg man, they followed him around, not falling one pace behind, and then arrived. Heidelburg man became from then on merely a textbook aid to the science of paleantology. Labour began to make man. Man began to make the stone axe. The stone axe began to do its work. Man killed mammoths with his stone axe, man killed man. This was intelligent work and serious existence. We sat on glaciers and boiled pine needles and skins. And then there's the instructive history of the bee. The bee flew off to Africa and came down in the Sahara. But there are sands in the desert and the poor thing was never to make it as far as the splendid jungles. And this was where transformation and formation of the species began. We all know that the bee has stripes. It took the bee two hundred and fifty years to adapt to the conditions of life in the desert. It shed its transparent wings and then flew further south. Its body gradually began to elongate, and the head started to swell up because of the harsh climatic conditions. So the bee turned into a striped snake – the cobra. The bee's sting became the snake's bite. But, no matter how far the snake crawled towards the splendid jungles, he got nowhere. Nature lent a helping hand. Another two hundred and fifty years went by and the cobra's body increased in size, its tail grew hairs, it grew legs, and hooves appeared on the legs, the face acquired two nostrils, and teeth grew in the mouth. The cobra became the striped zebra. The zebra soon ran to the splendid jungles and took a close look. But the splendid jungles did not turn out to be so splendid. They were swarming with snakes, crocodiles, rhinoceri, spotted panthers and other delights. So then the bee had to change its form once again. On the whole this was not so difficult. There was a struggle for existence going on in the jungle. You needed fangs, claws and muscles there. The zebra trained for two hundred and fifty years. And not without success – its fangs became bigger, claws appeared, the muscles developed – the main thing was that, as before, there was no need to change the skin. The coat stayed striped: the zebra became the tiger. What animal it developed into over the next two hundred and fifty years remains unknown to science. That's how it was. But it wasn't like that with people. The development of mankind went in leaps and bounds. Somehow people jumped out of the glaciers. They became – just look at yourselves! – not people, but – beauty itself! You know your thinking is really up-to-date and there are subconscious elements in it! After all, you all have big moustaches. And you too are sitting "doing time" in your ice-box and then you up and leap up the masts of your own accord. And up the masts there's the sunny present, and the bright blue cosmos!'

'And sailor Bal swinging by the neck,' added Fenelon.

'That's neither here nor there. He'll swing for a bit and then fall in the sea,' said Daniy, becoming really inspired. 'No, Fenelon! We're not what we were yesterday, neither is the sea, nor the ship. One way or another all ships are sailing towards happiness, but we're the only ones who'll get there, the others won't. And all because the structure of our ship is far superior to that of all the others. Our ship is always on course! Since the battle of Grünfelde [or Tannenburg] in 1410 our ship makes seven knots more than it used to!'

'Oh-ho! Now that's progress!' said the sailors in admiration.

'But in the old days our ship sailed without any aim – it just sailed on and on. Now, though, we have an aim – we're sailing to happiness!' concluded Daniy enthusiastically.

'Let's go and have a drink,' said the ship's cook, Piros, to Daniy, the philosopher, 'and we'll get smashed out of our brains.'

'I've never yet been drunk,' said the goose foot. 'Getting drunk is just a secret as far as I'm concerned.'

'Well, that's fine. You drink two bottles of brandy and in half an hour you'll solve the terrible mystery of your secret. Just think of the prospects, you little globule!'

'Drunkenness is not a form of reality.'

'What is it, then? What would we do on our ship if we didn't drink? Just you see what paradoxes we come up with when we're drinking!'

'But paradoxes aren't life.'

'Correct. Life is a paradox.'

'Life is the useful activities of the organisms. Stop it, Piros! Your deductions are chasing around in a vicious circle.'

'Only the dead man's fiancée is chaste.'

'Then if I'm chaste that means I'm the dead man's fiancée, does it?' Daniy pulled out his colt, his head – the little sphere – began to turn and his face puffed up.

Piros grabbed Daniy by the top button of his tunic. By now Daniy's body – the large sphere – was starting to turn as well. The outline of 'The Flying Dutchman' glittered on the button.

'Listen,' said Piros. 'Life isn't useful activity. It's also a jewel always hanging over a precipice by a spider's web. Don't blow on that web, Daniy.' Piros took Daniy's colt from him. 'A colt,' said Piros, 'is only a product of man's activity.' Piros seized Daniy by the throat. Daniy's head was now turning in one direction and his body in the other. 'This hand of mine,' said Piros, 'is mother to all work. And, you'll agree, it's not such hard work to grab you by the throat. If you take out that colt of yours once more in front of me to prove the primacy of your opinion, then all that'll be left of your gullet will be the vertebrae for the kids to play dice with.'

'Clear off, you mollusc!' said Piros.

[Then the crew mutiny.]

The day promised laughter and tears, blood and happiness.

Gamalay [the naval lieutenant] stood on the bridge like a statue of Hannibal.

This time the twelve buglers did not sound reveille. They sat like geese in wicker baskets and watched Gamalay with their turquoise eyes. Being bodyguards, they were guarding him.

They kept Gamalay in the sights of their twelve colts. How many times had the lieutenant warned the buglers not to point the barrels of their colts at him but at the usurper, Captain Gram? But the captain was sleeping his pre-death sleep and Gamalay stood on the captain's bridge, and Gamalay had warned the buglers to keep the bridge in their sights, and that was just what they were doing.

So Gamalay's nerves were tense. And his nerves pulsated at his temples and in other areas of his body. He understood the full responsibility he had.

The sailors had been singing for more than an hour, and so well that they had forgotten for what purpose they had come out of the cold stores.

The air was gentle and close. An oceanic garden; it was a morning for inhaling the scent of the roses of paradise; not for starting a mutiny, but for laying a wonderful girl, a princess, on a bed of debauchery.

But, leaving their coats behind, the sailors took up the struggle.

The decks were cleared.

So the mutiny was aimed at itself; each sailor was able to express his own particular opinion.

The sailor with the Leoncavallo moustache went up on the bridge. He addressed the officers, who were still asleep. In an angry voice of protest he said:

'You and I are people. Both you and we have jaws, cerebral matter, hip joints and spinal columns. But why are you the officers and we the men? Why do you have the sunny present in your cabins, while we only get the ice-age in the cold stores?'

'That's right!' roared the sailors. 'That's how it all really is! That's criticism, all right! Well said!'

'We protest against the artificial refrigeration of our talents and abilities,' shouted one inspired sailor. 'We don't want to fall victim to low temperatures! We want our thoughts to develop naturally. We want to create a happy life and cultural values for everyone.'

'I'm also a lover of freedom,' said the sailor with the Guy de Maupassant moustache. And he went up on the bridge, trembling with the urge to speak his mind. 'But wouldn't it be better to tell the captain and his toadies what the last speaker was saying? This is how it is: aren't they having a nice, pleasant sleep while we're talking to them?'

'That's right!' roared the sailors. 'They're asleep and don't give a whisker because they haven't any whiskers. And we have whiskers and we can tell them! Good lad!'

'We talk to each other and that's the way it should be, but there's only one thing to be said to usurpers – overboard!' said the sailor with the Leoncavallo moustache.

On all sides the crowd raised their fists. Shots rang out. It was the sailors firing their colts in the blue air.

Piros, the cook, came up on deck.

'What's all this, then; you're not staging the Olympic Games, are you?' The pansy was bringing the lion Maymun a bucket of fresh-salted cucumbers.

'We're having a mutiny!' boasted the sailors.

'Oh!' said Piros. 'I wish you success, then.'

Piros put the bucket a bit nearer the lion's mouth and wheeled out a machine-gun from a side box.

'While we've all been talking to each other,' said the sailor with the Guy de Maupassant moustache, 'Piros the cook has wheeled out a machine-gun. Look at the toady laughing bravely by the machine-gun!'

'He who laughs last laughs longest,' said the sailor with the Leoncavallo moustache. 'A machine-gun's no problem for us. There are no barriers to a mutiny for a just cause. Let him bring the statue of Ernst Theodor Amadeus Hoffman if he likes and laugh till he drops. Let him shoot. A mutiny needs sacrifices.'

'Traitor,' said Lieutenant Galamay through a loud-speaker.

'Who, who's a traitor?' said the sailors excitedly. 'Piros the cook or the one who's always asking questions?'

'That one,' said Gamalay, 'the sailor with the Guy de Maupassant moustache. I suspect he's a pupil of Fenelon's. Only their kind is capable of asking unforeseeable questions to distract us from action.'

'We haven't any names and that's disgraceful,' decided the sailor with the Leoncavallo moustache. 'You all have names, even if they're only short ones like "EF" [the ship's radio operator]. You all have names and we're nameless creatures. We don't want to be called "the sailor with the Colbert moustache . . .", "the sailor with the . . ." '

'What difference will it make if I call you *Desdemona*?' asked Fenelon.

'There, you see!' exclaimed Gamalay woefully. 'Fenelon's here! This part might have been written for him!'

Fenelon had made his way quietly into the crowd and had been standing there among the mass of sailors and listening to their twittering.

'If they give me a name I'll become conscious of my own self and I'll feel moral responsibility towards everyone,' replied the sailor with the Leoncavallo moustache to Fenelon.

'How clever you are, Desdemona!' said Fenelon. 'Where did you learn such beautiful words? To put it bluntly: is this a mutiny of semi-literate sailors or an international symposium of young poets?'

'Drop the grenades, Fenelon,' said Gamalay through the loud-speaker. 'Take the weight off your hands and we'll hang you.'

'That won't be necessary. If I drop the grenades I'll get blown up myself, but I'll blow up all your plebiscite as well. There's a thing or two I want to ask you about.' Gamalay did not lose face: 'I order you to leave the grenades on your person. Don't do anything with either yourself or your grenades. Ask away, toady, we won't make secrets of your convictions.'

'You want to move into the cabins. But you know there's not enough room in the cabins for everyone. Those of you who are left over, one way or another, will go back to the cold stores.'

'We'll convert the cold stores into cabins.'

'Then you'll starve to death because there'll be nowhere to keep the rations.'

'Don't worry. We've foreseen everything. We'll transform the ship. We'll take the rotten sails down. We'll make a fruit tree out of every mast. We won't have the unfortunate human victims of arbitrary rule hanging from our masts; we'll have peaches, apricots, oranges and pineapples.'

'But if you take the sails away the ship will go round and round on the spot like a dog chasing fleas on its own tail.'

'We have a sailor who all his life has felt the calling to stand at the helm. He's simple-hearted, handsome, ruddy, he has a moustache like the Duke of Alba. And we'll fix cork life belts to the sides of the ship so it will never sink. And everyone will have his own cabin and his own piano. And it'll be nice for everyone. And we'll all sail to happiness together.'

'But we're already going to sail to happiness.'

'But how? We don't want to sail the way you want to, but the way we want to.'

Piros had become bored standing by the machine-gun. He was combing his locks with a tortoise-shell comb and sighing. For want of something to do, the cook threw an occasional cucumber or two into the mass of sailors who were preoccupied with the mutiny, and then the agitation among the sailors increased and started to take on a more aggressive character.

The sun was high in the sky.

The sun warmed the world of living and non-living nature. Shoals of little fishes swam through the water like nail files.

Big fish lay on the surface and opened their gills – just as white lilies open their gills at dawn.

'That's right!' roared the sailors. 'Gamalay's right and the sailor with the Leoncavallo moustache, and the sailor with the Guy de Maupassant moustache, and Fenelon too. Good lads!' the sailors hailed them and fired their colts in the blue air. And they fired off insane swear words as well.

Just at that moment Captain Gram came up on deck. His entire body was, as always, covered in red, wiry hairs. If the captain were to turn into a dog, then it would be an airedale terrier. The captain was wearing leather shorts. The dirk hung on his red hairy chest on a gold chain.

'Look,' said the captain to Piros, 'what red curls I have all over! You ought to have curls like these!'

The mutineers surrounded Piros and the captain.

The sailor with the Tigranes III moustache said: 'It's too late, you barbarians. Stop your disagreements, you dictators and executioners. Hand over your weapons!'

'This sailor has never in his whole life hung on a yardarm. And yet he has a moustache like Tigranes III. That gives you pause for thought,' said the captain.

And it did give them pause for thought. The captain sat on the deck and paused for thought.

He sat on the deck and cudgelled his brains.

With his own fist he cudgelled the brains of the sailor with the Tigranes III moustache.

'What's going on here?' asked the captain, shaking himself. 'Why are they all making a noise and mumbling something?' Gamalay put his oar in. He was white faced and was wearing dark glasses.

'We're having a mutiny!' exclaimed Gamalay. 'We're people too, after all, and I'm not afraid to tell you straight to your face, captain: I can't see any difference between officers and men. The difference which you introduced is artificial and false.'

'You know what,' said the captain. 'There's still a great deal of difference between a good bottle of wine and a bottle of good wine.'

The sailors broke into applause. The applause gradually turned into an ovation. The captain knew how to pluck at the sailors' most intimate heart strings.

'That's right!' roared the sailors enthusiastically. 'Well said, captain! He's told 'em, the old dog!'

'We're having a mutiny!' Gamalay reminded them. 'Sailors! All as one!'

'We don't want to talk to you!' shouted the sailors. 'What the captain said about that bottle was right!' And to avoid talking to Gamalay all the sailors, as one, climbed up the masts.

'We're near to land,' whispered Sotl [the first mate]. 'Tell me something, Fenelon: is it at all possible to escape from this ship? Is it just possible to alter your fate? Maybe I have some talents that I don't know about? Could my talents come to light in adventures on earth?'

Dawn was breaking.

In the bows Maymun the lion was getting frisky. He started to rattle his chain, got up on his hind legs and yawned magnificently. Soon he would roar a bit so that his friend and mentor, Piros, would wake up.

Unfortunately Doctor Amsten [the ship's doctor] had dozed off. His head with the gas mask on it lent against the mizzen sail. Naturally he was dreaming about air defence. The book about curvature of the spine in children fluttered and was blown into the sea.

A huge, brightly coloured dragon fly beat its wings hysterically above Sotl's head.

Sotl waved his hands but the dragon fly would not fly away.

'No,' said Fenelon wearily. It was light now and you could see how unshaven Fenelon was. His whole face had grey stubble round it, like an owl's face has feathers. 'No one can escape anywhere from this ship. "The Flying Dutchman" is a legend. Mysterious, dark forces are involved in its movement, no matter how much Daniy goes on about happiness. Lots of people have tried to stop the ship, but they've all died a terrible, agonising death. And the ship still goes on with all sails set regardless. And the fate of its crew with it. Do you think you're the first one to think about escaping? You're not. They've escaped. But they've all come back again. And when they've come back they've all died. And, mark you, they've come back of their own free will and died of their own free will. They were driven back by those same dark and mysterious forces in our movement and these forces are in the soul of every one of us. We *love* our total theatre of the absurd, just as Christ loved his crucifixion, as the prisoner loves his prison. That's what it's all about, Sotl.'

Sotl stared at Fenelon with his blue, short sighted eyes.

'Something's changed in you, Fenelon. I don't know what, but something's changed.'

'I don't think so,' chuckled Fenelon. 'I'm still as independent and free in my thoughts as I was . . .'

'Oh no,' said Sotl, slowly turning away. 'Yesterday the top button on your shirt was undone and today it's the bottom one. That's all the metamorphosis you've undergone.'

'Oh, if only we knew yesterday which of our buttons would be undone today!' said Fenelon sadly. And he laughed the unpleasant laugh of an owl.

'Well, then,' said Sotl calmly and without turning round. He spoke as if into the distance. He turned his *pince-nez* once more to the dissolving moon. 'I understand now, it's good to sail on "The Flying Dutchman", on a mysterious sailing ship, like a pleasure yacht, with the blue air, all the sailors and the banquets. It's good that all thoughts about my bride, Runa, come together in my dreams, and in my dreams both Runa and I have lots of adventures under the cupola of the sea.'

'Let me tell you something, Sotl. And these will be my last words for today. I'm tired, I'm falling asleep, my drum won't play. These are the last words I'll say to you. Sotl, you never had any dreams, so there weren't any cupolas, no bride Runa and no adventures with her. You've made it all up.'

Sotl didn't turn round. He nodded indifferently. He repeated, like an echo:

'No, there weren't. No dreams. No cupolas. No bride. No adventures. I made it all up.'

As always, at twelve o'clock noon Captain Gram knocked on the first mate's cabin door, to give him the ship's bearings and the meteorological data.

The door was locked on the inside. The captain examined the portholes. They were barred and the curtains drawn.

Then the captain shot off the lock with his colt. He turned on the light.

Sotl lay on the carpet. He had lain down on the carpet and shot himself in the heart, and the bullet had gone into his heart. His whole, huge face was tear-stained, like a child's. On the white tunic, where the heart was, was a red stain which had already dried out. They could not find any personal belongings of Sotl's. He did not have anything, not even a pencil in the writing desk. Only under his bunk in some little plywood boxes they found a lot of books. And there were pictures in them all.

TO ALL!   TO ALL!   TO ALL!

To all admirals, captains of all ships, boatswains, helmsmen and ships' cooks.

To all sailors and all those who are even a little bit of a sailor!

To everyone else!

To the United Nations Organisation, all presidents of united republics as yet ununited! To a few kings!

I, THE AUTHOR OF THE LEGEND OF THE FLYING DUTCHMAN, TODAY, 15TH SEPTEMBER 1967, SANK THE SHIP.

My ship is sunk, all the crew have perished. Only the cook was saved and there will be a second part to this novel about him which I will never write.

I accept full responsibility for the act.

The sunny present rules the world.

Mankind has prospects!

So love the sun! But love dark bad weather too.

Love your colander and the theatre of opera and ballet!
Love merry-go-rounds and Hellenism.
Love only swallows from your own geographical area!
Love your own spiritual strength and your own tastes!
Love lily of the valley and the police dog!
Love your own family and your own prison!
Stroke lions and mistresses!
Love your own orators, generals and literary scholars! They are the salt of the earth.
Love your own syphilis and say: Our syphilis is the best in the world!
Love the Chinese!
Love life and love death! After all, whose life and whose death? Death is no one's.
My children, spit up in the air, but don't put the sun out!
It is my fault that there are shipwrecks and that there is this universal mania for persecution which is caused by the word combination 'The Flying Dutchman' – it was me playing the guitar. [A guitar has played mysteriously throughout the story.]
It is my fault that alcohol, fornication, police methods of re-education, philosophical systems and murders are regressive, and not progressive. I sang their praises in the legend of 'The Flying Dutchman' – it was me playing the guitar.
It is my fault that on earth there is rainfall, nervous breakdowns, suicides, prostitution; it is my fault that a man is a friend, a comrade and a wolf to another man; I was the one who spread all this false propaganda in my false legend of 'The Flying Dutchman'! I swear – it was me playing the guitar!
Now my ship has been sunk by me, and my legend has discredited itself in the consciousness of all humanity.
I realise that I have committed the crime of the century, that your judgement is wise and implacable, and that in the end they will hang me, as they did Fenelon, and it will be one of the most just acts in history.

So look at my corpse with joyful eyes.
How it convulses, swinging on the yardarm!
And say in the words of Captain Gram:
'ALL'S WELL THAT SWINGS WELL!'

Viktor Sosnora, *The Flying Dutchman* [*Letuchiy Gollandets*] (Frankfurt: Possev, 1979)

Further Reading

Among many useful studies of ideology and the Russian tradition are S. White, *Political Culture and Soviet Politics* (London, 1979), and D. Barry and C. Barner-Barry, *Contemporary Soviet Politics*, 2nd edn (Englewood Cliffs, NJ, 1982), chs 2 and 3). The Solzhenitsyn–Sakharov debate and related arguments are discussed in M. Shatz, *Soviet Dissent in Historical Perspective* (Cambridge, 1980), and in M. Meerson-Aksenov and B. Shragin (eds), *The Political, Social and Religious Thought of Russian 'Samizdat': An Anthology* (Belmont, NY, 1977).

The works of Aleksandr Zinoviev available in English include *The Yawning Heights* (Harmondsworth, 1981) and *The Radiant Future* (London, 1980). Other literary treatments of note include V. Aksyonov, *The Steel Bird and Other Stories* (Ann Arbor, Mich., 1979) and A. Sinyavsky, *The Makepeace Experiment* (London, 1965), as well as Irina Grekova, 'Ladies' Hairdresser', in the *Ardis Anthology of Recent Russian Literature* (Ann Arbor, Mich., 1975).

2
Stalin and the Stalinist Legacy

Stalin's 'revolution from above' after 1928 transformed the Soviet Union within a generation from a still largely rural and illiterate society into a relatively modern industrial superpower, but did so at an appalling human cost. Khrushchev at the 1956 20th Party Congress and afterwards sought to come to terms with this ambiguous legacy by trying to isolate the good from the bad. This left much unfinished business, raising at least as many questions as it answered. As a consequence, de-Stalinisation, which had initially bolstered Khrushchev politically, became an increasingly difficult tightrope act, splitting the nation rather clearly into those who wanted more discussion and those who wanted none of it. The responses to Aleksandr Solzhenitsyn's first published work, *One Day in the Life of Ivan Denisovich*, in 1962 (as surveyed in L. Labedz's *Solzhenitsyn: A Documentary Record*, Harmondsworth, 1974) showed this polarisation rather clearly. V. I. Lakshin, the then deputy editor of *Novy mir*, said that it was common in the Soviet Union to state: 'Tell me what you think of *One Day* and I'll tell you who you are.'

After Khrushchev's fall in 1964, the Soviet leadership consistently sought to play down the Stalinist past. Attempts to re-open the historical inquest were discouraged, whether they came from critics of the regime, such as Solzhenitsyn, or from diehard Stalinists. As *Pravda* expressed it on the centenary of Stalin's birth in 1979, 'the Party gave an exhaustive appraisal' of this 'complex and contradictory historical figure' in 1956, and the matter is now regarded as closed. Stalin provided tough and resolute leadership during difficult times, winning 'great prestige and popularity'. Subsequently, 'the praise heaped on Stalin went to his head', resulting in 'serious violations of Soviet legality and mass repressions' of many innocent Party and non-Party people. But the Party and the Soviet system itself 'were never pushed off the path of socialism'. The masses, led by the Party, 'fulfilled their historic mission', Stalinist deviations being 'swiftly overcome'.

As a rough political compromise, this formulation had some merit. There were certainly many people who, for good or bad reasons, had no wish to disinter the past. Yet the Stalinist legacy and the questions it raises have not been totally buried and probably never can be, if only because past and present are inseparable, as the extracts in this chapter illustrate.

The first extract is taken from a powerful short novel, *On the Irtysh*, by Sergey Zalygin, first published in Moscow in 1964 at the tail end of the Khrushchev period. Its subject is the mass collectivisation (i.e. nationalisation) of agriculture and the forced deportation of millions of peasants to almost certain death as kulaks [rich peasants] or 'class enemies' after 1929. This was a critical turning-point in Soviet history and one which continues to raise some central questions about ends and means. Many of the generation that carried out collectivisation certainly believed that their actions were justified. As Lev Kopelev in his memoir, *No Jail for Thought* (London, 1977), put it:

> With the rest of my generation I firmly believed that the ends justified the means. Our great goal was the universal triumph of Communism and for the sake of that goal everything was permissible – to lie, to steal, to destroy hundreds of thousands and even millions of people . . . to hesitate or doubt about all this was to give in to intellectual squeamishness and 'stupid liberalism'.

But the legacy of that era has been a sullen and inefficient agricultural sector, a peasant culture destroyed and mounting agricultural difficulties; what Solzhenitsyn called 'an ethnic catastrophe' and the Soviet economist Barsov 'an utter economic disaster'. A proper understanding of the Stalinist agricultural legacy therefore remains highly relevant even fifty years later, not least given the growing international implications of the Soviet Union's inability to feed its own people adequately.

Sergey Zalygin was well qualified to write about collectivisation, having been born in a village in the Urals in 1913 and witnessing the turmoil of collectivisation at first hand. An engineer by profession, Zalygin has published frequently since the 1930s, a novel of his about a partisan detachment in the Civil War, *Salt Valley*, winning a Lenin Prize in 1968. *On the Irtysh* is arguably a franker and more humane account of collectivisation than the better-known *Virgin Soil Upturned* by the Nobel Prize-winning novelist Mikhail Sholokhov. The novel is set in a small west Siberian village in 1931. The central figure, Stepan Chausov, is a natural leader and a supporter of the Soviet system, having fought against the anti-Bolshevik Whites in the Civil War. But he also has the peasant's proprietary instinct for and love of the land. He is willing to join the new collective, but refuses to risk starvation for his family by contributing his last ounce of wheat to the common store of seed grain. His very qualities of independence antagonise the new masters of the countryside, the regional organisers from the cities. Ultimately a simple act of compassion leads to Chausov's downfall. He shelters the innocent family of a saboteur, Aleksandr Udartsev, much to the horror of his neighbours. Badgered and cheated by the local authorities, alienated from his confused and terrorised fellow-peasants, Chausov is dispossessed and, with his family, sent into exile 'beyond the swamp'.

A similar fate of deportation and death befell at least 10 million other peasants who were, like Chausov, dubbed as kulaks (the other two classes of peasant being 'middle' [*srednyak*] and 'poor' [*bednyak*]; in practice the categories were arbitrary). No accurate assessment of the price paid in human lives exists. Registered losses of livestock during this period are fuller and more accurate. As the economist Alec Nove has written, this was an episode which 'by common consent must be a painful period, of which many men in high places must feel ashamed in their hearts'.

ON THE IRTYSH

Sergey Zalygin

[Stepan Chauzov has been summoned to an investigation following the incident in which the kulak Aleksandr Udartsev burns and sabotages the village grain-store. It is March 1931.]

So Stepan looked at the office walls, the windows, and he looked at the table and was astonished: it was as if he were seeing all this for the first time, as if it were all unfamiliar to him. It seemed like that because there was only one person sitting in the office and this man was completely alien; he did not come from these parts.

'Sit down . . .'

Stepan looked from side to side. Why the 'sit down'? Perhaps he was not the only one who had come into the office? But he was.

'Sit down!'

Well, if they were only talking to him, then it was only proper for him to reply politely: 'It's all right, I'll stand . . .'

'Sit down!'

'Thanks. I will.'

'Chauzov? Stepan? Yakovlyevich?'

'That's right!'

'Year of birth?'

'1900.'

'Were you born here in Krutyye Luki?'

'Yes, I was.'

'Russian?'

'Yes.'

'Can you read and write?'

'I went to school for three winters.'

'Married?'

'Yes, of course.'

'Any children?'

'Everyone's got children, haven't they? They're both living, thank God.'

. . . A minute or so went by like this, not just asking about Stepan himself, but about Klashka, the kids; it was all noted down.

Yet it was enough for him, the investigator, that there Law-yer. He was still asking questions and writing things down.

'What are you? A poor peasant? A middle peasant? A kulak?'

He must understand everything, yet he keeps on asking, just like a child: 'Kulak?' Well, if I'd been a kulak, I wouldn't be sitting here in front of you in Krutyye Luki – I'd have had to clear off long since to the other side of the swamp.

'Registered as middle peasant.'

'Simple middle peasant or upper middle?'

'Simple middle. That's to say, normal?'

'Completely normal?'

'Yes, completely, even . . .'

'All right . . . Now, you're a member of the collective farm?'

'Yes, I joined.'

'Long since?'

'Two months ago last Thursday.'

'Were you given a fixed quota [of grain to deliver to the collective] before you joined?'

'Yes, couldn't get round it.'

'Did you meet it?'

'Yes. The same day they gave me another lot.'

However, it was a waste of time talking about the second quota. He was not asked about it.

'Now tell me how you destroyed Aleksandr Udartsev's house.

How and why? Give me all the details as you recall them.'

'That house of his stands near a steep drop. About thirty or maybe fifty paces. No, it can hardly be fifty paces. Anyway, we ran off from the fire Aleksandr had started and shoved his house over the edge.'

'Go on.'

'Well, then he went himself. Down the slope.'

'I've warned you; give me the details!'

'Am I refusing, then?'

And they were silent again for a while.

'All right . . . Whose idea was it to push Udartsev's house over the edge?'

'Maybe it was his . . .'

'What do you mean – his?'

'Aleksandr Udartsev.'

'What, he spoke to you about it? Himself?'

'Why just me? He talked to everyone about it.'

'When?'

'He was talking about it that day. And before then – more than once. When he asked for his hut to be moved to its old place at Mitrokhino. So that it wouldn't fall down the slope by itself.'

'But he had just the opposite in mind, didn't he?'

'And it would have been just the opposite, if he hadn't burnt the grain afterwards. But he did burn it, so they moved his hut for him, only in the other direction.'

'That's the way you see this business, is it?'

'Not just me. That's how everybody sees it.'

'Very well . . . After the fire when everyone was going to Udartsev's house, who was in front? Was there anyone in front of you?'

'A couple of people. One was a bit taller, the other a bit shorter.'

'Yet others testify that you went first. Do you think that means anything?'

'Of course it does. It means I went along with everyone else. Only I was a bit more in front. Everyone saw me but, as it was, those who'd gone on ahead couldn't be seen by the others.'

'Who were those two, then?'

'Either Yegorka Gilev and someone else, or just two people. No, I can't say who. It were dark. They were a long way in front, those two.'

'And you didn't look carefully to see who it was?'

'No, I didn't. I didn't know I'd be asked about them later.'

'All right . . . You went into Udartsev's house. And there old Udartsev swung at you with a crowbar. Did he intend to kill you?'

'Kill me? Never in your life. He'd never had any reason to. He just intended to scare me out of his house, that's all . . .'

'Very well . . . Everyone ran out of the house and started to push it towards the edge. Were you shouting while this was going on? Were you giving orders? Were the people obeying you?'

'No. Though there was a lot of shouting by everyone.'

'Everyone was shouting, and what – you were quiet?'

'No, I wasn't quiet at all. I have to say, I was swearing.'

'Were you very worked up? Angry? Swearing at old Udartsev?'

'At that moment I'd forgotten about the old man altogether. I was swearing at the cat.'

'What cat?'

'Who knows what cat? It were dark. You couldn't see the people properly, let alone a little cat.'

'Why were you swearing like that? At the cat?'

'It had started scratching me.'

'Where had it come from? Was it all of a sudden?'

'Of course. It must have fallen off the top.'

Suddenly the investigator looked up from the paper and rubbed his eyes with one hand. He did it as though seeing had become painful for him, but was still anxious to look at something.

'Now, listen to me, Chauzov,' he said. And he started to speak smoothly as if reading from a prepared text, but quite quietly: 'Why are you denying everything? You had a fight with a cat – nothing else? Come on, there was something else besides. What happened? Why? I thought at first that this was the fact of the matter: old Udartsev tried to kill you and, after the fire, at which you nearly lost your life trying to save the collective-farm grain, you couldn't restrain yourself, you saw in that old man your class enemy and you called on people to destroy his house. That's destruction, disorder, because no one gives you the right to destroy property – it makes no difference whether it's state or private property. But, given the circumstances, it's not a serious crime if one bears in mind that the destruction of the house was in retaliation for arson, in retaliation for an attempt on your life by a class enemy. That's what I thought. But, judging by the answers you've given me, you're saving Udartsev senior from his just punishment. You don't even see Aleksandr Udartsev as a class enemy. And tell me something else: is it true that Olga Udartsev and her children have found refuge in your house?'

'She's spent the night there.'

'Is she going to spend any more nights there?'

'She don't even know herself. She's said she'll live there till the warm weather comes. After that she'll go off to her relatives.'

'Explain this to me: why was it your house that Udartsev's wife found shelter in?'

'Klavidya brought her. My missus. She's very soft-hearted.'

'And how do you view it? This is a very important question for you: how do you yourself view it?'

'How do I view it? What you have to ask is: if some woman with three kids comes into your hut, your home, are you going to drive her out again into the cold, or what?'

'I'll ask the questions. You answer them. And you only have the right to ask me to repeat the question if you can't understand it.'

Koryakin [an ex-peasant, who travels from village to village conducting a merciless campaign against kulaks and priests] looked at the investigator, stood up from the table, walked up and down stamping his huge felt boots on the creaking floorboards, and stopped behind him.

'Well?' asked Koryakin. 'Well, what more, then?'

'Nothing . . .,' replied the investigator without turning round. 'You must analyse the facts.'

'I know!' nodded Koryakin. 'To do that, to do the analysis, you need a higher education, don't you?'

'You need education. And you need our whole life as well.'

'I know! You're remembering those books you wrote about rural justice. Your political work among the peasant masses when you were in exile. Your length of service to the Party?'

'I remember that, too.'

'And I say: even with your Party service you're not going to turn me from the Stalin course! More than that – I won't let you flinch, either!'

'Haven't you forgotten: "An answer to the comrade collective farmworkers" and "Dizziness from success"?' [pronouncements by Stalin in 1930 shifting the blame on to local officials for the use of excessive haste and force in collectivising, which had resulted in the wanton slaughter of livestock and rural depopulation].

'Now, let me tell you: what does Stalin see the success of our cause in? Where are you to see any success if not right here in our attitude to the middle peasant? Any objections? No? Good, because of dialectics . . .'

Koryakin chuckled and tapped his forehead. 'Right, then, I've familiarised myself with the record of your interrogation. I realised immediately: you were presenting Chauzov in terms of the class conflict. As if he wanted to settle Udartsev's hash as a class enemy! Only it didn't work out like that for you – he didn't want to recognise

Udartsev as a class enemy. You thought we could prosecute Chauzov, give him about six months for destroying the property of a class enemy, and afterwards he'd come home again as if nothing had happened? It didn't work. And it won't work. I repeat: he is a vehicle of individualism and property-owning. Yet he'll always stand among us as a conscious labouring collective-farm worker. Your own record of the interrogation exposes Chauzov completely. All the peasants testify to Yegorka Gilev being the instigator when Udartsev's house was destroyed; they're protecting Chauzov – to put it bluntly, they're shielding him. Yegorka Gilev leading them all? Don't make me laugh! I wasn't at the fire, but I can well imagine who followed whom. Today Stepan Chauzov is the man who went to put out the fire, tomorrow he'll go and destroy the collective farm, and some peasants are protecting him just for that! People like Chauzov have to be isolated from the masses for ever; you have to get rid of their influence. You've explained to the peasants about the pasturage, about the baker's shop, about the dairy association. They know more about all that than you or I do! But I haven't seen where you've delivered a crushing blow at their petty bourgeois essence. There's been no such blow from you! You know we're creating a collective farm, and in a collective farm the atmosphere has to be absolutely pure . . .'

Koryakin rose slightly on his toes and then rocked back on the heels of his huge felt boots and suddenly, quietly and dreamily, said: 'Just like melting snow in spring – drip-drip! drip-drip! And nothing must cloud it; not the tiniest mote in it! Like a baby's tear.' He patted the investigator on the shoulder. 'This is the kind of ideology we're creating today. So that, after one five-year plan or maybe two, even the peasants will laugh at themselves, saying what inhuman desires they used to have for private property! Just think – they begrudged a whip-round of three poods [approximately fifty kilograms] of grain a head for their own collective farm? Today it's a battle to get them to do it. I'm not just talking about Chauzov – I've done something to prove his kulak essence.'

In Stepan Chauzov's hut flowers had been painted on the doors – light blue on dark red, and others, red ones on light blue, all along the support beam the length of the hut. And it was as if this were the way the peasants in Krutyye Luki had lived for many ages, since far-off times . . . and they had all accumulated ideas about their peasant life, from grandfathers to grandchildren those thoughts stretched, and they reached as far as that very door, as far as the blue and red flowers, as far as this support beam . . . They reached right down to this spot, and you, Stepan Chauzov, decide what peasant life is. What is it? Where has it been deflected to? How can it be lived any more? Can it be lived at all?

It was an endless Thursday morning when Stepan Chauzov sat silently gazing at those little flowers.

His kids, already dressed, were sitting on the bundles, while Olga's eyes stared down from the stove. Did they understand what had happened? Klashka was giving her kids a drink of milk straight from the ladle: 'When will you get a drop of milk to drink again after this? Never in your life from your own cow!' They drank. She made them drink some more. Then they sat there – as if stupefied by the milk . . . Klavdiya and Olga sewed up one last canvas bag with their stuff in, hurried, both weeping silently.

Without looking at them, Stepan went round the house with his pliers, trying to find useful things he could rip out.

He tore the handle off the oven tongs, the hooks from the yoke for the buckets. There were bolts on the windows – he ripped them off, too. The ring on the trapdoor was made of iron so he unscrewed it.

Anything made of wood they could manage without; as for these iron things, they may not seem up to much, but afterwards you'd kick yourself if you hadn't thought to take them with you.

And there wasn't really any time for feeling miserable. It hadn't come to that.

Rage, or something like that – that was for later on, so that then you could curse someone else for your fate and not yourself. He himself had done everything right, he'd done things as best he could, he couldn't have thought of anything else to do.

He stood on the stool and set about pulling the hook out of the main beam. It was a strong beam; he'd put it there himself and had once chosen the log of wood for it himself, so that there'd be no splits in the log. The hook was embedded firmly in it, the whole thing groaned, the blue paint flaked off it, but the hook barely gave way . . . Stepan bent the poker trying to get it out and broke out in a sweat under the strain . . .

How many years back had that hook been forged by a smith, if Stepan himself had been rocked in the cradle that hung from it? And to recall that probably Stepan's father when he was still taking his mother's breast used to stare up at that hook as he lay on his back in his cradle!

He ought to burn his hut now, splash kerosene all round the corners, and throw in a match, but instead of that there he was tearing the hook out of the main beam . . .

Klavdiya slipped an icon in her bosom, the smallest one, a dark one, which her mother had given her . . .

Maybe they wouldn't be able to load everything the women had sewn up in bundles on to the cart. They might have to throw out some of the sacks on the way to the place on the other side of the swamp. So just in case that happened Stepan had told the women to sew up the adults' clothes separately. They could throw that bag out before all the others: they'd get by with what they had on their backs. There again, they were workers, they were wanted everywhere, and no one had any reason to let them go barefoot and naked, but what were these workers going to eat and drink, what do you take a hot, cast-iron pot by, the tongs or your bare hand, how could they bar the doors from the inside so that other people couldn't get in? Who cared? Who was responsible to his wife and kids for all this? Well, they'd want some answers from him, wouldn't they? There was no one else responsible. You have to live . . . Olga Udartsev there is living. Not a tear in her eye. Seems to have more than the strength of a woman.

How much swampland would there be from Krutyye Luki? Five hundred kilometres? Even a thousand kilometres beyond the town of Tobolsk, Stepan Chauzov would still be the man of the house, wouldn't he? He'd still have to work and live? He'd still have to feed his kids, wouldn't he?

The women finished sewing the last bundle. They put on their outdoor clothes. They looked round the ruined hut. And Stepan looked at the door again, at the blue flowers. He'd hung that door. He'd thought: They'll carry me out through this door feet first when I'm an ancient old man, and now I'm walking through it by myself and going away . . . still alive, sort of . . .

You flowers, you flowers . . .

Mitya the commissioner [a young man dispatched by the village Soviet on Party work; when in Krutyye Luki, he boards with the Chauzovs] was sitting in silence on the counter; he didn't want to be noticed. And they didn't notice him. Let him worry about himself, what kind of a man he would turn out to be . . .

Only Olga was troubled by Mitya. Apparently she wanted to talk to Stepan, but Mitya was preventing her. But what was to be said now, if up to this day nothing had been said between them?

It was too late now.

Don't forget anything – the bolt.

Mitya snorted quietly by the stove and went outside. He was the commissioner, he was doing his job. Maybe he should have gone away altogether, but he wasn't allowed to.

As soon as Mitya went out Olga fell on her knees in front of Stepan. When they smashed up her house she was silent, but now her bawling filled the whole hut and shook it, as she wrapped her arms round Stepan's legs.

'It's all because of me it's happened, Stepan Yakovlevich! Forgive me, Stepan Yakovlevich, and you, Klavdiya, for God's sake forgive me! When your kids grow up don't let on that I probably knew what would happen when I came into your house!'

Stepan dragged her up off the floor and put her on her feet.

'You're crying for nothing. You're not a cow. Who's blaming you?'

He was silent . . . Better to chuck the bundles on the sledge, the trunk and the kids, and after that – well, it was out of his hands. Wherever they took you, whatever they did to you, it wasn't your business. Your place was beyond the swamp; then you could take hold of life again, and the joyless earth, build some hut or other . . . Most likely they'd have to start by living in a dug-out . . .

He said to Olga: 'Look, if I'd given them the grain yesterday, what would it have been next? There'd be something else I'd not given way on, or something else I'd said. Things would have turned out the same way anyway . . .'

Perhaps he would have said something more, but at that moment Mitya came back into the hut. What did he want now? Were the words stuck in his throat?

You could see he'd thought up something – his eyes were fixed on Klavdiya and he called her quietly: 'Klavdiya Petrovna!'

She didn't hear – she had other things on her mind.

He repeated: 'Klavdiya Petrovna!'

'Well! Who do you want?' asked Klavdiya without taking her hands from her face as she sat at the table . . .

'Klavdiya Petrovna, seeing as you're from a completely different class stratum you could make out an application . . . And your application could be viewed positively. And you could be allowed to stay in Krutyye Luki. Even your children, too.'

She didn't understand immediately what Mitya the commissioner was saying, but when she did understand she took her hands from her face and looked at him.

'You miserable little rat! And I used to wait on you hand and foot, put food on the table for you, darn your socks, and all for nothing. Was it all for nothing? Haven't you any soul in you? Stepan could do you in right now, you rat, and I wouldn't say a word – let him do you in!'

She turned away.

And sure enough at that minute he could have grabbed Mitya by the feet and bashed his head on the floor . . .

And no regrets . . . Only he had to think of the kids – if he'd done it, then they'd be left with no father at all.

'Klavdiya Petrovna,' said Mitya, 'I considered it my duty to tell you. I couldn't help saying it.'

There was one more bolt to unscrew. And the hook for the cradle . . .

Nechay the Lame came in wearing a sheepskin coat and carrying a whip.

He came and said: 'Ready, Styopa? All set for a new life?'

'Let's go, then,' answered Stepan.

Nechay looked round the hut, slipped up on to the stove to see if they'd left anything they needed. He went outside.

And when he came back he brought a small box containing five-inch nails.

'What's that, then, Styopa, eh? Have you forgotten? Maybe you can get started again with these nails, can't you? . . . Listen, I've given myself the job of taking you to the station. Myself. No one will take you, so I'll do it. We're neighbours. And friends as well.' He paused for a while and then asked Mitya: 'You tell me, Comrade Commissioner, is it true that Stepan Chauzov, a peasant of Krutyye Luki, is a kulak and an enemy of the people?'

'No,' said Mitya. 'Chauzov isn't a real kulak.'

'Then why are you exiling him for real?'

'It's the remaking of all life, Comrade Nechay. People have been divided into two opposing camps: those "for" and those "against". And there's some who are in the middle. And the most insignificant instance of someone in the middle can be pushed either one way or the other. Here we have such an instance. Him.'

'And in a similar instance would you exile yourself to the other side of the swamp? Yourself, instead of Chauzov! Would that suit you? Turn your own life inside out?'

'I'm not afraid, Comrade Nechay,' answered Mitya. 'I'm not afraid of anything, not of a kulak killing me or – worse still – that Soviet power should inadvertently take me for a kulak and send me beyond the swamp. You can't make omelettes without breaking eggs . . . I'm serving the cause honestly.'

Just see what a lad he is, though, this Mitya, thought Stepan, but he didn't even answer his own question as to what kind of a man he was. He looked at Klavdiya.

From under the shawl which she'd pulled down over her head as far as her brows she, too, threw a glance at Mitya.

'You talk about honesty? Honest things get done by truth, not by robbery!'

'Robbery, Klavdiya Petrovna, is for oneself, for one's own enrichment. But this is a struggle for the bright future. Your tears are the last tears. In about five years' time, when the class struggle is over, complete justice will be established. And there'll be no more tears. Never.'

'That Aleksandr Udartsev', said Klavdiya to Mitya, 'burnt the corn. There was no profit in it for him, either. Yet he's a villain and nothing else, and he's afraid to show his face. You ruin people, too, but you're in the right all the time and as bold as brass about it!'

But Nechay, almost as if agreeing with Mitya, sighed and said: 'I understand now you've explained it, Commissioner! It's quite clear. Only you're going far too fast. But don't you see that, for example, I'm grey-haired and lame . . . People like that live on the earth — neither war nor famine will carry them off. They live and they remember what has been promised . . . Well, let's go, then.'

Olga slipped out on to the porch wearing Klavdiya's shawl, and her kids were wearing whatever had come to hand, the smallest being quite barefoot . . . How could things have turned out like this? Olga left in the house while the Chauzovs were no longer there? Would Olga live long in the Chauzov house? Hardly long . . . Maybe a week. And maybe an hour . . .

Polkasha, the dog, was banging his ungainly head against the fence. They'd put him on a chain so that he wouldn't run after his masters.

It was only a minute's work to throw their things on to the two-horsed sledge.

Pavel Pechura ran up just as the sledge started to move off.

'Why is justice for us peasants set at such a price?' Pechura asked Nechay. 'And who needs such a price? Whose benefit is it for? Ay!'

Nechay didn't reply; he whipped up the horses.

Their own people, village people, were standing by the gates. Some woman was howling and they shouted at her: 'You're crying for the living as if they were dead. Shut up or it'll come true. I dare say they'll find land beyond the swamp!'

Terentiy, the deaf-mute, Yegorka Gilev's brother, tried to run after them along the road . . . He made inarticulate noises and gesticulated; he just couldn't understand what had happened.

How could he, a deaf and dumb man, understand?

The snow was melting for the first time that year. Icicles hung from the roofs, and the drops — large drops — struck the water forming on top of the ice on the ground and rang out: drip-drip, drip-drip!

Sergey Zalygin, *On the Irtysh* [*Na Irtyshe*], *Novy mir*, 1964, no. 2

The second extract deals with another critical turning-point in Soviet history, the German invasion of 22 June 1941, which marked the start of what Russians refer to as the second Great Patriotic War (the first having been against Napoleon). The Soviet Union was caught very largely unprepared at the time and her military collapse was swift. Within months 40 per cent of the Soviet people were under German occupation, leaving in enemy hands 2 million Soviet soldiers and nearly 18,000 tanks. Why this happened has been much debated. Stalin subsequently mobilised a great many historians to explain and justify this débâcle. At first the military leaders were blamed, then the sheer element of surprise attack was emphasised. Khrushchev in 1956 laid the blame squarely on Stalin's authoritarianism and lack of foresight, particularly his misreading of Hitler's war aims. After 1956 the Party leadership of 1941 was increasingly criticised while the generals were exonerated, not least by the historian Aleksandr Nekrich, in a study published in Moscow in 1965. By now the Party was in no mood for further criticism, however, and Nekrich's book, *22 June 1941*, was recalled and Nekrich expelled from the Party. To redress the balance and close the argument, the regime writer Aleksandr Chakovsky published between 1968 and 1973 a massive semi-documentary work, *Blockade*, which, though it had few literary pretensions, sought to act as an authoritative interpretation for mass consumption. *Blockade* does indeed offer a useful and relatively balanced insight into a highly charged affair, dealing as it does with the central question of Stalin's direct responsibility for one of the major and avoidable catastrophes of Soviet history.

Aleksandr Chakovsky (b. 1913) was a war correspondent from 1941 to 1945 and has been a literary functionary for many years, notably as editor-in-chief of the important weekly *Literaturnaya gazeta* since 1962. He is a member of the Central Committee of the Soviet Communist Party.

The extract which follows portrays Stalin and several major war figures, including Zhukov, the eventual victor at the 1942 battle of Stalingrad, a turning-point in the war. The Politburo, which includes Molotov, Kaganovich, Khrushchev, Zhdanov, Voroshilov and Kalinin, among others, betrays a certain awed sycophancy towards Stalin, in no way challenging his initial and disastrous decisions. Later Stalin went to ground for several days, only emerging to address the Russian people on 3 July, and Chakovsky attempts here to reconstruct Stalin's thought processes at this time.

BLOCKADE

Aleksandr Chakovsky

[The date is 22 June 1941, a Saturday, but a normal working day. The blockade of the title is the 900-day siege of Leningrad which started later in the year. The scene here is Moscow.]

. . . Stalin was silent again. So, too, was the general at the other end of the line, pressing to his ear the receiver of the Kremlin direct line clenched in his hand, and he saw vividly all that had happened twelve hours before in Stalin's Kremlin office.

'What's he thinking about, what?' the General tried to understand, to guess impatiently.

But Stalin sat on the sofa converted to a bed, leaning on the telephone table, half-dressed, feeling that some huge weight was dragging him down lower and lower to the ground. He put the receiver on the table, but still clutching it tight. He, too, saw the same picture which attracted the inner eye of the man who now, pressing the telephone to his ear with a feeling of huge alarm, was thinking in bewilderment: Why is Stalin silent? Yes, they could visualise each other at that instant, could see what they had been like when they stood facing each other twelve hours earlier, during their last meeting.

But each had his own thoughts.

It was a mistake, thought the General, a mistake that Stalin didn't believe that German soldier, didn't believe us, forbade us to issue the order to free the hands of the unit and formation commanders . . . Why is he silent now, why doesn't he issue, with his customary decisiveness, the only possible instructions? . . .

What's happening there, on the frontier? wondered at the same time the man clutching the receiver in the quiet, wooden house shielded from the forest by a high fence . . . Is it all panic? Is it hysterics, so characteristic of people incapable of penetrating to the essence of phenomena and able to see only their surface? Apparently they have no doubts that that soldier was right. But isn't it true that a lie often appears in the guise of irrefutable truth? Isn't it really that this bombardment, whose scale has surely been exaggerated by the panickers, is probably just a part of some well-thought-out provocation?

No, Hitler can't be so stupid as to start a war against the Soviet Union without finishing off England first. This bombardment is doubtless a provocation, and it has to be on such a grandiose scale as to make weak-nerved people panic. Hitler is probably waiting for some retaliatory action which will give him the opportunity to convince the Germans and all his satellites of the Soviet Union's aggression. After all, it's not out of the question that he's been able to reach an agreement with England, is it? Maybe that old fox, the sworn enemy of communism, Churchill, has persuaded the Germans to change the direction of the attack and now Hitler needs to justify his next step to world public opinion?

And the more Stalin thought about it, the more he became convinced of the rightness of his own suppositions. At last he lifted the receiver to his ear and said unhurriedly, but quietly, too quietly even for his usual manner of speaking: 'Come to the Kremlin immediately. Bring the People's Commissar with you.'

He hung up without waiting for an answer.

... Less than half an hour later sleek black cars slipped out of the open wooden gates. Warned in advance by walkie-talkie, the controllers in the traffic department hastily switched all the traffic lights along the whole length of Dorogomilovsky Street and the Arbat [near the Kremlin] to red; a warning bell rang in the guard's box by the entrance at the Borovitsky gates. The occasional passers-by who happened to be out on that early Sunday morning turned their eyes in respectful understanding after the cars which sped down the outside lane and had no doubts that Stalin was in one of them, and they thought: 'Work, work! ... It's so late and he's not asleep ... He's not asleep! ... Work! ...

People were hurrying home from visiting friends, from restaurants, from Saturday-night parties. Some were carrying record-players, cases of records, others were crowding around on street corners trying to catch a free taxi. They were all in a hurry to get home, dreaming about the coming day off, about how nice it would be to have a lie-in, and afterwards, if the weather were nice, go to Khimki or Serebryany Bor or the Agricultural Exhibition [popular excursion places for Muscovites] ...

They could do anything they liked because the people on whom their tomorrows, their future, depended did not sleep even at night. And among them, speeding past in one of those black cars, was Stalin, the wisest, the most energetic, the man who knew everything in advance, the man who knew neither sleep nor rest, protecting them from all dangers, from all hostile plots, the great man ...

When the Marshal [Timoshenko, People's Commissar of Defence] and the General of the Army [i.e. his deputy, the Chief of Staff of the High Command, General Zhukov] came into the Kremlin office of the Chairman of the Sovnarkom [Council of People's Commissars, i.e. Stalin], with its embossed wallpaper and oak panelling, the members of the Politburo were already sitting on both sides of the long conference-table.

Stalin had his pipe filled with tobacco but as yet unlit in his hand. He did not reply to the military men's greeting and said flatly: 'Make your report.'

The Marshal reported on the situation laconically: the enemy was bombing Murmansk, Tallin, Kiev, Mogilev, Odessa . . . his troops were attacking the border all along the western front.

He tried to speak calmly, without lending any emotive colouring to the words he uttered, but, all the same, here they sounded like peals of thunder. When the Marshal finished, silence fell. All eyes turned on Stalin. But Stalin was also silent, preoccupied with pressing the tobacco in his pipe with his thumb.

At last his voice resounded.

'Tell us, then, you don't think that this could all be provocation?'

It seemed that he pronounced these words in his usual, pale, almost toneless voice. But everyone who had had frequent occasion to hear Stalin could now detect in his tone some new, hitherto unthinkable, as it were, pleading notes.

This made the atmosphere in the room even more alarming.

Stalin waited for an answer. He looked questioningly at the military men, his head tilted slightly back and his chin jutting out a little; his hand held the pipe as it described neat semi-circles like the hands on a clock, and it went cold in the air.

And all those who were now in that large room – those sitting at the table and especially the two military men, one on the thin side with marshal's stars in his buttonholes, and the other stocky, thick-set with a huge head and a heavy chin, the general of the army – they all felt that Stalin wanted nothing more than to get an affirmative reply.

Whether by luck or by design, while he was waiting Stalin settled his gaze precisely on the General, who realised that he would have to reply.

The General knew very well that people often gave this short man in his grey, tightly buttoned coat and his soft boots which deadened the sound of his footsteps just the answers which they unfailingly guessed he wanted to hear.

Perhaps under the influence of that bitter feeling the General replied more loudly, sharply, more bluntly than he intended: 'How can it be provocation, Comrade Stalin? There are bombs falling on our cities!'

Stalin made an impatient gesture with his hand and said in dissatisfaction: 'The Germans are past masters at provocation. They could even start bombing their own cities to that end.'

He looked round at all those present, as if seeking the usual support.

But everyone was silent.

Stalin took a few silent steps about the room and stopped opposite Molotov [the People's Commissar of Foreign Affairs], who was sitting at the table.

'We must contact Berlin immediately,' he said, pointing the bent stem of his pipe at Molotov. 'You must ring the German embassy.'

Everyone seemed to breathe a sigh of relief: Stalin's words now contained some sort of action, and everyone was now waiting for some action, some order from Stalin.

Molotov got up hastily and went over to the table where the telephones were, next to the large writing-desk. Lifting one of the receivers he half-whispered an instruction to the duty officer at the People's Commissariat of Foreign Affairs.

Silence fell. Stalin renewed his continual movement pacing up and down the length of the wall. As before, he was walking to and fro with the unlit pipe in his hand, only occasionally turning his head, slowing down more as if listening for something. And it seemed to those assembled in the room that he was trying to catch the sounds of the distant gunfire.

The telephone rang. Molotov had not left the table; he picked up the receiver quickly. He listened in silence for a few moments. Then he said, 'Tell him to come,' replaced the receiver and, turning to Stalin, said with a slight stammer: 'Sch-Schulenburg [the German ambassador] wants to see me right away. He says there is an im-important message. I said he was to come over.'

'Off you go, then,' said Stalin brusquely.

Molotov strode out of the room quickly.

Once again silence reigned. The Marshal and the General were still standing in the middle of the room. No one invited them to sit down. But Stalin himself was on his feet, so it all looked quite natural. This was how they had stood twelve – no, now it was thirteen – hours ago when there had been the conversation about the deserter. They were all in the same places as before.

If only it were possible to turn back the clock, stop time, turn it back thirteen hours, thought the Chief of the General Staff, and at that moment his gaze met Stalin's.

And the General thought that Stalin had read his mind and was not taking his cold, penetrating eyes off him now, as if reproaching him: We'll just see, Comrade General of the Army! You know your way about in military matters, but you're not too hot when it comes to politics. You aren't able to see into the enemy's cunning intentions. But I, I can see right through them. And time will prove that.

The General knew that Stalin could not bear it when people

lowered their eyes when he stared at them. The ability of a man to hold his gaze and not look away was deemed by Stalin to be a sign of sincerity, of no ulterior motive.

But now the General of the Army, this short man with the broad, straight shoulders out of which rose the large head with its heavy chin, fixed his eyes on Stalin not because he was afraid for himself.

No, he just wanted Stalin to be right. The General wanted to read in Stalin's gaze certainty, knowledge of something of which the others present in the room were not aware, but which in the last analysis would radically alter the order of things.

At last Stalin shifted his look from the General and once more took a few steps along the wall and, although his steps on the carpet were completely silent, the General seemed to hear them sounding in his ears. Stalin walked to and fro and there was something pendulum-like in the repetition of his movements.

He was not looking at anyone now, but the eyes of all those who were there were glued to him and seemed joined to him by invisible threads. And when Stalin walked to the far end of the room all the heads turned in his direction. And whenever he came back everyone followed incessantly the expression on his face, waiting for some important, decisive words.

But Stalin was silent.

In the tense silence no one seemed to notice that Molotov had reappeared. In a dull voice, without addressing anyone in particular, he said: 'The German government has declared war on us.'

These words caught Stalin on his way to the far corner of the room.

When he heard them he turned abruptly. And at just that moment everyone saw that some indefinable but certain change had come over him.

He took a few uncertain steps, not along his usual route but into the middle of the room. Then, as if seeing nothing in front of him, he went up to the table and slowly, as if groping, lowered himself into an empty seat. He sat there hunched up, his head bowed, his filled yet unlit pipe lying on the table. This pipe, in the minds of millions of people, eternally moulded into Stalin's hand, as it were the natural extension of his hand, lay lonely and useless on the wide table – a small, bent piece of wood. At last Stalin raised his head and, pointing his index finger at the military men, said: 'Issue immediate instructions for our troops to repel the enemy's attack. But', he went on, raising his voice unexpectedly as if arguing with an invisible opponent, 'tell them not to cross the frontier for the time being.' He was silent for a while, then added in a quieter voice: 'Except the air force. Get going.'

The last words were pronounced almost in his usual calmly imperious manner, but none the less everyone sensed bitterly that this time his voice sounded somehow unnatural.

Stalin was crushed, oppressed, and they all realised this.

[Indeed, Stalin's orders 'not to cross the frontier' were almost comically beside the point in the circumstances, and indicative of his remoteness from reality. Later that same day, Stalin ordered the advancing German units to be 'surrounded and annihilated' – an order of considerable folly which led to the premature encirclement and loss of many thousands of men.]

Late in the evening Stalin and a few of the Politburo members accompanying him suddenly appeared in the People's Commissariat on Frunze Street.

Going into the Commissariat office Stalin was calm and confident. However, it was there at the very centre of the military management of the country that he felt for the first time in all its concreteness the scale of the danger hanging over them. Formations of enemy tanks were trying to take Minsk in a pincer movement, and it looked as if there were nothing that could stop them. Contact with our troops who were retreating under the blows of the enemy was broken . . .

Usually outwardly calm, slow in conversation and movement, Stalin was unable to restrain himself on this occasion. He heaped angry, insulting reproaches on the chiefs of the Commissariat and the General Staff. Then, without looking at anyone, drooping and hunched, he left the building, got into his car and went off to his house in Kuntsevo [Stalin's country dacha outside Moscow].

. . . No one knew what Stalin thought about during the next few dozen hours. No one saw him. He did not appear in the Kremlin. No one heard his voice on the telephone. He summoned no one. And none of those who during those days hourly expected his summons could resolve to go and see him unasked . . .

Immediately masses of business, great and small affairs, all connected with implementing military measures at the front and in the country, fell on the Politburo members, the Commissariats, the chiefs in the People's Commissariat of Defence, the General Staff and the Political Administration of the Army [i.e. the political watchdogs]. No one was idle.

Yet from morning till deep into the night, occupied with urgent business, they kept asking themselves: Where's Stalin, then? Why doesn't he say something?

Just what was the almighty and omniscient man doing and thinking about during those long, terrible hours? One can only guess. That night he left the Commissariat building as if in a trance, seeing nothing and no one. He got in his car. The traffic lights flashed, the 'cuckoo' horns sounded dully, telling any other cars to pull in. The blank gates of the Kuntsevo dacha swung open silently . . .

Perhaps he went through silently into the room which served him as a dining-room and study, moved aside a pile of papers and newspapers, sat down and felt a sharp pain in the region of his heart. Paid sceptical attention to it. He was rarely ill and like any strong, healthy man had no time for doctors.

True, once or twice a year he let a doctor examine him. In case of emergency there were a few medicine-bottles in the dining-room in the sideboard. But Stalin never resorted to them.

And now perhaps, for the first time in many years, he went into the dining-room to the sideboard, opened it, looked at the bottles and, without touching them, closed the door again quite automatically.

Slowly, with a shuffling gait unusual for him, he walked over the soft, deep-pile carpet – probably the only luxury allowed in the house – stopped by the window and looked into the garden.

He loved sitting and reading in the arbour at the start of the day, surrounded by cherry trees, loved looking at the white apple blossom.

He opened the window, breathed deeply but did not catch the usual scent of the blended aromas of the plants. The air seemed full of pungent burning to him. He closed the window, went back to the long table and sat down again.

How could it have happened? How? . . . Why are our troops retreating? Stalin wondered . . .

He sat there bending low over the table and asked himself these painful questions. He wondered: how could it happen that the most terrible thing about which he thought constantly, the danger of which he had warned the Party and the people more than once in his speeches and addresses, the possibility of which, it seemed, he was always taking into account – how could it have happened that this had still caught him unawares?

What was the mistake? Where had he gone wrong? Why were our troops retreating?

Maybe not enough attention had been paid to the defence of the country. Maybe it had been begrudged resources. Maybe they had not attracted the best minds in the country for the creation of the latest military technology. Maybe the army and the people had not been brought up in the spirit of constant mobilised readiness. Maybe they had underestimated Hitler, his army, forgotten the danger of German fascism, lulled themselves and the people with thoughts of the indestructibility of the Red Army.

No, no, answered Stalin mentally.

After all, not one serious decision had been made without taking into consideration the military danger. Every hour, every day, every month had been regarded only as a delay, a breathing-space, which had to be taken advantage of, sparing neither strength nor means. Had not our artillery increased sevenfold in some ten years, and our anti-tank weaponry seventeenfold? Seventeenfold! In actual fact, our tank troops had been entirely re-created, the number of aeroplanes had increased 600 per cent! The navy had got 500 new warships. Was that really inadequate? Could you really demand more from a people which had only had some ten years to create in a vast, beggarly, peasant country its own industry, create it without any previous experience by means of deprivation, suffering without any help from outside?

Had not the alarming thought of a coming war not figured in the writers' works, in films, not been heard in songs or been shouted from hoardings? Hadn't he himself, Stalin, made a single speech warning of the danger of war?

So why, then, why had war overtaken them like lava from a volcano? Why were our aeroplanes burning as they stood at the airfields? Why didn't the artillery deliver one all-destructive volley? Why were our soldiers retreating?

. . . With drooping shoulders he sat motionless by the long narrow table over an untidy pile of papers and books. The sun was shining outside the wide window, the garden was fragrant, not a sound from outside penetrated this country house surrounded by woods . . .

Perhaps the mistake was to be found in the Soviet–German pact [1939]?

No! That had been essential, unavoidable, that treaty. It had not been easy to make, but the interests of the country demanded it.

Hadn't the Western powers sabotaged our efforts over many years to create collective security against fascist aggression? Wasn't it they who had betrayed the world at Munich? Wasn't it Chamberlain and Daladier [the British and French leaders] who had sent pawns to Moscow who were not empowered even to agree to particular military decisions, let alone conclude an effective pact against Hitler?

What was the reply from these inveterate enemies of communism when we wanted to help Czechoslovakia and stop Hitler seizing it? What did France do? She refused Czechoslovakia miliary aid. What was the Polish government's response? 'Not a single Soviet soldier will be allowed to cross Polish territory!' How did Beneš [the Czechoslovak President] behave? He preferred to ignore help from the Soviet Union and capitulate to Hitler. England and France did all they could to 'appease' Hitler, if only he would turn eastwards, against the Soviet Union . . . So what else could we have done, what?

Yes, it wasn't easy to conclude that pact – but didn't it give us the opportunity of living in peace for nearly two years when war was already raging in Europe? Weren't we able to shift our frontiers a long way? Was it really a pact of submission? No, we kept a watchful eye on the enemy's advances. When necessary we weren't afraid to talk to him with the voice of a great power. Had Molotov really gone to Berlin as a suppliant? . . .

Then why, despite all the measures they had taken, had the German blow still caught them napping? Why? In fury, resentment and pain Stalin kept asking himself: Had we allowed some fateful oversight, or is there nothing I should reproach myself for? . . .

He found no answer to this implacable question. He couldn't find it at that time because the man was distinguished not only by willpower, tremendous political experience, intellect and devotion to the communist cause, but also by other characteristics which, it would seem, were logically incompatible with the first ones: year by year his growing faith in his own infallibility, and his suspiciousness and unjustified cruelty – not simply the cruelty necessary to fight the enemies of the Revolution, but the cruelty with which he struck so often at his own people, too . . .

No, it wasn't that they hadn't prepared for war – in recent years and months worries about the army were the chief concerns of the Party, the Central Committee, and the government. They tried to provide it with the most that the newly created socialist industry could produce.

And, of course, Stalin's oversight was not to be found in the pact with Hitler – this fragile treaty was forced on them unavoidably, predetermined by the treachery of the great capitalist powers at Munich when they took it upon themselves to free Germany's hands and set her on the Soviet Union.

The oversight was elsewhere. And it reflected precisely Stalin's contradictory character, the authoritarian nature of his thinking, the peculiar combination of creative and dogmatic elements in him.

From the moment Hitler came to power Stalin was convinced of the possibility and even the inevitability of his attacking the Soviet Union, and he hourly expected such an attack after it had become clear that England and France did not want to join forces with the Soviet Union and check Hitler, but on the contrary were trying to do all they could to enable the German dictator to attack the socialist country while having nothing to fear in the rear, and so when Hitler, against expectations, started a war in the West Stalin became unjustifiably calm.

He was alert again during the period of the phoney war between France and Germany when the German troops were suspiciously inactive on the Maginot Line [between France and Germany] – the thought that Hitler was conducting negotiations with the venal rulers of France sharpened Stalin's vigilance again.

However, when war broke out between Germany and England, Stalin became convinced that Hitler was going to be bogged down for a long time . . . One way or another, Stalin reasoned, if Hitler decided to carry the war over on to English territory it would give the Soviet Union a minimum of a year's grace. The possibility that Hitler would attack the Soviet Union while simultaneously waging a war of attrition against England was something Stalin considered unreal . . . Naturally, thought Stalin, there had to be another danger: that the rulers of Great Britain still had not relinquished their cherished, yet unrealised, idea of setting Hitler on the Soviet Union . . . The possibility of an agreement amongst the imperialists at the expense of the socialist state was something Stalin never ruled out. Consequently, he did not rule out the possibility of a situation in which England managed to persuade Hitler not to wait until the might of the Soviet Union had grown even more, but to treat with Britain, making her neutral or perhaps even an ally, and strike at the East.

Given such circumstances, it was Stalin's conviction that any overt military activisation of the Soviet Union, any decisive implementing of a mobilisation plan, would no doubt facilitate England's plans and would become a trump card in her secret game with Hitler.

Consequently, the present task was to play for time – time was on our side, on the side of the Soviet Union. The task was to utilise the extra year or eighteen months for a systematic re-arming of the army, and at the same time not to give any grounds for provocation. Such was Stalin's calculation. And he had his reasons – logical, political and strategic reasons – for such a calculation.

However, the most perfect calculation, when turned into dogma, loses its original sense. In that case all the new facts that come to light, if they contradict to any degree the decision taken previously, are rejected out of hand in irritation.

Soviet agents informed Stalin of the facts which pointed to Hitler's preparing for an imminent attack on the Soviet Union. He ignored some of these reports and did not accord to others the significance they warranted. Moreover, as he daily expected some cunning moves by the English or Hitler himself, Stalin sometimes saw in these intelligence reports evidence of ulterior motives, and was convinced that the authors of the warnings had become involuntary weapons in the hands of the enemy.

These secret intentions were certainly no mere figment of Stalin's imagination. He well remembered in his time the words Chamberlain had used in a circle of like-minded people: 'Of course, for us the best thing would be if Hitler and Stalin fell out and tore each other to pieces.' Stalin was right to be on his guard.

But he was wrong to close his eyes to all the new facts which contradicted his prognosis, his calculation . . .

Also there were limits to the analysis that this man ventured upon. He would not have been Stalin if he had always been able to evaluate directly and impassionately all his calculations and actions.

The belief, strengthened over the years, that Stalin had in his own infallibility, in the correctness of his foresight, in the ability which only he had to take the only correct decision, even now prevented Stalin from finding the correct answer to his question: 'Where was the oversight?'

For if he had found in himself the strength, determination and desire to weigh up all his actions objectively and mercilessly he would inevitably have had to recall something else: the fact that of his volition, because of his unjustified suspicions that went beyond the bounds of common sense, the army had suffered grave losses in its cadres in recent years [during the purges].

And there he is, sitting silently, absorbed in grave reflections, a long way away from the people in these minutes when his country is at its peril. So this country is doomed!

This was probably just what our enemy would have been thinking, foretasting victory.

But it would be a crude, fateful miscalculation. And not only because very soon now Stalin would find in himself the strength and decisiveness to head the Supreme Command of the Army and the country's Defence Committee. There was something else . . .

It was in those tragic days that it became irrefutably clear that the unconquerable strength of our country lay not primarily in Stalin, but in her social system, in the devotion of millions of people to the cause of communism.

Aleksandr Chakovsky, *Blockade* [*Blokada*] *Znamya* (1968–73)

The first two extracts in this chapter have focused on major turning-points in Soviet history: collectivisation and the fate of the kulaks, and the 1941–5 war and Stalin's culpable negligence in 1941 itself. The third extract takes as its theme the extent to which this past history is still unavoidably a part of everyday Soviet life. The younger generation may be relatively unversed in Stalinism and unburdened by any guilt feelings, though, as the poet Yevgeny Yevtushenko pointed out in an open letter to Brezhnev in 1974, protesting at the expulsion of Aleksandr Solzhenitsyn from the Soviet Union: 'The younger generation really does not have sources nowadays for learning the tragic truth about that period because they cannot read about it either in books or in school texts . . . The truth is replaced by silence, and silence is a lie.' (Yevtushenko had been shocked to discover that hardly any of the teenagers he had recently met knew one-tenth of the human cost of Stalinism.) The older generation however, is only too well aware of the legacy and of its complex nature, and this is precisely the theme of a novel by Aleksandr Kron, *Insomnia*.

Aleksandr Kron (b. 1909, Moscow) could be described as an orthodox Stalinist writer. Originally a dramatist, his earlier works, with such titles as *Rifle No. 492116*, *Navy Officer* and *The Party Candidate*, received considerable attention under Stalin. But the publication of *Insomnia* (1977), a rich and interesting novel, was a reminder that labels are all too easily applied and often at best oversimplify.

Insomnia (a title which conveys both a literal and a figurative meaning) consists partly of notes, partly of reminiscences, partly of diaries written by the central figure, Yudin, at night when he is plagued with sleeplessness. Yudin is an internationally celebrated scholar, a physiologist, eloquent and urbane. He is a key figure of an academic research institute in Moscow. The previous director, Uspensky, an even more renowned and revered scholar, had been Yudin's teacher and friend. Both are tortured, however, by qualms of conscience, for they have pasts marred by fears, compromises and indignities of many kinds. After the war Yudin, for example, as the following extract shows, largely wrote the thesis of a man called Vdovin, a Stalinist witch-hunter of the worst, opportunist kind. It is not clear why Yudin did this, but he did, and later, when Yudin and Uspensky are together in Paris, Uspensky attacks Yudin for his behaviour in 1948 in selling out his scholarly values for Stalinist orthodoxy. ('Scholars must tell the truth to their governments.') Uspensky himself, however, has even older skeletons in his cupboard dating from his betrayal of a friend in the great purge year of 1937.

Uspensky dies, possibly through suicide – a man who has held power from the 1930s to the 1960s and therefore, Kron implies, a necessarily compromised figure. Yudin the scholar and Vdovin the ex-witch-hunter are also, in different ways, compromised figures. Some kind of *modus vivendi* is established between them and, on the surface, the past is buried; but in private there lie some very uneasy heads, and arguments about whose course of action was the least discreditable remain unresolved.

INSOMNIA

Aleksandr Kron

[The narrator Yudin is writing in his diary in the late 1950s.]

The first of these episodes relates to the autumn of 1948, when a wave of officially inspired criticism [*prorabotka* is the Russian word here; literally a 'working over' of someone] swept over many scientific establishments. Formalist geneticists, opponents of the methods of the Academician Lysenko [the quack geneticist and agrobiologist], mendelists–morganists, over-zealous supporters of the theory of relativity and the then barely conceived science of cybernetics [i.e. unacceptable deviations] were all subjected to public malediction . . .

But I am getting away from old Antonyevich [the doorman at the Institute]. I think I have already mentioned that the old man always stood behind the screen of the cloakroom, leaning his hands on the oak counter. That is not quite accurate. On days when there were open meetings of the University Senate, public defence of theses and scientific examinations, old Antonyevich, while still keeping a sharp eye on the entrance and the cloakroom, would stand by the half-open door of the council chamber and listen. God only knows how much he understood. Even the most unbridled fantasists among the young staff members would not care to argue that the old man could fathom the language of our dissertations and synopses of papers; on the contrary, everyone knew that, even though he looked every day at the bust of Ilya Ilyich Mechnikov [the microbiologist, 1845–1916] which stood in the foyer, he never knew who he was. And probably I was not the only one to ponder about what it was that forced old Antonyevich, an active man for all his inertia, to listen attentively for hours on end to speeches in some incomprehensible language, rendered all the more arcane by the occasional appearance of some familiar Russian words in it. In the end I penetrated this enigma. And quite by accident.

It occurred on the second day of an extraordinary session of our institute, which was remembered in our collective as 'the anti-neo-Malthusian session'. Just why eminent scholars and talented youngsters at this session were utterly trounced and accused in particular of neo-Malthusianism remains somewhat unclear to me to this very day; with similar success they could have been accused of neo-Kantianism, surrealism or exhibitionism. Now I have a deeper understanding of the meaning behind what went on – but more of that when the time comes. Contrary to tradition, the inaugural meeting took place not in our modest council chamber but in one of the largest concert halls in Moscow, with a motley confluence of the public at large attracted partly by the morbid interest we all inherently have in the problems of the physiology of ageing, partly by the sumptuous buffet and the books and consumer-goods stands in the lower foyer; participants and guests could buy Shakespeare's sonnets in Marshak's translation, imported ballpoint pens, and stretch-nylon socks. But perhaps it was the yearning for a spectacle which attracted people most of all. And they got one. In the praesidium illuminated by hot arc lights you could see many distinguished people with their glittering medals and insignia; they completely swamped the humble members of our senate. Of the three main speakers, only Uspensky was a physiologist. I had recently reread the transcript of his lecture with a peculiar feeling: less than ten years had passed, and a lot of what he was saying then now sounded like medieval scholasticism. I could find a lot to say about the course of that discussion which played such a sorry part in the life of our institute, but it is enough to say for now that it was a three-day *corrida* in which the bulls had their horns sawn off in advance so that, if you wanted to be a matador, you needed neither skill nor courage.

There was no real discussion, either: neither at that first meeting nor at the subsequent ones, which took place less ostentatiously in the council chamber of our institute. Perhaps the most depressing memory I have was of the evening meeting on the second day at which my protégé, Kolya Vdovin, whose thoroughly mediocre dissertation we had knocked into shape by our joint efforts, fulminated against and savaged one of the most talented postgraduate students, Ilyusha Slavin. Balaam's ass suddenly started to speak and in such a powerful bass voice that many hearts shuddered with ill bodings. Vdovin was standing on the rostrum beneath the marble plaque which bore in gold letters Marx's famous dictum that there are no highways in science, and trampled on Ilyusha for attempting to lead the physiology of ageing away from the highway laid down by the labours of Soviet scholars. He fulminated against his recently completed dissertation, which had not gone beyond the four walls of our laboratory and which, though controversial in places, was brilliant in its boldness and talent. I glanced at Uspensky. He was in the chair, a squeamishly estranged expression on his face. I left the hall immediately after Vdovin's speech. I do not smoke, but just then I found it easier to breathe in the smoke-filled foyer. As I passed old Antonyevich, standing in the doorway, our eyes met and it was suddenly revealed to me that the old man knew what was going on in the chamber, understood as well as I did, or, it seems to me now, even better than I did. Of course, he did not know what a constellation was or why Lamarckism was bad, but he could clearly identify the spite, rivalry, suspicion and fear which ruled our peaceful council chamber in those days.

At that time I was so naïve and presumptuous that after the meeting I called Vdovin into my room and tried to get him to see sense. It was a complete affront. Vdovin, hitherto having revered my scholarship and my having been a general in the army, replied politely but firmly, and even with a sense of superiority. He gave me to understand that he had spoken according to the dictates of his civic and scientific conscience and it was strange for him to see me trying to shut him up, given my constant championing of free scientific discussion. As with his single-handed battle with Marx, the score was one-nil to him.

We left the Institute when everyone else had gone. As I went along the dimly lit foyer I glanced behind the screen of the cloakroom and noticed Ilyusha sitting on the shoe-box. He was munching a piece of salami, and an empty quarter-litre vodka-bottle lay on the floor. Old Antonyevich was standing next to him; he had tried to hide Ilyusha with his coat tails when he saw us coming. So this skinflint and teetotaller had done what had not occurred to any of the boy's friends to do: without further ado he had got hold of some vodka from somewhere and was administering an antidote to the shocked lad. The old man looked hatefully at Vdovin, reproachfully at me.

I spoke on the last day at the morning meeting. At the time a lot of people, and first and foremost I myself, thought that my speech was an act of high civic courage. Without going to the heart of the dispute I said that no one had the right to pontificate on an unfinished piece of work which had not yet been presented for public discussion; in passing, I managed to call into question several particular remarks Vdovin had made, exposing his elementary ignorance and making the audience laugh, but even this diffident attempt to inject some dignity into the proceedings prompted angry yells; Vdovin had his acolytes among those who had been quiet up to then. As always, Uspensky was sitting upright; and fury could be read in his strong cheekbones. It had been unpleasant for him to listen to Vdovin, but listening to me was worse. It was unbearably stuffy in the crowded council chamber, the doors to the foyer were thrown wide open, and from the rostrum I could see old Antonyevich's off-white coat the whole time.

Another episode relates to the comparatively recent life of the Institute, immediately following the publication of the decisions of the 20th Party Congress [in 1956]. A two-day Party meeting was held, the people who had previously kept quiet got everything off their chests, the most loquacious fell silent. It was a closed meeting, and old Antonyevich could only listen to the excited voices from a distance as they carried outside the council chamber. The time had come for Vdovin and his yes-men to pay for their erstwhile triumphs. They were accused to their faces of destroying scientific cadres, of ignorance, of poisoning the atmosphere of the Institute and putting it back ten years. Uspensky was not at the meeting; two days before he had flown off to Prague to some congress. Vdovin bore himself with dignity, admitted his mistakes, but without the terrible self-flagellation which his opponents had gone in for when in their time they had confessed and renounced their correct views. He never once referred to Uspensky. Voices were raised to expel him from the Party. But at this juncture the secretary of the Party bureau intervened, saying that we should not mix up a discussion of fundamental decisions with the personal case of one individual Communist Party member, and everyone agreed with him. It was also obvious that Vdovin would leave the Institute, and that suited everybody.

[Yudin recalls a conversation of the 1960s with Uspensky [Pasha] when they were in a Paris café. Uspensky starts the conversation.]

'We've known each other for a good thirty years, but "known" is only a turn of phrase. We've been moving in one direction but on different levels; we don't get the same readings from the instruments. We came into the world of science at different times and with different luggage. What do you know of the time when the scientific intelligentsia was committing acts of sabotage, while ideas of materialist philosophy were openly reviled by people holding university chairs? And I felt myself to be above all a Party fighter, drafted in by the Revolution. In Koltushi I was considered by many to be the *enfant terrible*, a real fanatic. What a joke to think I once argued with Pavlov [physiologist who discovered the notion of conditioned reflex, 1849–1936] himself. I really did. I stood to attention in front of that genius, horrified at my own impertinence – but I argued. He loved me. You only saw Stalin standing on the Mausoleum, but I saw him as I see you now. Seeing Stalin at such close quarters means seeing more and seeing less than others.'

'Did you argue with him, too?' I had no malicious intention in saying this, and Pasha understood that.

'No. But . . .' He chuckled. 'It all started with an argument. We met at Gorky's house [Maksim Gorky (1868–1936)]. He used to go there, and I dropped in by chance. Stalin asked me if my family had been clergy. I said no, my father had been a village schoolteacher.

' "Your surname gives you away," he said. [Stalin's gibe refers to the Uspensky sobor (Cathedral of the Assumption) in the Kremlin.] This niggled me, and I answered that I couldn't vouch for my forefathers but I myself was educated at a workers' college and not in a church seminary [as Stalin was]. Everyone around almost died, but for some reason Stalin was amused and began asking me who I was and what I did. We started talking about physiology, and once again an argument ensued. I saw him many times after that. I'm obliged to him entirely for the transformation of our laboratory into the Institute. But you're right – I never argued with him any more. Though I loved arguing. There was a time when I thought that there was nothing more important and absorbing than the political battle. I liked open polemics best of all. I would seek out ideological opponents just to test my strength. I no longer have the pleasure of delivering the last words. Monsieur!' he shouted to the passing waiter, explaining to me, 'I can't for the life of me call a grown man "garçon". In Germany the waiter is called "Herr Ober" – that's more substantial somehow.'

'Do you want more coffee?' I asked.

'Yes, and cognac. Otherwise I won't get to sleep.'

'You were talking about discussion,' he went on when the waiter had brought the order. 'These days I understand as well as you do that discussion has both welded and disunited scientific strength; it has inflamed dark passions and it's poisoned the atmosphere at the Institute for a long time. It would be base of me to contend that there was someone who forced me to conduct discussions in precisely that way. I did everything off my own bat – both the things I wanted to do and those I didn't want to do. After the war a great fermentation of minds and reassessment of many values began in the Institute; it was as if people set themselves the task of outdoing each other in the novelty and contrariness of their judgements. Everyone was seized by the desire for publicity; our lads started making speeches everywhere where people wanted to hear them. In my view, as it was then, this all got completely out of hand. In the administration the signals were there: I'd be summoned and told, "Your chaps are preaching philosophical idealism, toadying to bourgeois authorities and attacking the prestige of the signposts of Soviet biology." Well, you understand whom they had in mind. One of our people was giving a talk on Malthus and, instead of giving the establishment view and damning him, burbled that, despite all his fallacious conclusions, the old man still deserved our gratitude, if only for formulating the problems of demography so clearly. Good gracious, the fat was really in the fire! In my view there could be only one conclusion: order had to be restored in people's brains; free but skilfully directed discussion would purify the air, and the very presence of the enemy would help us sharpen our ideological weapons. At first I thought about doing it at our annual general meeting, but in the process of consultation the magnitude of the issue grew and it became a question of an All-Union forum and, as you can guess, for that you need to get the go-ahead in extremely high places. And it was in one of these places that I cravenly chickened out.'

He stopped talking and turned away. For a minute he contemplated the turning of the windmill [they are near the Moulin Rouge] decked with fairy lights and frowned. One might suppose that he was regretting having talked too much and our conversation would stop here. He began to speak suddenly, when I no longer expected a continuation of our talk.

'I probably laid it on a bit thick when I made my report. I said I needed money, a big hall in town, hotels, and entrance by ticket only, and a lot more besides. To get all that, I had to convince people that the game was worth the candles. They listened to me attentively. When I'd finished, the man chairing the meeting, a very powerful man in those days, said: "We would like to know, Comrade Uspensky, is it really that serious? If it isn't, then you're wasting our time. You have adequate means and powers to settle your own internal issues yourself. If indeed it is that serious, then these half-baked formulations of yours are impermissible, and the issue will have to be raised with all political pungency, as it is in agricultural science [by Lysenko]". It was a point-blank question – yes or no.'

'And you said "Yes".'

'You're a good guesser. I said "Yes", and from that moment I fell into the trap which I had set for myself. While preparations were being made for the meetings, the situation internally and externally changed appreciably, the storm clouds gathered, the Cold War began . . .'

'And against that background appeared that humble candidate of science, Vdovin.'

[In the 1970s after Uspensky's death, Vdovin and Yudin discuss Vdovin's possible return to the Institute. Vdovin defends his Stalinist past with remarkable vigour.]

At last the kettle boiled. Vdovin made coffee, broke the French loaf and proferred these gastronomic delicacies to me. He was very fussy and I could guess why. There is an ancient conviction alive in every one of us that a man who 'breaks bread' with another will thus endorse an unwritten agreement with him. I chewed the bread and cheese and in due course tried all the other things: a refusal would have seemed like a demonstration of something. Vdovin wanted to drink, but without me he felt too inhibited and settled for pouring some cognac into his coffee. He was trying his utmost to behave as though the main part, the most difficult part, of our conversation was already behind us, and all that remained was for us to relax and agree on the details.

'Well, then?' he asked with a benevolent smile. 'Have I answered all your questions?'

There was no mockery in his tone of voice but there was an obvious implication: You needed this conversation, not me. And you needed it to make it clear that you're not a pawn in the game but a person in a position to make conditions. Make them. That way you get what you regard as the essential points. You have them. Last of all, just to clear your conscience, admit that I've met you halfway over everything. But now that all the conventions have been observed let's get down to business.

'No, not all,' I mumbled, trying not to betray my mounting irritation.

'I'm listening.' He expressed his accession to my will with an inclination of the head.

'You just said: in a year's time . . . In a year's time no one will think your return to the Institute strange. True. But there are one or two things which can't be forgotten in a hurry. Like Ashkhen Nikitichn being taken away with a heart attack after your speech, or your destruction of Pogrebnyak's laboratory . . .'

'There's no need to go on,' said Vdovin. 'You've already read me a list of my misdemeanours at the Party meeting, and I'm not complaining about being reminded. I admitted my mistakes then. I spoke of my deep-seated guilt at Pasha's open grave, and you know what he meant to me. Listen, Oleg.' He came over to me and stretched out his hand as if to shake mine firmly. 'Drop all this. Times have changed, there are other songs to be sung and you can't turn the clock back. You know the old folk-saying: Let bygones be bygones.'

'I don't like that formula,' I said.

'Why not?'

'There's something threatening about it. Like losing an eye.'

Vdovin laughed. He was capable of appreciating a joke, even a malevolent one. But my sense of humour suddenly deserted me.

'I've had enough of this talk,' I said, practically shouting. 'My dear Nikolay Mitrofanovich, I used to be an army surgeon and I know a thing or two about wounds. Wounds have to be treated, not concealed. And they have to have salt rubbed in them. In 1942 when I didn't have any pencillin I put a very strong salt solution on wounds and saved them from turning septic that way. And until people understand this . . .'

I think I achieved my end. Vdovin staggered back and I could see his face darken with rage.

'What do you want from me?' he snarled. 'Do you want me to go down on my hands and knees? And who do you think you are to pass judgement on me? I caused his heart attack! There was a battle to be fought! You can argue about whether I was right or not, but you couldn't expect me to get a report from the clinic on the state of his cardiac muscle . . . Yes, I trod on Ilyusha, but what did you do? You defended him, and all the ladies of academe ooh'd and ah'd: Isn't he brave, isn't he highly principled! So what? Did your defence help Ilya? You weren't defending him, you were defending yourself. Your reputation. You defended him as far as your own circumstances reasonably allowed you; you had Uspensky behind you, and you knew that he might grumble but he would stand up for you. And what then? Were you, the goodie, a lot of help to Ilya [Slavin]? I'm the baddie, but I gave him a crust of bread and now I'm breaking my neck to get him out of here. Do you think I've forgotten the way you laid into me at that meeting after the plenum [1956]? I wasn't even angry with you. I just thought: Why didn't you, the goodie, speak like that at the anti-Malthusian session [1948]? Because it's allowed now, but it wasn't then? And then – I've never said this anywhere before, but I'll ask you straight now – who ordered the attack, me or Pasha [Uspensky]? You got all indignant about Pasha, but, incidentally, you didn't refuse a jaunt to Paris with him, yet at his funeral you thought shaking my hand was a big favour on your part . . . Oh, what the . . .'

He waved his hand and turned away. No doubt he was sincere at that moment, and sometimes sincerity makes more of an impression than being right does. I did not feel crushed, but I had hit the canvas. He had become no closer to me, but as his honest opponent I had to confess that I had received a few hard knocks.

'Think about it, Oleg,' said Vdovin, and I could tell by his voice that he was just as weary of our conversation as I was. The conversation was not exhausted; it had just got out of breath. We both realised this and, without exchanging a word, started to get our things together for the journey.

Five minutes later we were turning off the smooth swishing gravel of the driveway and on to the bumpy forest road.

Aleksandr Kron *Insomnia [Bessonnitsa] Novy mir*, 1977, nos 4–6

Further Reading

Among the best recent studies of Stalin and Stalinism are A. Nove, *Stalinism and After*, 2nd edn (London, 1981), and R. Tucker (ed.), *Stalinism: Essays in Historical Interpretation* (New York, 1977).

Literary portraits of Stalin include those by A. Solzhenitsyn in *The First Circle* (New York, 1968), V. Serge in *The Case of Comrade Tulayev* (Harmondsworth, 1968) and V. Voynovich in his story, 'A Circle of Friends' in the collection *In Plain Russian* (New York, 1979). This last item provides a satirical alternative view of the events covered in our extract from Chakovsky's *Blockade*.

Fictional works which deal with the purges include L. Chukovskaya's *The Deserted House* (London, 1967) and Yu. Dombrovsky's *The Keeper of Antiquities* (London, 1969). On collectivisation, M. Sholokhov's *Virgin Soil Upturned* (London, 1935) should be compared with Zalygin's treatment of the subject.

Important memoir accounts include N. Mandelshtam, *Hope against Hope* (Harmondsworth, 1975) and *Hope Abandoned* (Harmondsworth, 1976), and N. Khrushchev, *Khrushchev Remembers* (London, 1971).

The hounding of dissident academics, as described by Kron, was not unknown in the 1970s: see, for example, E. Etkind, *Notes of a Non-Conspirator* (Oxford, 1978).

One work of Zalygin's in translation is *The South American Variant* (New York, 1979).

3

War and Militarism

Defence of such a vast territory as the Soviet Union – twice the size of China, two and a half times that of the United States, ninety times that of the United Kingdom – is complicated and difficult. She borders directly on twelve countries, and her sea coast is exceedingly long. Despite high mountain ranges to the south and east, her frontiers elsewhere, particularly to the west, have little natural protection. Russian and Soviet history have thus been characterised by a series of major invasions, from the Mongols in the thirteenth century, to the Poles and Swedes in the seventeenth and eighteenth, and Napoleon in the nineteenth, to the Germans twice in the twentieth century. Nor should the British forget their two invasions of Russia in modern times – the Crimean War (1854–5) and their intervention in the Civil War (1918–20). During the German invasion of 1941–5 over 20 million Soviet lives were lost. This momentous fact, coupled with the need to protect a vast and vulnerable territory, helps to explain the heavy Soviet emphasis today on defence, with a huge arms budget, a large programme of national service compulsory for all young men, and much military propaganda ('the army is the school of the nation'; defence a 'sacred duty of the regime'). The Soviet Union spends a higher percentage of its gross national product on defence than any other modern industrial state, and suffers a consequently lower standard of living – the price that is paid not just to overcome a persistent national sense of insecurity *vis-à-vis* the encircling outside world, but also because history has apparently shown it to be necessary for sheer survival.

As the previous chapter indicated, the Great Patriotic War, 1941– 5, has long received saturation coverage in the Soviet media and is a traditional theme in contemporary literature. The 1945 Victory over Fascism was a critical turning-point, a famous victory for both regime and people, and the prerequisite for the Soviet Union's proud status as a world superpower. War, too, is a prism through which writers can explore relatively easily the more heroic issues. Generally it continues to be treated with great reverence for the millions who perished, but a number of writers have been able to depict episodes with considerable realism and raise questions of continuing political significance. Several noted writers, including the Byelorussian Vasil Bykov and the Russian Yuri Bondarev, have quarried richly from this subject in recent years. Bykov's work, for example, has often defended the ordinary soldier, the unsung hero. Most real heroes died in the war, often without getting medals on their chests, he argues. Military orders issued 'according to the plan' were sometimes fatal in their lack of common sense or basic strategic awareness. If the only alternative is death, collaboration with the enemy demands analysis and explanation rather than bald denunciation.

Both the extracts which follow illustrate how the Great Patriotic War can be used to reflect more recent political and social developments. They were originally published in the early years of détente. The first piece, by Pyotr Pavlenko (1909–1951), though written in the early postwar years appeared only in 1972 in the edition of *Literaturnaya gazeta* which celebrated the 27th anniversary of the Victory over Fascism. In it Pavlenko argues the case for a common cultural heritage, and points not just to the barbarities committed by the Nazis, but also to the existence of German opponents of fascism. As literature, it is a characteristically unremarkable piece from a writer who, in his day, was a successful populariser of the Stalin cult, with novels such as *Happiness* and *In the East*, but politically it is noteworthy in presenting the relatively balanced view of the Germans that the Brezhnev era of détente required. In this respect it contrasts markedly with the second and much more anti-détente extract in this chapter by Vsevolod Kochetov.

MARIA
Pyotr Pavlenko

The battle for Schöneberg started in the morning. Tsvetkov's company, reinforced with three light tanks, outstripped the rest of its regiment and burst on to the streets of the little town as the last columns of German carts were setting off from the main square. The Russians had not been expected to arrive before the Wednesday, and this last Sunday in April, warm and rainy, with blossoming narcissi and hyacinths in small front gardens, seemed to represent a natural transition from war to peace.

At midday the church pastor was to deliver a sermon on the theme of loving one's neighbour, and afterwards a few members of the town council were to assemble in the town hall to exchange opinions on the encroaching events from the east.

During the last days of the war Tsvetkov knew perfectly well how important it was now to cut off the enemy's retreat and to penetrate as far as possible behind the lines, and he assumed that for some time he would receive no support, either from the regiment or from the division, which were operating at incredible speeds over a huge area. True, he had been informed some two days before that workers from the political section were hurrying to him, specially detailed for work with the local population, but Tsvetkov well knew from his own previous experience how many headaches and how much business they had in places more important than Schöneberg.

'There is a German element here . . . a woman,' said the company sergeant-major, a stout Kazakh with large, crimson eyes. 'She understands a bit of Russian. She asked me to tell you that she is willing to interpret.'

Immediately Tsvetkov saw in the shadows of an old building with a sign outside, obviously a bar, the thinnish figure of a girl standing next to Lance-Corporal Zavileyko.

Dressed in a grey travelling-suit, coarse yellow shoes, and with a large bag reminiscent of a map-case over her shoulder, she gave an impression of great efficiency, perhaps a little too emphatically. Tsvetkov gestured for her to approach.

The girl ran up, greeting him with a raised clenched-fist salute.

'Is there a town council here?' he asked, without any preliminaries, reckoning on discovering what sort of person she was and how to behave towards her during the course of the conversation.

'Oh, yes.'

'Fascists?'

'Yes. All of them!' And she shook her little fist vigorously. 'Apart from Dr Harneck, but he's in prison.'

'I see. By the way, where is . . .?'

'Oh, here we are,' she said, immediately understanding his unuttered thought, and, smiling, took out of her bag a guidebook with a small street-map of the town.

Tsvetkov raised his eyes from the map. Before him stood a beautiful, stern and very restrained girl, though shaken to the depths of her soul. She had the hands of a child with closely clipped nails. While showing him the position of the prison, the radio station and the police station she still found time to tell him about the proposed meeting at midday and the sermon in the church.

'What's your name?' he asked.

'Maria.'

Tsvetkov ordered a squad to occupy the prison and release those held, told Sergeant Karambaev to occupy the radio station and went into the town hall; its doors were flung wide open and it was cluttered up with piles of documents, ration cards and notices on blue and pink paper.

About twenty people released from the prison appeared in the square. They could scarcely stay on their feet and did not carry so much as drag behind them along the ground, with their last ounce of strength, their dirty bags and rucksacks containing their personal effects.

'What's up with them?' Tsvetkov asked the mayor.

The latter shrugged his shoulders. 'The Gestapo ran the prison.'

'Maria, who are they?'

'Anti-fascists.' She got up from her typewriter and, running out into the square, spoke to them excitedly. In a child-like fashion her face expressed all her emotions. It now looked both frightened and joyful.

'Dr Harneck isn't there,' she reported, striking the palm of her left hand with her right fist. 'But . . . I don't know . . . there's another camp . . . we must look right away . . . .'

Sergeant Karambaev took a squad of men and three of the ex-prisoners and clambered on to a tank – to go to the camp.

'How do you plan to organise the town's food supplies?' Tsvetkov asked the mayor and the pastor, and in reply heard: 'Just as you like, Herr Commander.'

'I don't want the population to suffer any special difficulties.'

Corporal Zavileyko dashed up and reported: 'Hestimated forty-seven bodies, Comrade Lieutenant, five of what is locals.'

'Get the local people to bury them.'

The mayor mopped his brow with a handkerchief; his huge bald patch was ingeniously decked out in sparse hairs combed forward from the back of his head.

What an old woman, thought Tsvetkov. A serious person wouldn't be bothered with such nonsense now.

'The local people,' repeated the mayor. 'I don't know what you mean. Mobilise them? How?'

Behind his back Tsvetkov heard Maria's fist striking her palm. He got up and so did the Germans.

'Have you finished typing the order?'

'Oh, yes,' answered Maria.

'Baryshev, take the pastor to the radio transmitter, have him read the order to the population in your presence. Next, have the mayor and the members of the town council duplicate the order and post it up all over the town. Go on. And you . . .' He turned to Maria.

'Would you please have a word with the prisoners who've just been released? Sergeant Karambaev will help you give them something to eat. Put them up here, in the town hall, close to hand. Make me out a list of who they are, where they are from and why they were inside. OK?'

'Yes. Right away.'

'Wait a moment. That's not all. Organise through the council's administration the burial of the dead German soldiers and the civilians.'

'But how?' she asked, at a loss, repeating the mayor's question.

'I'll tell you how. Organise regional groups to help you. Appoint supervisors throughout the town ... Take them from the most respectable people ... and, well, I'm appointing you mayor of the town. Take over the premises on the first floor. Report to me in an hour on how things are going.'

Late in the evening Tsvetkov returned in the captured Opel car from Weber's clinic, which was the concentration camp's 'experimental base'. In the 'school equipment' section he had seen neat rows of skeletons, shelves of childrens, women's and men's skulls, preserved hearts and kidneys, but in the 'economy' section he saw packets of powdered bone and preparations of ash for botanical nurseries. Schöneberg's dahlias were blooming on the ashes of Slav lives, and perhaps it was to this circumstance that their exceptional beauty and strength, described at such length and so tenderly by the guidebook Maria had given him, were to be ascribed. As the old inhabitants had pointed out that day, before you got to the prisoner-of-war camp there was the camp for politicals. The bodies of communists were thus transformed into asters or narcissi or, in the form of skeletons, demonstrated the perfection of Aryan bone in German schools. And any schoolboy in Berlin or Dresden, when answering teacher's questions on anatomy, as he touched those scientifically demonstrative ribs, might have been touching the remains of his own father. The preserved heart of an underground resistance fighter destroyed by suffering could probably serve as an example of how a life unregimented and, therefore, bad, which did not look after itself, could be seen in the blood vessels and muscles ....

He sat at the wheel of the Opel, steering it carefully through the narrow, empty side-streets all similar to each other, distinguishing between them by the odd lorry abandoned by the Hitlerites, or the bodies of horses at the crossroads, or a smashed shop-window – by all that his eye could retain most quickly and easily.

'Stop, stop, Comrade Lieutenant,' said Corporal Zavileyko behind his back. 'We ought to turn down that street where there was that seven-ton truck with the German stuff on it.'

They went back a bit and slipped down the next side-street, but the seven-tonner, the landmark for where they should turn off for the town hall, was not there. Then they climbed out of the car and investigated the suspicious-looking expanse around, torches in hand. There were signs that the seven-tonner had actually been there recently; but had then been taken away, far off into those almost impassable streets, where it had finally disappeared.

As they quietly walked about shining their torches, the life of the apparently dead town unexpectedly exhibited itself. People in the houses were bustling about, moving furniture, banging doors, shifting ladders and clattering pots and pans.

'They're getting themselves fully kitted out,' said Zavileyko. 'I reckon a lot of people have cleared off; the flats are unattended so the neighbours aren't going to hang back . . .'

There were crowds of people by the town hall, just as during the day. Some of them wearing white and red armbands were giving orders, others without armbands but with white rosettes on their chests were obeying, writing things down in notebooks, and asking those in charge to repeat things.

In the town hall Tsvetkov saw an embarrassed Karambaev carrying a tray covered with a serviette.

'Must fortify Maria, Comrade Lieutenant,' he announced confidentially and went up to the first floor, his Herculean feet labouring under the weight of the unfamiliar burden, the cutlery clattering away.

The mayoress was asleep, curled up on the divan. A leg dangling over the edge revealed a darned stocking and a shoe with a neatly patched sole.

Karambaev patted the girl paternally on the back and tickled her behind the ear.

'Chairlady, come on, stoke up!' He said this several times in his growling whisper and then laughed when he caught the lieutenant's eyes.

'She's one of us [*nash element*],' he said, nodding at the sleeping girl.

Maria woke up lazily and unsuspectingly, like a child who knows that everything around will be favourable to its wakening. She hunched up a little, tucking her head in and smiling, as though she wanted it understood that she was not being woken at the proper time and that she intended to sleep as long as she liked; but, suddenly realising where she was, she jumped up quickly and, in embarrassment, started to tidy her dishevelled hair.

Meanwhile Karambaev reported that while the commander had been away there had been a number of serious incidents – a stock of liquor, half of it pilfered, had been discovered, two torch-bearers had been arrested, people looting a perfume shop had been detained, a few Hitlerite officers who had changed their uniforms for civilian clothes had been caught, and from the next morning there would be ration cards for the sale of bread.

Tsvetkov was pleased that Karambaev had taken such a personal interest in the restoration of civil order. Maria noted timidly that the representatives of the local council would be present not only when the bread was distributed but when it was baked, too. And that drinking-water could not be supplied to domestic users in their homes because of an accident at the pumping station. That there would be lighting until around midnight. And that . . .

'Don't you live locally?' asked Tsvetkov. 'Why don't you go home to rest?'

'Oh, Mummy would be frightened. I'm the mayoress, aren't I? You don't understand, yes? It's impossible for you to understand. And the other reason? I'm afraid myself.'

'What of?'

'Oh, I would be alone there. The mayoress can't rest so well there as here.' And she laughed shyly, as if apologising for taking the liberty of dozing on the divan in an official room among complete strangers.

The sound of breaking glass and the explosion of a hand grenade which followed it threw Tsvetkov into a corner of the hall. Karambaev dashed up to the broken window. Acrid smoke was swirling about the room and the heavy curtains at the windows blew about in the air, as though caught in a strong current. Tsvetkov rushed to the stairs and, groping for the banister, felt that his right hand was heavy and weak and that he could hardly clench his fingers.

The doctor, a thickset man with a grey, spiky crew-cut on a large, wrinkled head, who had been on duty at the commandant's office, bandaged the wound and assured him that the splinter had not damaged the bone.

His hands shook and great sticky beads of sweat ran down the wrinkles of his face.

'What are you so agitated about? Fräulein Maria, ask him why he is so worked up.'

She stood in the doorway looking at Tsvetkov and then anxiously towards the corridor, where those released from prison were discussing heatedly what had happened.

'He's afraid.'

'What of? Does he think we're going to shoot every tenth man? Or shoot you, Maria? After all, you are the mayoress, aren't you? You're responsible for civil order, aren't you?'

'Better to shoot me,' she answered, with such sincerity that even the doctor, who had not understood a word of their conversation, raised his astonished eyes to her.

'I made a mistake,' said Tsvetkov. 'I shouldn't have appointed you mayoress, Maria. It should have been an old person. And insisted on him handling all the riff-raff himself. But the mistake's been made now. You're the mayoress . . . . Who's responsible for your district?'

Without replying, Maria went out into the corridor and spoke to the people released from prison and the supervisors of each district. A minute later a few people wearing red armbands came out of the town hall, accompanied by soldiers.

Having finished the bandaging, the doctor wiped the sweat from his brow and asked Baryshev [the military interpreter earlier indisposed] to interpret for him.

'Any idiot can throw a bomb,' he said. 'My son – fifteen years old – he could also do it. You might ask why would he do it? It's the war. You've occupied the town. We're the defeated ones. People in defeat bear a lot of grudges, resentment. Their souls burn with revenge.'

Tsvetkov interrupted him. 'That's not true. It's my soul that is burning with revenge. Your sisters haven't been killed, your old father taken out and shot, your own home burnt and hundreds, thousands of other houses nearby.'

'I'm not talking about politics.'

'Neither am I talking about politics. Do you think banditry is normal?'

'I don't think anything, Commander. I'm just afraid that hundreds of innocent people will answer for the stupidity of just one man.'

'Yes, well, that's the way things are. The whole of Germany is answering for your Hitler.'

'I didn't like that gentleman, I didn't belong to his party and I don't bear responsibility for its policies.'

'Which party did you belong to, then, Doctor?'

'I'm outside politics.'

'So you hid in your hole and sat it out until we broke Hitler's backbone? Answer, Doctor.'

'Yes.'

'And you're proud of that?'

'I'm just stating a fact. I didn't like Nazism.'

'What would you prefer? If there was just a bit of Nazism, then you wouldn't be against it, eh? You're just against large doses of it. You're like a political homeopath: a grain of fascism is all right, useful; a handful is harmful. Is that it?'

'I'm not well up in politics, Commander; I've never had to conduct political discussions.'

'What's politics got to do with it? It's your fate, your life, your conscience. Or do you think that politics equals whatever's going on beyond the bounds of your conscience?'

'You're probably right, Commander. But I'm a man of a different culture and of an older generation than you.'

'What other culture, I'd like to know? What ideals were you brought up on, Doctor? Goethe, of course. Right? Faust? The striving of the spirit towards the celestial. Dreams of immortality. Well, Schiller, then probably? Which of his plays is your favourite? I prefer *William Tell*. I can still remember his soliloquy to this day.'

And Tsvetkov, with wrinkled brow and his gaze turned to the ceiling, recited eight lines almost without hesitation.

By now a lot of people had crowded into the room.

'Now let's get on to music. You're a Wagnerian, no doubt? But I've always preferred Schumann of the German composers – or even, if you like, Bach. I say "if you like" because I suppose Bach is a bit old hat from your point of view. But, most of all, I love Tchaikovsky. You people know him well.'

'The Fourth Symphony is marvellous,' whispered Maria.

'Oh, yes, yes,' confirmed the doctor.

'You see, we even have common tastes in music. Now painting. You won't know the ones I like – Repin, Serov – and if we go back to the classics, then probably Michelangelo is closest to me: I find Raphael too calm, devoid of strength. I don't know Rembrandt very well – we have a few of his works in the Hermitage – but he affects me with the force of the truth to life. You don't have any objections to Rembrandt, Doctor? I am glad.

'And now let's get on with the job!'

Pyotr Pavlenko 'Maria', *Literaturnaya gazeta*, 1972, no. 19

The second extract is taken from a work of some notoriety, *What Is It You Want, Then?* by Vsevolod Kochetov, published in 1969. Kochetov (1912–73) was a literary functionary, editor of the influential monthly journal *October* [*Oktyabr*] and the quintessence of ideological ultra-orthodoxy in Soviet letters after the death of Stalin. The son of a peasant, Kochetov worked as an agricultural scientist on collective farms in the 1930s. Wartime service on an army newspaper on the Leningrad front introduced him to journalism, a profession which he followed until the end of his life. Kochetov first made his name immediately after 1945 with the publication of collections of stories based on his experiences during the siege of Leningrad and with a novel, *The Zhurbins* (1952), the story of three generations of a Russian working-class family. Subsequently, in 1958 Kochetov published *The Brothers Yershov*, notable in that, amid the de-Stalinisation and liberalisation of the Khrushchev thaw, this book sounded a clear note of reaction and nostalgia for the old certainties of Stalin's days. As editor of *Oktyabr*, Kochetov strongly opposed the relatively liberal line of Tvardovsky's *Novy mir*, which championed Solzhenitsyn and other anti-Stalin writers.

His novel, *What Is It You Want, Then?*, serialised in Kochetov's own journal, is a remarkable tale. With its complex net of plots, stratagems, double-crossing and dirty tricks that are hatched by Western spies and saboteurs against the good, honest simple folk of the Soviet Union, it might appear to lack both credibility as well as literary merit. But Kochetov was remarkably skilful at playing on the fears and resentments that lurk just below the surface in the minds of many Soviet people in their attitudes to the West. His chauvinist neo-Stalinism also represented a strong current of opinion among the Soviet managerial and working classes.

Kochetov's world may seem very two-dimensional – and he was officially rapped over the knuckles for producing this effort in an era of détente – but does, however, provide a real insight into some aspects of Soviet thinking. There is the continued focus on 1941–5, on the existence of present-day enemies, and on the risks of again being lulled into a false sense of security. The novel argues that there is still every need for both political vigilance and high military expenditure. There is also an awareness that the younger generation might be less than wholly committed to the struggle.

WHAT IS IT YOU WANT, THEN?
Vsevolod Kochetov

[The year is 1969. Feliks the hero is an intelligent and idealistic man, who has chosen to work in an aircraft factory as an engineer.]

They often struck up conversations like this. Questions of literature and art excited the workers, technicians and engineers in the factory. It was as if they could discern beyond these specific issues, so remote from the production process, great political questions, as if you could hear the echoes of the struggle between two diametrically opposed worlds. Feliks listened to these discussions with great interest. To his mind, the lads from the workshop sometimes over-simplified, or occasionally made hasty judgements, but on the whole they understood everything correctly, exactly, and put a sound, practical interpretation on everything.

Feliks's factory was not one of those with its roots in history, in the eighteenth or nineteenth centuries. It had been built a few years before the outbreak of the Patriotic War, so as to provide the Red Army with aeroplanes of the latest design as fast as possible and in as great a quantity as possible. There were not as yet any second- or third-generation workers who might have settled round the factory in whole dynasties as they had at the old factories in the Urals, in Leningrad and even in Moscow itself. But, in addition to the factory collective being well run and having been in existence for three decades now, it had done a lot for defence during the war years, and had acquired its own style of work, its own culture. Practically no one working there had completed less than seven classes. And some had done eight, nine, or even the whole ten. [Basic education in the Soviet Union in the 1960s lasted eight years from age 7 to 15; two more years at a 'polytechnic' makes up the so-called ten-year school.] How many went to evening classes or did correspondence courses from the technical colleges or institutes of higher education! Of course, there were some dunces, a bit loutish, badly behaved, drink-ing, idling their lives away. You find that sort everywhere, even among engineers and above. But it was not those, the mediocrities, shiftless men, who set the tone at the factory. The people there thought, argued, wanted to sort out the problems of the day. Every-thing was their concern because they were the genuine masters of life, masters of the country, the creators of its present and future. Feliks liked the bubbling, busy factory atmosphere, the spirit of working comradeliness, the willingness to help each other, support each other, the spirit of rigorous justice applied when solving complex, acute human conflicts. Feliks had never seen anyone at the factory being patronising, patting someone on the head, but the workers' collective stood up for its own people. In the company of those around him Feliks felt confident, reliable, just as he did at home with his father.

The girls at the factory were marvellous. They were so different from the affected, dolled-up secretaries in other institutions, or from shop assistants whom he'd chanced to meet at times in a crowd round a table! Here they were not just creatures of a different sex, they were genuine equals of the men. If you went up to talk to one of them, she did not start swinging her hips in front of you, pulling enigmatic faces, putting herself forward one way or another as an object to be courted. She was just a person like any other, straightforward, unaffected, no airs and graces, no playing to the gallery. Even when one of them asked, 'Well, then, Feliks Sergeyevich, still single, then?' it didn't mean that he was being offered a fiancée, but that they understood the difficulties of his bachelor life. They might add: 'Don't worry, don't rush to put your head in the noose. Enjoy yourself. There'll be time enough later.' It was all joking, of course. The factory workers liked joking.

[At home Feliks and his father discuss modern youth and other topics.]

'But aren't you exaggerating, Dad? After all, those "National Democrats" have only 2 or 3 per cent in the German regional assemblies. You haven't mentioned the Italian fascists. In the last elections to parliament [1968] they won not just 2 or 3 but 5 whole per cent of the votes! They're having a torch-lit procession in Rome. They —'

'Italian fascism is Italian, and German fascism German. And they're both bad. But German fascism is the main danger for humanity. Experience has shown that. And, as regards percentages, you'll never deceive yourself with statistics that are here today and gone tomorrow. What do you know about Hitlerism?'

'What d'you mean? I know a lot . . . I know that —'

'I realise you can tell me about how the Nazis came to power and how they used it. Yes, you've read about that all right. The embers of the world war the Nazis started are still smouldering. More than twenty years afterwards. No, I'm not talking about that; it's well known. I'm talking about it sprouting again. And these are the shoots. The National Socialist German Workers Party – the NSDAP – was a gigantic machine. And what did it start with? With Anton Dreksler – incidentally a real worker, metalworker – who put together a little gang of regulars from one of the pubs in Munich. There were only six of them including him. Note that figure. Six! They called themselves "The German Workers' Party". One more turned up and joined those six. That was Adolf Hitler. They gave him party card number seven. Seven! And ten years later new members of the NSDAP had six-figure numbers on their membership cards. And in another ten years the Hitlerites had covered the lands of Europe with millions, tens of millions of corpses, as they translated Hitler's "party programme" into reality. Today they're marching again, Feliks, under their red banner with the white circle in the middle. All you need now is a black swastika in that white patch. The programme's the same, the same, if you ignore the minor tactical differences.'

'And do you think . . .?'

'I have to think. If we hadn't thought about the threat of German fascism back in the early 1930s the outcome of the Second World War might have been very different. As it was, everyone thought about it – from the Politburo of the Party, from Stalin, right down to the Pioneer groups, to the Octoberists [youth movements], not people just putting their hopes on one person, thinking individually about everything. You must think deeply today as well. West Germany is full of revanchists and nationalists. There are ample resources for the neo-Nazi party's growth. If those fine lads get any power, they'll only need a toehold in the Bundestag and the bugles of a new war will start ringing out. So you lads must be careful. You've put all your energies into pleasure and entertainment, that is, into consumer goods. The enthusiasm of consumerism! Of course, it's nice, pleasant. Enjoy yourselves. We weren't just making plough-shares, as they say. We weren't monks: we brought enough of you into the world. But let me tell you, Feliks, we weren't careless: night and day, at work, on holidays, we were preparing ourselves, preparing ourselves for the eventuality that sooner or later they would attack us; we learnt how to fight, to uphold our power, our system, our present and your future.'

'They attacked you suddenly, all the same, and you read everywhere that Stalin wasn't prepared for war; he lost his head.'

'I realise you're consciously raising the temperature of the conversation, fanning the flames, Feliks. After all, you're not stupid, you're clever. And so you must understand that, if it were really the way you say it was, that is, as you've read it was somewhere, you and I wouldn't be sitting here happily today by a window with newspapers in our hands. Your father and mother would have been burnt in one of the crematoria designated for the systematic extermination of Soviet people. And you, young man, and your friends would be working for the Germans as long as you had the strength, like oriental slaves. Don't repeat, Feliks, the conscious slanders of some people and the everyday twaddle of others. The main thing was done: our industry was prepared for war, ready to produce the most up-to-date weaponry on a massive scale, and our agriculture which produced the bread had acquired extraordinary strength – because it had been completely collectivised. There was no "fifth column" since the kulak had been liquidated in good time and all aspects of opposition in the Party smashed. That was the main thing, and that wasn't lost on anyone, Feliks.'

'So?'

'So, just this. Your job is to work towards our being outstandingly strong economically, outstandingly superior to the enemy ideologically, utterly convinced by the truth and rightness of our cause, and our being completely uncompromising in our struggle against those who seek to shake our confidence, undermine it and weaken it.'

'Quite a neat, clear-cut programme. But what is it that troubles you so much about contemporary youth? Let's get back to that question.'

'I'm telling you: carelessness, that is, not realising the dangers all around you, and, if you like, demanding too much, running ahead of yourselves; it's premature.'

'Feliks,' said Raisa Alekseevna, who had been listening in silence to their conversation, 'can you explain one thing to me? Why is it that kids today, for all the noise they make discussing everything freely, bandying all sorts of words about, when you look closely at them, they all look horribly alike and uninteresting?'

'Who are you thinking of, Mum?'

'Well, a crowd of them get together in our yard, laughing for hours on end right under our windows. Or you meet them in town, or among holidaymakers. They sometimes come up to you. Or you see films about them at the cinema, some miserable, dreary film.'

'You've been unlucky, Mum. There are all sorts. Including the kind you've been talking about. But there are others. There's quite a few kids who really think a lot about life. There's a lot that disturbs us, a lot. But it's true there's one or two people who are empty, colourless. You must have heard of the theory of reflection?'

'You mean how we perceive the exterior world?'

'You've heard, of course, that our brain doesn't produce anything itself?'

'Sorry, I hadn't. So you're saying the mind doesn't exist or something?'

'It's more complicated than that. The mind exists all right, don't worry. But the brain isn't the same as the mind, and by itself it doesn't produce anything, it only reflects reality.'

'Why is it in convolutions then?'

'Everything accumulates in them, in the convolutions, in the convolutions' cells. And the more that accumulates there the cleverer a man is, so to speak. So what does this mean, then? It means that when something new enters the brain it correlates one way and another in the enriched brain with what is already stored away there, and gets properly assessed accordingly. And if something new enters a brain which is unenriched with knowledge, then it correlates to nothing, and bounces about like a button in an empty tin can. There's a lot of truth in the saying "A little learning is a dangerous thing". Whatever a man's experience is, Mum, that is what is stored in his brain. Whatever I acquire, that's what I have. If I read Pushkin, I reflect Pushkin. If I read *The Week*, I reflect *The Week* [*Nedelya*, a popular Sunday magazine]. So if a brain receives real things, then it reflects real, deep, substantial things. If it receives nonsense, then it reflects nonsense, rubbish, trivia.'

'But you keep saying "I read, I read". But the written word is only a product of reflection,' said Sergey Antropovich.

'Even more to the point. Those who have heard, seen, experienced something then reflect it, inevitably distorting reality by reason of the individual peculiarities of our perceptive apparatus; and when we read the distorted reflection we in our turn distort it . . . Therefore a man's own life experience is absolutely essential for objectivity to be reflected in his brain without any intervening factor playing a part. We all need our own social, professional, political, scientific activity. That is the surest and most accurate way of enriching the brain with genuinely valuable material. Do you understand, Mum?'

'This is what I understand. That the kids we were talking about just now are still wet behind the ears, they haven't experienced anything themselves, and yet they know it all, because they've read it all, heard it all, seen it all in the cinema a dozen times. And what they've been fed has not, in its turn, been created by the most mature minds, but also by people who've seen nothing, experienced nothing and have also read and heard all sorts of distortions a dozen times.'

'Exactly. Well said, Mum! But, let's face it, maybe I've distorted a lot in explaining the mechanism to you. It was a simplification, an approximation.'

'Fair enough. But it's a pity to forget the idea that our brain is nothing more than just a sort of reflective device.'

'That's all right; we can come to terms with that,' chuckled Sergey Antropovich, 'as long as it reflects accurately.'

'Another thing,' said Feliks. 'You and Father often get worked up about what's on at the cinema or what gets published now and then in journals, and you're dissatisfied with certain books. You're right; it's just cluttering up the brain. And like any blockage you have to pay for it. If lakes and rivers are blocked, the fish die. Block up a flue and the room gets full of smoke and hurts your eyes. Clutter up the brain and you'll have trouble. We are always being told that gangster films in America help to increase the crime rate there. It's true. It can't be otherwise. Films like that must be reflected in man's brains and affect his consciousness. And those films of ours which are just grey, feeble, talentless, empty also have their effect. All right, they may not encourage gangsters. But they encourage greyness, feebleness, lack of talent and emptiness. Why blame youth, Father? Blame yourselves, dear adult comrades. Blame the people who allow state money to be spent on making empty, talentless films. Those who write glowing reviews of films like that and confuse the audiences. All those who are responsible for putting such products on the market. And you say we are careless! First of all you're the careless ones. Why have you opened the door to all this? It wasn't we who did it, was it? It was you, you! And why? You were apparently afraid that you'd be accused of conservatism, dogmatism . . . I hope you understand that when I say "you" I don't mean it personally? You were scared and retreated, withdrew from the commanding heights you held over the ideological enemy, into the liberal, swampy lowlands. And now, if you like, you're neither one thing nor the other. Neither conservatives nor liberals, and now you and all the halfway houses like you who've lost their heads just make people sick. That's what it means to grow old: acquiring nothing new while losing what's old or, more exactly, letting loudmouths and demagogues take it away from you.'

[Meanwhile, a former SS major in Nazi Germany, Uwe Klauberg, has been commissioned to find a specialist in Russian art who will take part in an expedition to the Soviet Union to collect material for a book on medieval Russian art. The project is being funded by a London publishing house and has official UNESCO approval. Klauberg finds his specialist in Italy, in the form of a Russian émigré. The two meet their project organisers and the remaining members of the expedition, the Americans Portia Brown and Eugene Ross, in London. Except for Saburov, the émigré, all have some ulterior motive for going to the Soviet Union. In an interview with one of the organisers, Klauberg is told about the underlying purposes of the trip. The organiser is speaking.]

'I've already warned you that we have nothing to do with espionage. We don't need any codes, and if we do talk about them we're only joking. Please listen carefully to me. It might be a little tiresome perhaps, but it's essential. The possibility of atomic and nuclear strikes against communism, which the generals are always making a song and dance about, is becoming more problematical year by year. We would suffer an attack similar to any we could deliver, possibly more powerful, and in a nuclear war there won't be any winners, only bodies. Or, more precisely, only their ashes. We don't as yet possess any new, more powerful means of destruction to use in a war to wipe out communism and, in the first instance, the Soviet Union. As it happens, there may never be such means. But, leaving that to one side, whether such means do or do not come about, it is our duty to finish off communism. It is our duty to annihilate it. Otherwise it will annihilate us. What didn't you Germans do, Klauberg, to defeat Russia? You tried mass extermination of the people, a scorched-earth policy, merciless terror, "Tiger" tanks, "Ferdinand" guns. And it was still you who were smashed, not the Russians. And why? Because you didn't undermine the Soviet system beforehand. You didn't attach any importance to it. You ran up against a monolith, against firm stone walls. Maybe you were hoping for a spontaneous rising of the kulaks, as the Russians used to call their rich peasants? But the communists had by then expropriated the kulaks and you had only the remnants of them – the appointed village elders, *polizei* [Russians who collaborated, as policemen, under the German occupation], and others like that. Were you putting your hopes in the old intelligentsia? By then it had no influence. It had dissolved in the new worker-peasant intelligentsia and had long since changed its own views in so far as the communists had created all the conditions for its life and work. Were you putting your hopes in the political opponents of Bolshevism – Trotskyists, Mensheviks and others? The Bolsheviks had promptly smashed them, spread them to the four winds. Yes, it's right and proper I should be doing your reasoning for you! You didn't even think about any of this. Your secret documents said only one thing: destroy, destroy. A pretty stupid, ham-fisted programme. If you destroy one man, the ten left behind who've seen what's been done will resist even more desperately. Destroy a million and 10 million will start fighting you with three times the bitterness they had before. An unreliable method. The best minds in the West these days are working on the problems of how to dismantle communism, in advance, and, first and foremost, how to dismantle present-day Soviet society.'

The speaker poured himself some soda water, took a few sips and then dried his lips with his handkerchief.

'So,' he continued, 'the work is coming from all directions and going in all directions. The communists have always been exceptionally strong ideologically, they have the upper hand as regards the unshakeability of their convictions, as regards a feeling of being right in literally everything. Their awareness of being encircled by capitalists has bolstered their sense of unity. It has mobilised them, kept them tense, ready for anything. You could not fault it anywhere. These days there are one or two hopeful signs. We exploited the dethroning of Stalin with exceptional skill. Together with the over-throwing of Stalin, we managed to ... But that, gentlemen, demanded the work of hundreds of radio stations, thousands of publications, thousands and thousands of propagandists, millions and millions, hundreds of millions of dollars. So with the fall of Stalin, let me go on, we managed to shake the faith that certain minds had in the cause which had been everyone's for thirty years under the leadership of this man. A great wise man of our time – forgive me for not mentioning his name – once said: "De-Stalinisation is a fulcrum which we could use to topple the communist world." Of course, the Russians realised all this, too. In the last few years they've renewed the communist offensive. And that's dangerous. They mustn't be allowed to win our minds again. Our task today is to keep up the attack, use it to bring down the "iron curtain" and, as they say, build bridges everywhere. What are we doing to this end? We're trying to flood their cinema with our own products, we're sending them pop singers and dancers, we— In a nutshell, their strict communist aesthetics are being eroded. And your "operation", Herr Klauberg,' he said in faultless German, 'is to serve as one of the bridges, one of the Trojan horses which we are constantly presenting to our Party friends in Moscow [i.e. de-Stalinisers]!'

[In Italy, Lera, a Russian girl married to an Italian communist lawyer, Benito Spada, whom she met when he was a student in Moscow, meets a visiting Soviet writer, Bulatov. Lera is deeply unhappy in her marriage and very homesick.]

At the end of the evening Bulatov spoke. He spoke of the features common to the Russian and Italian peoples, of the solidarity of workers throughout the world, of how he believed in a system on earth whereby there would be no frontiers between states, and then people with different languages would start to communicate more often and would produce a single language common to all mankind. And no one, no hostile publishing houses, no monitoring organisa-tions, could prevent the free exchange of what was best in the cultures of different peoples.

Then they all embraced again and no one wanted the party to break up.

On the way to the hotel, Bulatov started to tell Lera how marvel-lous the people had been today and how good it had been that they had arranged the get-together.

'The worst thing, the most useless thing, is when you visit another country and you don't meet the people, don't see their real life. Being just a tourist and seeing only what the guides and guidebooks tell you. But obviously you must see that, too. For example, is there anything in Turin that one really shouldn't miss?'

'Yes, there is. A lot. It depends how much time you have.'

'Maybe a day. Two with a bit of luck.'

'Oh, so little! Then at least visit the Royal Palace . . . No, better still, the Egyptian Museum. It's very interesting. The richest collection outside Egypt. The local museum here isn't as well known as, say, the Louvre, or the museums in London, like the British Museum, but they can't hold a candle to the one here as far as the Egyptian collection is concerned. It was made up by various people from things brought back from Napoleon's Egyptian campaign. Please see it.'

'If you agree to be my guide, I can spare an hour or two tomorrow morning. Can you make it?'

'Of course! Don't even ask. It's so miserable here far from home, from Moscow. You can't imagine how glad I am.'

Before returning to the hotel, Bulatov gave Lera a lift to her block. She glanced up at the windows of her flat – dark. Damn him, damn Benito, let him demonstrate his displeasure. Come what may, he couldn't spoil her excellent mood today. Today she had been with the real people of Italy. Not Benito's parents and his infrequent visitors and white-collar friends.

It was one o'clock; there was nothing to lose and no point in hurrying. Lera walked up and down in front of the house in the dark, thinking and thinking. What kind of a communist was Benito really? Her husband seemed the most commonplace Italian, Mr Average. Benito Spada and the communists of Italy – nothing in common! She'd seen real communists today. They were people with whom she found a common language so easily; they were people who were interested in everything that went on in the Soviet Union, who saw in the Soviet Union an instructive example for themselves. And people like Benito only ruin the cause of the Party: they doubt everything; in their opinion everything is wrong; they disapprove of everything. Why had Benito joined the Party? Was Maria Antonioni really right, that it was just the fashion?

Lera's thoughts followed a long and complicated path from her Benito to Bulatov, whom Benito had referred to with such acute distaste. Bulatov? How easily he had talked with that group of Turin workers, how they had all liked his simplicity and sincerity. Where was the 'darling of the personality cult' in him? What a way to run down someone without knowing or even trying to know him!

When Lera went into the house, Spada asked in the dark: 'Well, then, did you rub shoulders with your fellow-countryman? Flaunt yourself in front of the eminent man-about-town?'

'Yes,' she answered calmly. 'He likes me. Tomorrow we're going sightseeing together. He said he doesn't need a better guide.'

'You're not going anywhere!' shouted Spada suddenly, turning on the light. He was lying on the divan, still with his clothes on. That meant he'd been waiting, fuming.

'Yes, I am. We've already fixed it.'

'I won't let you. I'll lock the doors and that'll be the end of your trip. That's all there is to it. And I'll write to Moscow, to the Writers' Union, to their Party organisation, to the Central Committee. I'll tell them what that . . . that gadabout gets up to here. Where have you been with him till two o'clock in the morning, you tart?'

'Where do you think, dear? You know about these things. You get about, too. We were in a restaurant, then in his hotel room. Drinking coffee. In the Liguria on Carlo Felice Street.' Lera told him they were in the best hotel in Turin, although the group that Bulatov was with wasn't staying there at all but in the second-class Great Mogol Hotel.

Humming a catchy little tune, Lera started to undress, trying by all manner of means to pretend that she had really just done all the night-spots in Turin with a man.

'I'll give you a good hiding, you hear!' said Spada, leaping towards her, his fists raised.

'You? Hit me?' she laughed. 'I'll go and tell your boss that you beat your wife, and they'll reduce your salary. You can't beat your wife in a free country, dear, in the land of genuine democracy. And, anyway, you're a communist, a revolutionary, the bearer of a new morality. You can't, you can't.'

He started to swear in Italian. The dirtiest oaths, such as only that sonorous language knows, rained down on Lera. But swearwords in a foreign language don't seem at all the same as they do in your own language. Lera started to laugh. Spada snatched the pillow from the divan and was about to hurl it at Lera but then threw it on the floor. He grabbed a china Martini ashtray from the table and smashed it on the ground. The pieces went everywhere. He was having tantrums, throwing everything in sight on the floor.

Every knick-knack that was smashed just made Lera more amused. And, strangely enough, she didn't mind any of it. Not a single article in the house, it seemed, could she regard as hers; it was all alien, foreign, belonging not to her, but to this pot-bellied little nutcase with black spots in his eyes instead of pupils.

Lera hated staying at home. For days on end often with Tolik [her little boy], but sometimes leaving him with Signora Antonioni, she wandered the streets. All around her she saw a heavy, stone, alien city, with its monuments, cathedrals, palaces, parades of shops. She remembered her first days in Italy when she couldn't tear herself away from the shop windows crammed with bright, beautiful things, all of which she wanted to buy, put on, bring home, admiring them and herself wearing them in the mirror. Now she went past without even glancing at this garish, glass-encased, consumer tyranny. There in the shop windows, they were real Italian things – Italian! – shoes, the best in the world, fashionable, just asking to be bought. In Moscow the very thought of such shoes had driven her and her friends mad. And the cosmetics, imported from Paris – perfume, lipstick, nail varnish, eye liner, mascara. Lingerie, just like the sea foam that Aphrodite, goddess of love, sprang from. All the colours, the shades, frilly or plain, loose or close-fitting. Lots and lots of it, so much it was too much. And she didn't need any of it; it could all disappear without trace. Just to go home, home, to your own people, to your family who understood you and who really need you. Usually when she spoke about her parents Lera said, 'My mother', 'My father'. But now she thought about them as in the old days when she was a little girl: 'Mummy', 'Daddy'. She wanted with all her heart just to get back to Mummy and Daddy. 'Mummy!' Tolik squealed at her side now and then, clutching her skirt. 'Mummy!' Everything inside Lera cried: 'Whatever have I done? Why am I here?' The scenes of the repulsive scandal that Spada caused that day when he locked her indoors kept coming back to her relentlessly. He'd come home as usual after four o'clock.

'Yes,' he shouted from the doorstep. 'You can curse at me if you like. I accidentally popped all our keys in my pocket. Funny thing.'

'Yes, a pretty disgusting funny thing,' agreed Lera. 'We had a similar case about fifteen years ago in the Soviet Union, in Kiev. Some jealous idiot left the house and nailed up the door so that his wife couldn't get out. There were articles in the papers about it. Then he was taken to court.'

'Pardon me, but what for?' inquired Spada with exaggerated gallantry. 'In your country they like taking people to court for works of literature [a reference to the Daniel–Sinyavsky trial in 1966]. So what was it for in this case?'

'For cruelty, for having the morals of a serf-owner, for violation of our Constitution.'

'Ha, ha, are you going to summons me?'

'No, I won't. In your country you'll never get at the truth. I had plenty of time today. I poked about in those books you keep ordering from Paris, London and New York. You read Trotsky.'

'Yes, Trotsky! That name's like a red rag to a bull. You start seething with fury when you hear anything about him. But he called for a more sensible relationship between the classes: without blood, barricades, and without some people crushing and coercing others.'

'Of course, he was against the dictatorship of the proletariat, and that's all there is to it,' said Lera mockingly. 'Oh, you really are a great Marxist, aren't you!'

'No, he wasn't against the dictatorship of the proletariat! That's slander!' shouted Spada even more furiously.

'Do me a favour!' said Lera and thumbed through a book he'd just received from London by some 'expert' on the history of the Communist Party of the Soviet Union, one L. Shapiro [*The Communist Party of the Soviet Union*, London, 1959; generally regarded in the West as the most authoritative book on the subject]. 'Here's what Trotsky had to say at the Second Congress of the RSDLP [Russian Social Democratic Labour Party, 1903; the predecessor of the Soviet Communist Party]: "The dictatorship of the proletariat will not be a conspiratorial 'seizure of power', but the political rule of the organised working class, comprising the majority of nations." Where is there such a situation and is it possible for the working class to comprise the majority of nations? What rubbish! If Lenin had waited for this, for the majority of the working class, Kerensky [1881–1970, Prime Minister in the Provisional Government of 1917] would still be in power. He's still alive, so it seems. And what does "a conspiratorial 'seizure of power' " mean? Oh, stop hopping up and down, stop it! Sit still or stand still for just a minute. That's enough jumping about. Let me say something. Or are you the only orator here? This Trotsky of yours was against the party Lenin created. Lenin created precisely a conspiratorial party which might work amongst the masses unbeknown to Tsarist power, and prepare the revolution. But Trotsky wanted parliamentary, legal chit-chat and no action. Lenin called him "Balalaykin"! And Balalaykin would have ruined everything and there would have been no proletarian revolution in Russia.'

[Through the good offices of the writer Bulatov, Lera returns home to Russia and eventually marries the hero, Feliks. The art-history delegation collapses. Portia Brown, who turns out to be the daughter of an anti-Soviet Russian émigré writer who collaborated with the Germans in the war, is expelled for pursuing her task of undermining Soviet morality rather too vigorously, mainly late at night. Klauberg, the ex-Nazi, leaves, haunted by the crimes he committed during the war. Saburov, the returning émigré, sadly realises that he has lost his birthright and goes back to Italy. Another plot involves the son of

Aleksandr Zarodov, the affluent editor of a Moscow journal special-
ising in art history. He leads an idle life and devotes much time to
black-market activities, notably in the role of go-between in the
illegal sale of icons. In the end he gets his comeuppance at the hands
of Klauberg, in the form of a brutal physical assault and a long
lecture from the fundamentally decent émigré, Saburov, querying his
values. 'What is it you want, then?' asks Saburov. 'Do you want your
country to be rid of the Soviet regime? Do you want another war to
begin so that you will suffer defeat and be subjected to a new order
established by some neo-fascists? Do you want the Russians and
other Soviet nationalities to be made into fertilisers for European or
American soil?']

Vsevolod Kochetov, *What Is It You Want, Then?* [*Chego zhe ty
khochesh?*], *Oktyabr*, 1969, nos 9–11

Further Reading

A useful general account of 1941–5 is A. Werth's *Russia at War* (London,
1964). An excellent discussion of the military and its importance in Soviet
politics is to be found in T. Colton's *Commissars, Commanders and Civilian
Authority* (Cambridge, Mass., 1979).

Soviet literary treatment of 1941–5 is almost endless, but among works
available in English are K. Simonov, *The Living and the Dead* (New York,
1968); A. Solzhenitsyn, 'Incident at Krechetovka Station' in *We Never Make
Mistakes* (London, 1972); Yu. Bondaryev, *The Hot Snow* (Moscow, 1976);
and V. Nekrasov, *Front Line Stalingrad* (London; 1962).

A notable account of the German occupation of the Ukraine is *Babi Yar* by
A. Anatoli (A. Kuznetsov) (London, 1970). This incorporates in heavy type
the sections censored when it was originally published in the Soviet Union in
1966.

Two works by V. Bykov in translation are *The Ordeal* (London, 1972)
and *Pack of Wolves* (New York, 1981). *What Is It You Want, Then?* by V.
Kochetov has been abbreviated and edited by M. Glenny for the Open
University in *Selected Readings in Soviet Literature* (Milton Keynes, 1976).
There are a number of tales of army life in V. Voynovich's *In Plain Russian*
(New York, 1979).

A rather more critical account of the Soviet occupation of Germany than
in Pavlenko's extract is to be found in the memoir *No Jail for Thought* by L.
Kopelev (London, 1977; published in Philadelphia, Pa, 1977, as *To Be
Preserved for Ever*).

4

The Communist Party and Political Leadership

In theory the powers and functions of the Communist Party are very clear. As Article 6 of the 1977 Soviet Constitution spells out, the Party is 'the leading and guiding force of Soviet society, and the nucleus of its political system', directing 'the great constructive work of the Soviet people' and imparting a 'planned systematic and theoretically substantiated character to their struggle for the victory of communism'. This view is long established, deriving at least in part from Lenin's directive in *What Is To Be Done?* (1902) that the Bolsheviks should be a disciplined, organised party, the vanguard of revolution. It is also a description of the Party that is widely understood and accepted in normal Soviet life. The Party in general and its leaders in particular are invested with great power and authority. Party membership, too, bestows status and privilege and is much sought after.

In practice, of course, things are somewhat more complicated. The relationship between Party and people and between Party and state organisations is complex and shifting, having changed in quite significant ways since the death of Stalin, as well as since the fall of Khrushchev. Furthermore, a party with over 18 million members inevitably includes a very large majority with little real power, and raises serious questions about exactly where such a party begins and ends. In addition, the theoretical role of the Party to 'direct but not supplant' specialist state agencies does not always operate in practice, if only because Party and state are not separate and parallel but interdependent and overlapping structures.

Indeed, it is at least arguable that the Soviet Communist Party, far from being a *sui generis* totalitarian machine, functions in some respects like political parties in pluralist systems. Despite the Party's monopoly of ideological rectitude and ultimate political power, it cannot take its position or authority for granted. Both depend in

large measure on the Party's continuous ability to govern successfully, as measured, for example, by political stability or economic
growth. The routes to such success, however, are far from clear; a
complex modern society leads to the creation of a great variety of
specific interests, some of them in conflict with others. As a consequence, the Party increasingly appears to act as the mediator
between powerful interests rather than as the fount of all political
wisdom.

One explanation for this apparent loss of dynamism by the Party
may be the nomenclature system, the recruitment of personnel on the
basis of political loyalty rather than proven talent or specific expertise, which has been described as a syndrome of 'bureaucratic degen-
eracy'. But equally it is a reflection of the fact that the Soviet Union is
a complex polity with some intractable problems. The Party has
power and authority beyond measure, is heir to a long tradition of
arbitrary centralised rule and, through its control of the media, the
law and the secret police, affects the lives of all Soviet citizens. At the
same time, it appears increasingly as a conservative rather than a
radical or initiating force, and often lacks the ability to translate into
reality a coherent and distinctive set of policies 'for the victory of
communism'.

In the extracts that follow we seek to give concrete illustrations of
these related themes of power and impotence, which are of course
also analysed in the abstract by Aleksandr Zinoviev in the passage to
be found in Chapter 1.

Daniil Granin (born 1918), the author of the first extract, is a noted
and long-established Leningrad writer, currently much concerned
about the problems of modern technology and the environment. His
first book was published in 1949; *The Picture*, from which the
extract here is taken, in 1980. Granin wrote one of the key works of
the Khrushchev thaw, *An Opinion of One's Own*, in 1956. Its
central theme – that one should stand up for what one believes to be
right, that courage and conscience are essential attributes – is one
that Granin has frequently explored. *An Opinion of One's Own* told
of a man who, even when he reached a position of real power, found
that he had not the courage of his own convictions and could not
speak out for fear of retribution from above. Granin's portrait,
though critical, was sympathetic to the problems of individual conscience and power, and *The Picture* similarly seeks to deal with the
conflicting pressures exerted on a public figure.

In a sympathetic portrait of a man called Losev, a provincial Party
boss, the mayor or chairman of the town Soviet, Granin highlights

the complexities and uncertainties of leadership. Losev encounters conflicts over priorities and clashes with hierarchical superiors. He also has inner worries brought on by the knowledge that, like many Party functionaries, he is not a breed apart, but has to deal with the lives of people he actually knows. Losev's town is remote and in poor shape economically. A picture of the town by a famous artist unexpectedly becomes the town's property. Inspired by the picture, Losev seeks to preserve the old creek area it depicts, even at the expense of losing a new calculator factory planned for that very site. Meanwhile he must also fight for more housing and better wages, for concrete short-term benefits, as well as deal with the broader issue of the town's environmental heritage. Losev does eventually achieve his immediate ambitions, but at the price of his earlier certainties about life, and at the cost of his job. The novel raises some central questions about leadership, not least the need to juggle conflicting demands. As *Literaturnaya gazeta* pointed out when *The Picture* was published, 'the novel can't help reminding you of Lake Baykal' (the most celebrated Soviet environmental controversy of modern times, and a clear example of the Party's left hand not knowing how to control its right hand).

It is worth noting that the question of housing, discussed here, is nationally one of the largest problems facing the Party. Within the past twenty years most urban Soviet citizens (now two-thirds of the nation) have moved into new apartments – an enormous achievement. However, for several reasons, including continued heavy migration from the countryside, early marriage and a rapidly increasing divorce rate (itself partly a by-product of inadequate housing), demand appears to be insatiable.

THE PICTURE

Daniil Granin

The sun was not dazzling. You could look at its dull surface, and it was as though the sun itself was scanning the earth and the day not yet begun through which it was to roll and roll right to the other end of the earth. You could see a long way from the bridge. The roofs covered in lathing had a silvery, lively sheen that was not enough for the grey, opaque slate. In the new block of flats opposite on almost every floor there were flowers in green boxes turning towards the sun. The block, decorated with flowers and curtains, looked even newer than it was. The spirit of being lived in had improved its appearance. Its lower part was faced with brown tiling. What made the block look especially nice were the decorative iron railings on the balconies; it had taken a lot of time and trouble to get them. The block was Losev's pride. A dozen more beauties like this one and the town would be transformed. Two years earlier Losev had been reprimanded over this block, but the reprimand had been revoked recently, while the housing block remained and was still standing there, the better to comfort him should similar trouble arise. Losev stood admiring it, and it warmed the cockles of his heart. If he were asked what the main worry of his life was, or the main business, or, rather, the main desire, without a second thought he would answer: to have a housing block like this *to spare*. Literally, *to spare*. So that there would be the keys to the empty flats in one unoccupied, spare block hanging up in the glass cabinet in his office. If a family or a visiting specialist arrives in town, you just say: There you are, have a flat!

Everywhere in his job he kept running into the bloody problem of housing. The shortage of living-space tormented him relentlessly day in and day out. The building programme, the materials, the housing applications, and the majority of people who came to his 'surgeries' – it was all to do with finding a place to live. People waited for flats, for a room, for several years; the queue did not get any shorter. It was a kind of curse. Housing blocks were built one after another; old wooden houses were demolished and reinforced concrete, prefabricated ones – faster and faster – appeared in their place. They brought in wall panels and ready-made sections . . . Sometimes by putting on a spurt they managed to shorten the waiting-list, but afterwards it just grew longer again, like a sort of hydra. He was in despair. No town had grown so much as Lykov. Worse still, the population had grown up in a flash. All the neighbourhood kids, who had only just been born, were suddenly shaving or putting on make-up and then getting married, and sitting in his office – plump, doleful madonnas and strapping great lads with moustaches – all asking for flats. Their rapid growth and their fecundity horrified him. He was besieged on all sides by queue-jumpers; everyone's circumstances were urgent, catastrophic, unique. After each surgery he felt drained. They shouted at him, threw hysterics in front of him, wept quietly, not even honouring him with acrimonious words. They looked at him in supplication, brought their children to him, banged their crutches on his desk. His own impatience wore him out, the impossibility of helping them when help was essential. A tuberculosis case who had to be kept separate from children . . . The perilous state of the roof in an old wooden house . . . The father-in-law's always getting at me, keeps fighting, I'm at the end of my tether, if you don't do something, I'll hang myself, I'm not joking, you'll see I'll hang myself, I can't go on living like this any more . . . My husband's divorced me and has moved the other woman in – and in the same room as the children and the old folk . . . He calmed them down, made promises, started scraping the barrel for them, but then, for example, the head doctor of the maternity hospital, of the very one that is now under construction, comes along and announces that he has been offered an excellent job in the Urals, in a new town, a detached cottage, etc., etc., but he is prepared to stay if he can be given a three-roomed flat. What could you do? He's an excellent doctor; you can't let him go. They shouted at Losev and told him the doctor was a liar, a blackmailer, greedy, how dare he, but all the howling was in vain, the three-roomed flat had to be given – and everything came crashing down, all the calculations, the promises, all turned to dust. He himself was prepared to abuse the doctor, but what for? The doctor had a wife and two sons. Why should they turn down a cottage. What for? Then came the collective complaint about the chairman of the town executive committee, who was not fulfilling his promises, was improving the housing conditions of a certain party at the expense of those who were already on the waiting-list, at the expense of war invalids . . . The complaint was examined, he was summoned, given a warning. How could you? For such a breach of regulations, you ought to be . . . And he listened and agreed and promised to take note, yet they still took his name, because they could not let the matter go just like that.

He noticed people being ruined by long-term overcrowding and congestion, constantly getting irritated over having to share a kitchen or a washbasin, and never having any privacy. He sometimes suffered nightmares – wooden houses bulging with people, the roofs being forced off, pushing and shoving, floorboards cracking. Children flying out the windows, residents hanging on at the doorways as on an overcrowded tram . . .

Strange as it may seem, sometimes it was easier to refuse a flat than it was to give one. When one of those who had been longing for a flat finally received one, there was a brief flash of joy, but how he had had to stretch and strain himself and his staff before that, demanding to know all the pros and cons, why it should go to so-and-so and not to someone else, and who was in greater need; he longed to be able to weigh up on inconceivably accurate scales degrees of justice which cannot be weighed – illness, domestic grounds or worse: mouldy damp on the walls, or the darkness of the basement rooms, or the draughts coming from the cracks in the temporary masonry. Every time he was stuck with an impossible choice – either old people who at the end of their lives deserved to live out their days in a dry, spacious flat, or youngsters who worked hard all day, who sometime, if not now, ought to have a bit of enjoyment . . . The trouble was, he knew them all, both the old folk and the young: the town was too small.

There were days when he sank into gloom: it seemed to him that all in all he was to blame; he could not get round the allocation grants, could not persuade the house-building consortium to play ball, could not find any carpenters.

No, out of all the wishes in the world, out of all the miracles, he would choose just to have an extra housing block, built and set aside, completed ahead of schedule – a magical, unchangeable rouble. One day there would be a block like that in Lykov. His dream would come true – for some other mayor.

At the end of the bridge by a street-lamp stood a long-haired lad in a nylon windcheater whom he did not know. He had a scarf round his neck.

'Give us a smoke,' he said.

'You don't ask like that,' said Losev, looking straight at him. 'Say, please!' and he went past.

The path led him over a hillside by the edge of some sheds, vegetable plots, boarded toilets, chicken runs and iron garages. The honeysuckle bushes shook heavy dew on him. The old houses rose up one behind the other on the incline; they were former private residences decorated with carved wood and, behind them, a bit newer, were one-storey brick houses with little mansards and a main entrance. Now the towpath started, cobblestones, poplar-trees and lilac. Here there were quite old estates, pretentious, with verandas, little triangles of stained glass, houses with turrets, little balconies, fancy windows, shutters. Each time Losev picked out and mentally restored the most beautiful of them, painted them blue and white, coffee and yellow, so as to highlight the carved wood, the protuberances; he re-covered the roofs with iron. Now his houses were becoming as smart as those in the old picture postcards he had admired at Polivanov's [an old art collector]. There were also houses remaining that were remarkable for something; interposed here and there, they preserved the old character of the town. They conserved its usual appearance, the well-known view from the river. He delighted in their restoration, although he knew they were doomed. A block of four-storeyed houses and a central nine-storeyed high-rise were already planned for this site.

And all those, in turn, plot by plot would be cleared away, bulldozed into a heap, and the mechanical diggers would dump them on the tip-up trucks. A heap of discarded wood, a jumble of bricks and dust – that's all that would be left of this house, its rooms, its stairs, its creaks in the night, its winter warmth, its carvings on the door jambs, its attics, stones, its porches, benches . . . He himself had grown up in that house, had loved its homeliness with all its nooks and corners, lumber rooms, and window sills. The attic where all the unwanted junk accumulated over the years – the kids' delight, an attic smelling of onions, apples, raspberries, drying here every autumn, the smell of the beech-twig besom, old magazines, unused wallpaper . . . With the cobwebs thick with dust, like grey flannelette. The basement cellar with the staves from old barrels, something dripping, scuffling, a spare Dutch tile for the stoves . . . A house is not just a hut. A town house always has a long history, the various owners . . . For example, the priest Nikandr used to live in their house; he left behind the iron lamps of dark-blue glass and a large press whose purpose no one knew. And after the war the priest's sister showed up and started to look in the garden for chronicles her father Nikandr had once buried there. And each house was a personality, each had its own story to tell; you could tell the owner's tastes and endeavours by his house.

Losev loved these houses and did not love them. All the hassle and headaches the owners of that one with the tiled roof had given him until he had had the old outhouses removed which were spoiling its appearance. And next door, behind the house of the retired colonel, there were four strands of barbed wire instead of a fence. All his persuasion had had no effect. Losev had asked him in a friendly enough manner, via the military commissar as well, and then tried to embarrass him in front of everyone: people at the front defended themselves from the fascists with obstacles like that! And in reply the colonel said: When you can guarantee some educational work for the youngsters so that they stop coming after my blackcurrants, then you can start demanding . . . It took police intervention for something to be done. Then for more than a year afterwards he was having to defend himself against the complaints made against him.

His felt gym shoes were damp. Losev had put them on to go out into the yard first thing that morning, feeling worn out after a sleepless night ful! of buzzing gnats. He stood there, hanging around, and then, without noticing his shoes, strode up the street, led on by the colours of the dawn.

Slipping off the gym shoes, he walked on, barefoot. The cold of the dew stung his feet. Pad barefoot over the ground at the crack of dawn, pad, pad, and the joy of having no one nagging you about watching your health, or pestering you with their questions and inquiring glances.

He could feel the pine needles on his bare skin, soft, always warmish, the cones, the gravel, the tickling, prickly grass. How long ago it had been the last time he had walked barefoot along the river bank. Or, no, how recent it had been.

Could this silence, filled with pink hue, this fast-growing sun, this beauty, all really be created every morning? The dawns, the sunrises, took place while he was sleeping; year in and year out this magnificent occurrence was achieved without him. He had clean forgotten what the sunrise created each morning. And this would continue, long after Losev was no more. Just as this morning did not exist for his mother. He saw his own absence with absolute clarity in the fresh, morning world, this town glistening with dew, all without him. His town, now preoccupied with other worries. The residence by the post office would become an ordinary housing block, and the brown tiles and balcony railings which were now well nigh impossible to get would become commonplace.

Of course Losev wanted people to remember him, but for that, he reckoned, you had to be a creator, an artist or architect, for example. And a mayor is not a creative character. But then he remembered Zhmurin [a pre-revolutionary governor of the town and a gifted architect] and again felt sympathy for this man he did not even know. Losev, as it were, felt his presence in the preserved beauty of the town, in the elegance of the Uspensky church, in the park with the long, overgrown pond . . . See, they remember Zhmurin, only a few, but they still remember, and he, Losev, recalled him today through this beauty. It was quite possible that Zhmurin used to walk along this very path of an early morning, and had the same dreams about his town.

Suddenly he had an unpleasant feeling; it had come from somewhere definite and he turned round and met a gaze from under a grey headscarf, pulled well down. The eyes followed him sullenly, with a stubbornly nasty expression. The woman nodded, grunted something indistinctly, and Losev answered mechanically. He went on several paces, then thought for a moment and turned round. The woman was going down the hill, towards the wooden pathway, and she was holding a large basket of laundry. The canvas coat hid her figure, which was usually clad in a dark two-piece costume, and she always wore a hat on top of her abundant hair, a little cap, a nice little thing. She always said hullo to you cheerfully, greeting you with her friendly smile. She was unattractive, and was shy because of this, but at her job in the library she felt more confident, and even as a little boy with a certain shameful pleasure he used to watch her moving between the cramped bookshelves in the library, her breasts brushing against them. It was an infatuation, and such that on one occasion he spilt ink on her desk. He could not for the life of him understand now why he had done it, but he remembered rushing to finish a book so that he could go back to the library sooner. Over the years her figure had become heavy and angular, but it had happened gradually and even now Losev still saw the shy, unattractive slip of a girl in her. She came from the Ukraine; her husband, a submariner, was killed towards the end of the war, and so she had stayed here. Now Lyubov Vadimovna was in charge of the town library, and set up all the exhibitions. A few months ago she had sent in an application for a pay rise. Losev noticed immediately that she had not come along in person, although she had come on other people's business more than once, and he was on the point of taking up cudgels on her behalf when it became clear that it could only be done either by finding her a special establishment post or getting the library up-graded to a higher category. The regional bosses asked him to postpone the question and he did; there were plenty of things that had to be put off. Now he remembered that since then he had managed to get a few people pay rises, but he was still postponing Lyubov Vadimovna's case, knowing that she would not kick up a fuss; she was too tactful for that sort of thing. Say what you like, it always worked out that the people satisfied first and foremost were the persistent, cheeky, pushing complainers whom he did not respect but who might give him trouble. Lyubov Vadimovna could not cause any trouble; she only knew how to petition for other people. She once applied for a garden allotment and suffered and worried so much, her strained, sheepish face was so flushed, her voice so quiet that you could not make out what she was mumbling. He had always reckoned that she would wait. It was easy to refuse people like her; they always understood, were always prepared to see the other side of the problem. And, anyway, where would she go? She was one of those activists who were dedicated to the town and to their work to such an extent that they needed no incentives and were always thought of last [i.e. a member of the *aktiv*, a distinct category of the most active members of the Party and other organisations, usually those in 'responsible posts']. When Losev tried to alter this foolish rule it turned out that a flat had to be given to so-and-so because in answer to his letters there had been phone calls from the regional authorities, they were afraid that someone else would take to drink, and a pay rise had to be found for a works superintendent who was threatening otherwise to get a job in a factory . . . And almost every time people like Lyubov Vadimovna were passed over . . .

She had not been able to check the look in her eyes in time; he had caught her unawares, but that was the whole point; she had not been embarrassed, had not looked away, had carried on looking at him quite calmly with the same cold expression, so out of character for her. You might have thought it was hostility. But why? What for? He just could not imagine Lyubov Vadimovna like this . . . Only recently he had met her at the town committee [*gorkom*] and they had said hullo as always and exchanged smiles.

He watched her down there, kneeling on the wet boards rinsing out her washing. For ages now the townspeople had been sending their washing to the laundry. The new automatic laundry served most of the inhabitants perfectly well, and it upset him that Lyubov Vadimovna, a person in a managerial position and on the town committee [*deputat*] was doing her washing there in the same way as simple peasant women did a hundred years ago.

Cursing and swearing, he started to go down to her. Lyubov Vadimovna's hostility had wounded him. He wanted to hear from her lips what the matter was, let her say it, come out with it. She straightened up, saw Losev coming towards her, but gave no indication. Losev slowed down, biding his time. He thought that Lyubov Vadimovna knew why he had not petitioned Kamenev [his superior] about her case. No one could have known why he had not, but Losev thought that, if she did know, then his questions would be a charade and Lyubov Vadimovna would detect the dishonesty in him, and would throw in some haughty remark like 'There's no point in your . . .' With that scene in his mind's eye Losev stopped. He was used to people catching him in town; some actually grabbed his sleeve, looked him in the eyes and sought his attention. Why should he have to explain himself, justify himself? What was she imagining, this moss-covered old goat? He called her more violent names, but even this did not help. The feeling of guilt would not go away. He could not walk away or walk up to her; he was stuck – with no way out. He stood there in his wet, rolled-up trousers, with his gym shoes under his arm, unshaven, wheezing, staring in front like a stupid bull. He stuck out there in front of them, not knowing how to turn round and go away. With every passing second his situation was becoming more ridiculous. His ears were burning. What a state this book you're returning is in, Sergey Losev! And you're so handsome; look at yourself . . . If only she would say something like that! As she used to. It occurred to him how irrevocable it was. Nothing could be returned. The fleeting excrescences of childhood meant nothing now; he was a seventy-kilo man, while Lyubov Vadimovna was getting on in years and had wrinkles . . .

She did not turn away, did not get on with her washing, did not lower her eyes. Mercilessly she kept looking at him, and both the other women there also looked as he retreated clumsily, withdrew, turned, while the eyes burnt into his back.

At home when he was shaving in front of the mirror, one after another, phrases, each one slicker than the last, came into his head. But this only made him more bad-tempered, not with himself, but with her. It would have been better if she had abused him, attacked him in front of the other women, told him he should be ashamed of himself, threatened him. Anything would have been better than that haughty pride, the restraint of these refined intellectuals. They had ruined the morning for him. Whichever way he considered that morning it still left a bad taste in his mouth.

Daniil Granin, *The Picture* [*Kartina*], *Novy mir*, 1980, nos. 1–2

In contrast to the rather gloomy but sympathetic realism of Granin, the second extract is taken from a comic extravaganza by Vladimir Voynovich. Voynovich, now in the West, was born in 1932. His father was a journalist, his mother a teacher. After army service and some years working as a carpenter, Voynovich joined Moscow Radio in 1960 where he wrote a popular cosmonaut's song. His early published work, including *I Want to Be Honest* (1963), gained him much critical and popular acclaim, for he was not only a talented writer but working-class, too. After the trial of the writers Daniel and Sinyavsky in 1966, some people found it increasingly difficult to retain their position within the literary establishment. Voynovich was expelled from the Writers' Union in 1974, and in 1980 allowed to emigrate.

The extract that follows is taken from the second volume of Voynovich's comic masterpiece, *The Life and Extraordinary Adventures of Private Ivan Chonkin, Pretender to the Throne*. Chonkin is a naïve hero, a village idiot, who innocently gets everyone else at cross-purposes and in the process reveals their hidden motives, making nonsense of the Soviet system. Voynovich satirises the pomposity and incompetence of authority and the delusions of ordinary people, and does so by fantasy and exaggeration. The Chonkin saga is set in the 1941–5 war. Chonkin is ordered to stand guard over a crashed military aeroplane in darkest rural Russia. He does so, but gets quite forgotten until a secret-police detachment, on a tip-off, goes to investigate and vanishes. Rumours of a 'Chonkin band' of terrorists then spread. The army captures Chonkin, believing him to be none other than a prince, albeit a red-eared, bow-legged one, and the leader of a massive White Guard movement acting in league with Hitler to restore the monarchy. Hitler and Himmler, Stalin and Beria all figure in the novel. It is, as the author warns, impossible to say definitely whether it all really did happen or not: 'I've collected everything I've heard on the subject and added a little something of my own as well; in fact maybe I've added a little more than I heard.'

The point to note here is that, unlike Granin, who focuses on the relative impotence of Party leaders and the complexity of their problems, Voynovich depicts a simple world of little Stalins, powerful and feared precisely because people let them be that way. But, though it may be a burlesque of institutionalised fear and absurdity, like all effective satire it has some truth behind it.

PRETENDER TO THE THRONE
Vladimir Voynovich

While the members of the Bureau were arriving, Andrei Eremeyevich Revkin, First Secretary of the District Committee, paying no attention to the general hubbub, had been preparing for the upcoming session. He was reading through the drafts of the resolutions prepared on various questions and, where necessary, making corrections. From time to time, without looking and without himself rising, he would thrust his hand out to the latest arrival and then plunge back into his papers. Sometimes he would press his buzzer and Anna Martinovna would appear silently and immediately. A tall, elderly woman with glasses on her impassive face, she could miraculously divine her boss's slightest wish even at a distance. Revkin had only to reach out to one side for the very paper he needed to appear in his hand. At that moment he was handing Anna Martinovna another paper in which something had to be retyped, giving her brief, whispered instructions, and at the same time observing who had arrived and calculating if there were enough to begin.

As a group, the people present in Revkin's office represented the ruling élite of the district and belonged to the so-called nomenclature. What set these people apart was that they had been appointed to direct, and without a twinge of doubt they had undertaken to direct firmly and decisively whatever it was they had been appointed to direct – vegetable growing, hog breeding, any industry, any art, any science. And if by chance it so happened that someone displayed skill or knowledge in some area of human endeavour, he would immediately be booted to another field until, by degrees, he was brought to that field where he did not know his ass from his elbow, where he swam as in a boundless sea with no points of reference before him except for that lodestar known as the Daily Directive. The imaginary line connecting the swimmer with that star was known as the Party line, to which absolute adherence was required.

It seemed that everyone had already arrived, but the session had not begun. They were still waiting for someone. Now they had begun talking about their illnesses, the weather, the harmfulness of tobacco, the value of vitamins, all sorts of subjects which no one there found the least disturbing, while they said nothing at all about what was truly disturbing them – the situation at the front, ration cards, the rumours that certain posts might lose their military deferments, people's usual concerns. Suddenly Anna Martinovna appeared in the doorway.

'Andrei Eremeyevich!' she said excitedly.

As Andrei Eremeyevich went to the door, the others pressed against the windows. They all saw a luxurious Zis-101, polished to a gleam, roll gently up to the main entrance of the District Committee building. The car looked like an ocean liner mooring at a dock on some insignificant little river. Running up just in time, Revkin flung open the front door. Climbing out towards him with a friendly smile was a portly man in a gray gabardine raincoat and a soft hat with its brim turned slightly up. They kissed three times, long and hard for some reason; the newcomer pounded Revkin's back while Revkin, though he considered himself the man's close friend, did not pound his in return. Instead he made a gesture of invitation and the newcomer began walking leisurely up the stairs. The members of the Bureau instantly recoiled from the windows and resumed their places; smiles appeared on their faces now turned towards the door as if they were expecting a famous movie star or simply some beautiful woman to walk in. But it was not a woman who entered, it was the man who had driven up in the Zis-101, the Secretary of the Regional Committee, Comrade Piotr Terentevich Khudobchenko. The smiles in the room were directed at him, not because he enjoyed their respect for his merits (little was known about them); it was the position he occupied which demanded the respect. And, had this position been occupied by a turkey or a crocodile, they would have smiled at it exactly as they were now smiling at Khudobchenko.

As soon as Khudobchenko appeared in the doorway, everyone rose to his feet. But Piotr Terentevich lifted a hand courteously. 'Sit down, comrades,' he said in his native half-Ukrainian language.

He then removed his gabardine raincoat and hat and handed them to Revkin, who hung them both on his personal peg. Khudobchenko was dressed in semi-military attire and box-calf boots. The top button of his field jacket, with its patch pockets, was open, revealing the collar of his Ukrainian shirt.

'Well,' he said, smoothing down his sparse hair, 'looks like I'm a little late.'

'The authorities are never late, they are detained,' said Revkin, offering a little joke.

Khudobchenko had expected this jesting reply, and, as always, it was met with Khudobchenko's benevolent smile and the approving laughter of all. It happened every time Khudobchenko was late, and he was always late.

He wasn't late because he had so much to do (though he did have quite a bit to do), and not because he was disorganised and could not find the time; he was late intentionally, assuming that the longer subordinates waited the more respect they would show him.

'Please, Piotr Terentevich,' Revkin offered him his own seat at the table.

'No, no.' Khudobchenko raised his hand. 'You're in charge here, you sit down. I'm a guest, I'll go sit in that little corner over there.'

He sat down in that 'little corner' by the window on a soft leather armchair which had been placed there especially for him.

Pshenichnikov, his general assistant, a young man around thirty with a painfully pale face, settled himself down beside Khudobchenko in a chair. It was said of this Pshenichnikov that he knew six languages, had a profound understanding of physics, mathematics, economics, and knew something of all the other sciences. It was also said that he not only knew *Das Kapital* and *Anti-Dühring* but also had a good grasp of local problems, knew by heart all the figures for the indices concerning industrial and agricultural production, from the amount of steel smelted in each province to the laying hen population of every *kolkhoz*. People called him a walking encyclopedia and said that with talents like his he should join the circus, but everyone knew such a career was closed to him, for, with all his knowledge, he had become indispensable.

'Well, then, comrades,' said Revkin with a glance that took in everyone, 'I guess we should begin.'

They closed the doors and disconnected all the telephones. A closed meeting began – that is, one kept secret from others, or, to put it another way, an underground session. Why closed, why underground, I will not take it upon myself to explain, it must just be a tradition. The Party held underground sessions before the Revolution and therefore held them after it as well.

The first item on the agenda was Borisov's report on the progress of the grain harvest.

Although everyone knew that due to the rain there had been absolutely no progress in recent days, Borisov read his report with the most serious of expressions and everyone listened to it with the most serious of expressions. The great successes achieved by the village toilers were noted, but certain individual shortcomings were noted as well. Here everyone understood that the shortcomings were not at all individual ones but were, one might even say, rife and rampant, but even this part of the report was heard with careful attention. Borisov severely criticised a certain *kolkhoz* chairman who was guilty of carrying out decisions obediently – he had sowed too early in the spring and the frosts had killed the shoots. (Others who had only reported that they were carrying out the decisions – as they were now again during the harvest – and had in fact not carried them out were currently in favour.) Among those lagging behind, Borisov mentioned the name of Ivan Timofeyevich Golubev, but at once announced that Golubev's case would be taken up later that day.

Several rather stupid resolutions concerning the progress of the harvest were adopted, not because the people at the meeting were all fools and had no understanding of such matters, but because to speak out substantively required courage, whereas stupid statements were encouraged.

They passed from the progress of the harvest to the question of preparing for the wintering of the livestock. The question was resolved in a most original manner – of all the possible alternatives they selected the worst. But what precisely it was has, unfortunately, slipped my mind.

At that point Revkin rose again and announced that Comrade Filippov would now make his report.

Comrade Filippov rose, straightening his field shirt. He was a bit nervous. It was the first time in his career that he had ever spoken in front of such an important audience. He had heard that experienced speakers, to make their speeches smooth and convincing, choose one person from out of the mass of listeners to address in particular. Filippov decided this was good advice. He began by saying that they were all Communists and so there was no need to beat around the bush. It was war and war was hard. Taking advantage of having struck the first blow, the enemy had seized important territories and was still on the move. The Red Army was fighting with extra-ordinary fortitude but at times had been forced to retreat before the onslaught of the enemy's superior forces. In such conditions the strength of the rear had become more important than ever before. Only if the rear were strong could our troops hold the enemy on the ground already taken and then, that accomplished, switch to a decisive counterattack. Speaking about one part of the home front in general, the limited territory of their own district, Lieutenant Filippov characterised their position as, on the whole, satisfactory. The workers of the district were accomplishing miracles of heroic labour behind the slogan 'Everything for the front, everything for victory'. Warm socks were knitted for the front, scrap metal collected, large sums of money donated. The lieutenant told the meeting of a certain heroic *kolkhoznik* who had built a heavy bomber at his own expense.

At that point the Bureau members began shifting their chairs, stirring, and coughing. None of them could help but think. What kind of *kolkhoznik* was that and where did he get so much money? If someone had told them that the *kolkhoznik* had earned that money from [their quota of] daily work, then all the members of the Bureau would have convulsed in silent laughter. But Lieutenant Filippov himself knew that it was too much to come from daily work and offered no details as to where the heroic *kolkhoznik* got his money, the important thing being that he had donated it when he could have kept it in a cash box or a sock.

As he spoke, Filippov kept looking at Boris Evgenevich Ermolkin, who thought that perhaps Filippov suspected that he, Ermolkin, instead of building a bomber or a biplane, was hoarding his money in the larder. Ermolkin immediately reached into his pocket, raked out everything it contained, which, all told, was four rubles and change. Ermolkin held the money out on his palm as if to say that he did not have one kopeck more but, if with this four roubles and change even a small bomber could be built, then he, Ermolkin, would be more than happy.

Lieutenant Filippov cited other examples of selfless heroism but, at the same time, noted (again looking directly at Ermolkin) that among the workers in the rear, and in particular among the population of their district, definite negative signs had begun to appear. Among the more backward elements, said Filippov, the most absurd rumours were circulating, possibly incited and spread by covert, hostile elements (another glance at Ermolkin).

The rumours about Chonkin and his so called gang were among those rumours.

The lieutenant confirmed that such a gang had, in fact, existed but it had been fully uncovered and rendered harmless. Chonkin himself was in prison awaiting a stern trial and justice.

'But Chonkin is not the point,' explained the lieutenant. 'I think we are all Communists here and know how to keep our mouths shut. This I am telling you in secret – an enemy even more dangerous than Chonkin is at work in our district, a certain Hans, the personal agent of the German Chief of Intelligence, Admiral Canaris.'

Ermolkin cringed at the mention of the word 'Hans'. He had at once recalled that Lieutenant Colonel Luzhin had asked him about this Hans not too long ago. Ermolkin fixed his honest eyes on Filippov, his entire expression demonstrating that he had no connection whatsoever to the Hans just mentioned. But, in turn, Lieutenant Filippov fixed his eyes on Ermolkin, which Ermolkin could not endure, and, giving himself away completely, he averted his eyes and looked over at Military Commissar Kurdyumov. Kurdyumov, deciding that Ermolkin suspected him, looked over at Neuzhelev the lecturer; a chain reaction of terror spread through everyone there, each of whom had no belief in the actual existence of any Hans, but neither did anyone possess any proof that he and Hans were not one and the same person.

However, it seemed that Lieutenant Filippov still did not suspect anyone in particular. He explained that one spy could inflict more damage on the country than a regiment or even a division, and asked all present to show utmost vigilance, not to divulge state and military secrets, to keep a close eye on those around them and, if even the slightest doubt or suspicion arose, to inform the Right People [i.e. the secret police] at once.

Chairman Golubev was among those waiting in the reception room. He was sitting by Revkin's door with a school notebook on his lap, working out his upcoming answers to all the possible accusations.

The poet who will someday undertake to sing and celebrate Soviet life will not be able to avoid the theme of the Personal Case.

A personal case is when a large human group closes ranks in the course of an interspecific struggle, to suffocate one of its members, out of sheer foolishness, out of malice, or for no reason at all.

A personal case is like an avalanche – if one falls on you, you can explain all you want; you're dead either way.

Golubev knew all that full well when it concerned other people. But now he was making the same error thousands before him had made and thousands after him would make. He was preparing answers to the questions which would be asked him; that is, he was hoping that, in the specific case at hand, his arguments and the considerations of common sense would prevail.

A few personal cases had been scheduled for that day. An elderly teacher from the local school, Shevchuk, a small man with red sclerotic veins on his cheeks, was sitting beside Golubev. He wore glasses, quilted felt boots, galoshes, and a patched quilt jacket tied with a thin belt.

On his knee there was an old Budenny hat missing one of its earlaps. Golubev knew Shevchuk casually; they'd met once in the tearoom. Shevchuk's face looked frightened; he kept crumpling his hat in his hands and mumbling to himself: 'I'll repent . . . I'll confess. What do you think?' he said, turning to Golubev.

Golubev shrugged his shoulders.

'What to do?' Shevchuk continued to mumble. 'I have four little children. I married off my daughter but the others are like this.' With his hand he indicated the approximate heights of his remaining children.

'What are you here for?' asked Golubev.

'For my tongue,' said Shevchuk, sticking out his tongue, pointing a finger at it to drive the point home. Golubev thought the teacher would tell him just what trouble his tongue had caused but, staring off, into space, he said no more.

There were two other people there for personal cases. One, Konyaev, was the Party organiser from the XVII Party Congress *Kolkhoz*; the other man was a stranger to Golubev. The former was accused of squandering Party funds and the latter of rape. Both their faces were tense and aloof, and neither of them spoke to anyone.

Konyaev was called in first. He had not been inside long when he came back into the reception room, crossing himself.

'What happened?' asked Golubev.

'A reprimand.'

'Did they give you a tongue lashing?' asked Shevchuk.

Konyaev took his measure, then answered through his teeth: 'I don't answer enemies of the people.'

Shevchuk flinched in confusion and fell silent. The rapist came out next. He was a bit more talkative.

'Don't be afraid,' he said to Shevchuk, slipping his Party card in the pocket of his field shirt. 'They're not animals in there, they're people too.'

The secretary peeped out of the room. 'Shevchuk, you're next.'

'Oi, heaven help me,' said Shevchuk, crossing himself.

He hopped to his feet and dropped his glasses. As he bent over to pick them up, he lost his balance and stepped on them. Completely confused, he began picking up the pieces.

Vladimir Voynovich, *Pretender to the Throne* [*Pretendent na Prestol*] trans. Richard Lourie (London: Jonathan Cape, 1981)

Further Reading

General texts on the Communist Party include L. Schapiro, *The Communist Party of the Soviet Union* (London, 1970), and R. J. Hill and P. Frank, *The Soviet Communist Party* (London, 1981).

A useful study of the housing question is H. Morton, 'Who gets what, when and how? Housing in the Soviet Union', in *Soviet Studies*, vol. 32, no. 2 (April 1980), pp. 235–59. It complements the account of Granin. So, too, but from a different perspective, does V. Voynovich in *The Ivankiad* (London, 1978), a minor classic about power and influence which relates the true story of how Voynovich's neighbour, an influential man, seeks to acquire an extra room in order to accommodate a magnificent American lavatory that he has brought back from his travels. Another literary treatment of housing problems is 'The exchange' by Yu. Trifonov in *The Long Goodbye* (Ann Arbor, Mich., 1978).

The first volume of Voynovich's Chonkin saga is *The Life and Extraordinary Adventures of Private Ivan Chonkin* (Harmondsworth, 1981). There is an account of Voynovich versus the KGB in *Kontinent 2: The Alternative Voice of Russia and Eastern Europe* (London, 1978).

5
The Planned Economy

The Soviet achievement in transforming a backward rural economy into a modern industrial superpower within two generations is well established. Equally, it is clear that this achievement was based on central planning and tough state control, and bought at a considerable human cost. Such methods, although they might have been essential in the formative Stalin years of industrialisation, are less appropriate for the more complex economy of a modern industrial society. The need for reform, generally in the shape of decentralisation and a greater role for the market, has long been recognised by Soviet economists if economic growth is to be maintained. The Brezhnev era, however, persevered with the traditional system still largely intact, and it may be that history will come to judge the Soviet economic system as one which proved able to cope successfully only with the first stages of industrialisation. Soviet growth rates, a key indicator of success, inexorably declined, from 5 per cent per annum in the 1950s and 1960s to little more than 1 per cent, a virtual stop, in the early 1980s. This was despite a traditional and continuing commitment to quantity rather than quality.

There are many reasons for this decline, including insufficient or misplaced investment, a poor record of innovation or risk-taking, and extraordinarily low levels of productivity. The centralised and bureaucratic nature of the economic system has meanwhile been unable to eliminate the pressures that lead to corruption and black marketeering. At the same time, it has engendered a lack of personal commitment and responsibility, encapsulated in the common saying: 'The state pretends to pay us and we pretend to work.' This is clearly seen in agriculture where, as the weekly *Literaturnaya gazeta* has put it, 'in order to destroy the private agricultural system we also destroyed the peasants' love of the land'. The annual need for grain imports, for officially run weeding campaigns, and extra workers drafted in from industry to help with the harvest (when over 20 per cent of the labour force is already on the land) all indicate that there are some central structural problems of incentive and efficiency.

Yet the agricultural sector also clearly illustrates a major 'plus' aspect. Despite population growth and increased expectations, people eat relatively better than they did a generation ago. It is the gap between people's expectations and a rather slowly changing reality that is the real problem, and the immediate legacy of the Brezhnev regime, which, though it was aware of the problem, was also acutely conscious that economic reform might involve an unacceptable price. More efficiency implied unemployment; more incentive and innovation suggested democratisation and *political* reform. The political logic of a relatively simple, centralised economic system remained strong. In a sense, therefore, the difficulty is not so much that the system does not work as that the political will to make it work better has been lacking. When it is not lacking, as in the case of the military–industrial complex, it is a very different story.

In this chapter we have taken two extracts from contemporary Soviet writing, one dealing with industry and one with agriculture, which put some of these matters into a more immediate perspective. The extent to which Soviet writers are mobilised to discuss the shortcomings of the nation's economic performance is now very marked and understandably so. To the extent that political stability depends upon economic success, the subject is a crucial one.

The first extract is taken from an industrial novel by Aleksandr Avdeenko, *The Sweat of One's Brow*, published in the journal *Novy mir* in 1978. Avdeenko, the son of a miner, is a writer of the older generation, born in 1908. After the Revolution he was one of the thousands of homeless orphans (the *besprizorniki*) who swarmed across the land in gangs, living as best they could by begging and stealing. In the 1930s Avdeenko worked in the steel complex at Magnitogorsk, one of the 'hero projects' of the Stalin era. His first published work appeared in 1933, and he has been published regularly since then. Although hardly in the first line of Soviet letters, Avdeenko none the less provides an interesting example of much contemporary writing, dramatising key issues of the day in a highly critical manner but in such a way that the reader draws the correct conclusions. Since the publication of Dudintsev's key thaw novel, *Not by Bread Alone*, in 1956, Soviet writers have increasingly been used to attack industrial inefficiencies in this manner.

The Sweat of One's Brow deals with a huge industrial complex forced by the current plan to produce more and more ('the plan has the force of law') to the long-term detriment of all concerned. A portion of the pig iron produced in the steel mill is falsely declared to be 'flawed' and is stored up, thus providing a reserve against emergencies. 'Sometimes there's a discrepancy between what we have to do and what we're capable of . . . That's why we . . . are forced to use cunning, to break existing . . . rules . . .' Regular overhauling or reconstruction is perpetually postponed because it affects the all-important current output levels. The plant director is in these circumstances, not surprisingly, rude, arbitrary and vindictive in his actions. The local Party organisations are well aware of this, but are not empowered to remove him. Such plant directors are responsible to their central ministries first and foremost. In order to dispose of the director, Avdeenko strikes him down with illness, but makes it fairly plain that the problems discussed, which are all too familiar to Soviet managers, are unlikely to go away very quickly.

The novel therefore not only illustrates the existence of widespread crucial defects in the planned economy, but also suggests an official willingness to dramatise such matters in order to focus public attention not on the need for reform but on the necessity of making the system work better. The particular passage that follows also highlights the often complex relationship between Party and state.

THE SWEAT OF ONE'S BROW
Aleksandr Avdeenko

[The narrator, Golota, secretary of a province committee [*obkom*], a key post in the Party apparatus, has been sent back to his old 'patch' to investigate friction between Bulatov, the director of the industrial complex [*kombinat*], and the local Party official, Kolesov. First he hears Kolesov's side, then he meets Bulatov.]

'I eat when I get hungry, often as not in works' canteens.'

'You what?' said Bulatov. 'You're living in the ninth five-year plan, not the first. And you're not twenty years old any more. At our age you must eat healthy food three times a day. After all, we're responsible for you . . .'

He picked up the phone, called the catering manager and asked him to make sure that the guest at the hotel – that is, me – was getting all he needed.

I tried to extricate myself from this embarrassing situation and continue to talk business.

'For four years now the people of this town have been going past a huge red-brick structure in the centre on the right bank, and every day they've hoped to see workmen, a crane, to hear the sounds of building going on on that derelict site. Tell me—'

He didn't let me finish. 'You're not the only one, dear comrade, who thinks that huge monstrosity is an eyesore. I do, too. I'd be glad to turn it into a beautiful Palaçe of Culture, but for the time being . . .'

'There's no money, you mean?'

'The money has been allocated to more important projects – housing. There is a waiting-list of seven thousand workers and clerical staff in the complex expecting notification to move into flats. We're going all out with the building programme like never before and we still can't solve the housing problem.'

'If I understand you correctly, Andrey Andreevich, you place less importance on an unfinished Palace of Culture [a Soviet equivalent of a leisure centre] than on houses?'

'Yes, I do. At this stage. As you know, there are two palaces of metallurgists in town, on the left and right banks. On top of that, the builders, the hardware workers, and the gauge-setters all have their own palaces. That makes five Palaces of Culture. Five!' For greater emphasis Bulatov stretched out the five fingers of one hand in front of his face. 'The workers of this complex now need houses and not yet another Palace of Culture which will be empty six days a week. People wouldn't understand me if I finished off that white elephant by curtailing the housing programme. That is what my strategy stems from, from this vital need the people have. There you are, dear comrade!'

I didn't agree, but I said nothing. I hadn't come to argue with the director, but to learn his side of the story.

'Have you any more questions?' Bulatov asked.

I had to change the subject. We would come back to the business of the postponed building project later.

'I happened to be in the Kamenka settlement yesterday.'

'Lots of complaints from those old Cossacks, I suppose,' said Bulatov, flaring up. 'They're trying to get special privileges for themselves; they're not interested in justice. They want to by-pass our laws. They're trying to get flats in the new blocks without taking their turn on the waiting-list – at the expense of the miners, steel-founders, rolling-mill workers. Yes, there are gas fumes in the village where they live. But do you think the metallurgists are working in a rose garden? Don't they have to put up with gas, fire, slag fumes every day?' Bulatov slapped his palm down on the shiny, polished table. 'I'm not going to give way to a lot of shameless complainers. I'm going to stand up for the metallurgists!'

And he went on to repeat almost word for word what I already knew. He said nothing new about the notorious injunction regarding the flats.

'This industrial complex isn't a bright sunny day – it can't keep everyone in town warm. And there's no way I can get this simple truth, as simple as two times two, across to Comrade Kolesov. Support me, dear comrade! I can't stand working any more with that . . . petty schoolmaster, Kolesov. Of course, you're familiar with my letter to the province committee?'

'Yes, I have read it. I came here to sort out who's tutoring and repressing whom.'

'Then do so . . .'

So judge, then which of them — the secretary of the town committee or the director of the complex — was best expressing the interests of the working people, who was most fruitfully following the general line and carrying out the decisions of the 24th Party Congress.

I recalled Fyodor Kramarenko, the senior blast-furnace worker, wringing out his sweat-soaked shirt, and I told the director of my conversation with him and about the working conditions in No. 10 blast furnace. Bulatov listened and smiled enigmatically. When I stopped talking he jumped up, strode across the office, stopping in front of me, and said in bewilderment: 'I honestly don't understand what it is that has you so worked up. A furnace worker's modesty? His pride and joy in work? His unwillingness to let difficulties get the better of him and grind him down?'

Not so. He understood everything correctly. I could see that by the calm expression in his burning eyes. He understood and was utterly opposed to my point of view. It was a great pity that a demagogical bayonet was levelled against me. I wasn't going to follow his example. I said calmly: 'Can you tell me, please, why the new capacities of the oxygen plant have not been brought on stream in the complex, as envisaged in the five-year plan?'

'That's not our fault. The equipment suppliers let us down.'

'And does the Ministry of Ferrous Metal know that?'

'The State Planning Agency [*Gosplan*] knows about it as well.'

'What else?'

'I don't follow.'

'You asked a question about amending the plan for the blast furnace plant.'

'My dear comrade, when the State Planning Agency wields a pen the director has to produce the goods. The five-year plan has the force of law. We are doing all we can to fulfil it. And, thank God, we're not coping too badly with the task.'

'No, you're not, but you could do better if you had enough oxygen.'

'Things will never be perfect.'

'So, as I understand it, you haven't even tried to adjust the plan for the blast furnace plant and make it more realistic?'

Bulatov sighed and rubbed his face with the palms of his hands.

'Do you think I'm my own worst enemy? I sent in reports, I spoke to all the chiefs. The people at the Ministry understood my position very well and were sympathetic, but . . . they didn't amend the plan. We were told that we had to carry on and there must be no slip-ups. The country needed cast iron. Every ton was vital. They told us that there had never been a difficult situation in the whole history of the working guards of the complex to which we couldn't find a solution. It was difficult not to agree when they put it like that.'

'Yes, very difficult,' I said knowingly. 'You might have been suspected of lacking confidence in the strength of our working guards [i.e. workers, a commonly used military metaphor from the Stalin era].'

Bulatov laughed merrily. 'Exactly!'

Dmitry Voronkov [Bulatov's deputy and the chief engineer at the plant] turned up with a bottle of Armenian cognac, a piece of cheese, some apples and two bars of chocolate. He wanted to have a feast with me. OK, so be it, though I was no great lover of spirits.

With Dmitry's arrival my usually quiet hotel room was filled with life and youth – laughter, the powerful, joyous voice of an energetic, happy and talented man.

As he prepared the feast-table he asked me, not without some irony, if I had had time to look at the blast furnaces and open-hearth furnaces without any promptings and explanations from a higher authority.

'Yes,' I said.

'And what do we look like to your fresh and enlightened mind?'

'Not too bad.'

'Is that all?'

'The cognac's losing its aroma. Cheers, Mityay!'

We clinked glasses, emptied them, ate some cheese and chocolate, cheered up a little and talked shop again.

'So you say, my dear chap, that our complex doesn't look too bad. That's faint praise.'

'I can be more expansive. You are great, marvellous, the first-born of the five-year plan! The factory of all factories! The flagship of the ferrous metal industry! The armour plating of the homeland during the war! But, my darling, why is your territory so cluttered up with rubbish today? Why have you gathered so much moss, so much dirt, you grey-bearded patriarch? Why so worn out? A good wash and brush-up is long overdue.'

'You've stopped loving this kid of yours, my dear chap!'

'I still love her! That's why I can't bear to see her so scruffy. For many years she was strong, good-looking, hard-working beyond belief, no wrinkles, fresh, blooming with health, but now . . .'

'All good things come to an end. In its time our complex has turned out 200 million tons of cast iron and a quarter-milliard of steel. An immeasurable amount of hot metal. It's reared thousands and thousands of heroes of labour. In the harsh time of the war with fascism it threw itself across the homeland to protect it. It's borne eight five-year plans on its shoulders, now there's the ninth. There's no disgrace in the patriarch's expressing himself a bit by his outward appearance. But his strength hasn't diminished.'

'Whose words are those, Mityay?'

'Whose? My own!'

'But in fact you think very differently. You're a talented engineer, an experienced Party worker; you know full well that the complex needs a thorough spring clean, renovation of old workshops, fundamental reconstruction.'

'That's true, but that's another ball-game . . .'

'No, it's the same ball-game. In pursuing the plan day by day, month by month, Bulatov is losing sight of the long-term strategy, and, whether you like it or not, you're helping him to do it.'

'It's my duty to help him.'

'You have a head of your own on your shoulders. A clever one.'

'The head of the deputy and chief engineer has no judicial or moral right to go over the director's head . . .'

He lightened the tones of these sombre words with a mischievous smile, but it didn't help him.

'Whose benefit is all this false modesty for? Why? I've known you a long time.'

Mityay was quiet for a moment, thinking, and then, becoming serious, he said: 'Yes, it's true . . . I know as well as you do that our blast furnaces, open-hearth furnaces, blooming mills are all worn out. They're getting older every day, with every melt of cast iron and steel. All our production units are in urgent need of renovation. All of them. It's like a slow death. Today the complex can deliver the plan, and tomorrow and next year. But we'll find it difficult, a strain, to fulfil this five-year plan. We squeezed all we could out of our equipment a long time ago. We've exceeded the capacities for which we were designed. We've been using up internal reserves. Today our complex is the flagship of the ferrous metal industry. But soon we'll be overtaken by other complexes where new, more powerful, more technically perfect blast furnaces and oxygen converters have been built. We must rearm immediately if we don't want to fall behind. The scientific–technical revolution [a Brezhnev era cliché] is knocking on the doors of all our workshops . . .'

Voronkov smiled again and looked at me through the thick lenses of his glasses with his crystal-clear eyes.

'I don't understand you, Mityay. Who, if not you and Bulatov, should be raising the question of the complex's reconstruction with the people above?'

'We have raised it! We are reconstructing! But it's far short of what should be done. And this is where we come to the most complicated part . . . The reconstruction of any enterprise under present conditions is, to put it bluntly, a heroic and sometimes thankless business. That kind of initiative, as a rule, will find support in the State Planning Agency, in the town and the province committees of the Party. So far so good. But all the difficulties and obstacles are yet to come. Those organisations which are supposed to plan the reconstruction of the metallurgical enterprises are reluctant to meet our orders. It's not to their advantage, you see, to start fiddling about! Next. The organisations which are called upon to service the metallurgists avoid like the plague "small-scale", "lightweight" jobs in the reconstruction of the workshops. The organisations in charge of the material supplies don't take into account the requirements an enterprise rash enough to embark on major reconstruction may have for metal, cement, timber, equipment; in their judgement the supply quotas go down. But it's not only other ministries and departments which make things difficult for anyone who dares to go in for reconstruction. Even the parent ministry maltreats an enterprise under renovation: "You've gone in for reconstruction," they think up there. "Fine. That's all to your greater glory. But be so kind as to fulfil your quotas of cast iron, steel and rolled metal as you did previously, before reconstruction began. If you don't improve your basic work in the next few days, we'll tighten the purse strings." And they do. They cut bonuses. Or don't give them at all . . . That's what reconstruction means if you look into it! So don't be too hasty about accusing me and Bulatov of the anathema of bad time and motion when it comes to reconstructing the complex. We're guilty. But we deserve sympathy and understanding . . .'

'I agree, you do. How do you get on with Bulatov?'

'Not bad.'

'Have you a good working relationship?'

'We couldn't help but have when we have the same yoke round our necks, could we? We pull the cart along friendly enough, don't goad each other . . .'

'All right. Let's look at it another way . . . Do you feel satisfied working with Bulatov, under him?'

'Not with everything, of course, but in the main, yes. He's an energetic man, no mean specialist, fanatically dedicated to the cause, demanding, doesn't like people who take their time turning out hot metal.'

'Do you really think that these days, in the age of the scientific–technical revolution, all these qualities you've just listed are enough to make a good director?'

'You're never going to get people without any shortcomings! Take me – I have plenty more than Bulatov has.'

[The narrator goes to see Leonid Kramarenko, a recently retired blast-furnace worker.]

'I don't understand anything,' I said. 'Why have they suddenly pensioned you off?'

He sighed deeply. 'I'll tell you . . . Only you must understand me correctly, Sanya. I'm not complaining. Not at all . . . Well, then. The ladles take up a lot of room: a big area with side alleys, nooks and corners. One day the director came in to us. He walked around a bit, had a look, made a few criticisms and then took me to one side and made a little speech: "Leonid Ivanovich, you have a lot of free floorspace here going to waste. We'll have to fill it up with any cast iron over and above the plan that comes off the conveyors. Put two or three hundred tons aside today, tomorrow a hundred or two. But only do it if the cast iron isn't up to standard. Understood? A good boss doesn't just think about yesterday, he looks far ahead as well. We need lots in reserve in case the blast furnaces run into any snags." As I saw it, he wasn't only talking about sub-standard cast iron. He was implying something . . . Anyway, the director of the complex is the director of the complex. He can see more and further from where he's sitting up there, I thought. I did as he had instructed me. I accumulated several thousand tons of sub-standard iron. From that time on, in the reports, on paper, there were never any hold-ups in the blast furnaces, even if in actual fact there were . . . Everything was fine. The director's fund showered me with gratitude and bonuses. Then, as they say, one rainy day some comrades from the town committee came to see us. They were checking up on how the Party organisation was working and, as if by the way, asked: "Leonid Ivanovich, why are all your alley ways and bays stacked up with pig iron? This won't do. It's untidy . . ." I didn't feel guilty of anything. I had nothing to hide from my own Party. Quite candidly, I said: "It's not untidy, friends; it's good orderliness. We use this sub-standard pig iron to plug any accidental gaps in output. But not without the customer's knowledge. It's with his full agreement." That's the way it was and that's what I told them. I haven't been trained in military cunning. I'm a worker, not a soldier ...

'The comrades from the town committee took due note, as the saying goes, of what I'd said, and went away. The same day the director rang me up and ordered me to see him that evening in his office for a friendly chat. He didn't get up to greet me as he usually did. No handshake. Didn't offer me a seat. Looked at me sideways, like he might at an enemy. "Well, then, Leonid Ivanovich, been informing on me to the Party, have you? Kolesov rang me and asked officially: 'Comrade Director, on what grounds have you created an illegal reserve of iron round the ladles?' " I interrupted Bulatov: What's illegal about it? The pig iron's not up to standard, is it? Neither you nor I have been lining our own pockets, flogging it on the side. We used it as and when it was necessary. I was talking about the matter in hand, but he just turned a deaf ear. He just snatched one phrase out of all I was saying: " 'As and when it was necessary'! 'As and when it was necessary!' Leonid Ivanovich, either you really are as innocent as a newborn babe or you are a crafty swine. Goodbye!" For the time being he just turned me out of his office. Then, a bit later, he turned me out to pasture. Put his signature to a certificate of gratitude, shook my hand, gave a smile and a farewell speech: "Thank you, Leonid Ivanovich, for your lifelong, honest, ardent work. We all bow in great respect to you ..." '

When I heard this story, so jolly in form and sad in content, I asked in bewilderment: 'But why didn't you protest? Why didn't you tell the director he acted immorally?'

'What was there to protest about? That I was being pensioned off at the right time quite legally?'

'I'm going to have a word with Kolesov today ...'

'No, you won't. I won't allow it.'

'Why?'

'It's already broken my heart. If they start stirring things up, I won't be able to bear it, I'll give up the ghost. So let sleeping dogs lie.'

It was difficult to agree with this argument. And I couldn't. So what was to be done? I asked him: 'Who took you off the blast furnaces and put you in charge of the ladles?'

Kramarenko threw his head back and laughed. 'I don't know. I don't remember ... That's all, Sanya! I'm not going to tell you anything else.'

'OK, don't then ... I'll go to the town committee.'

'Don't do that, Sanya. Respect my request!'

'I can't, Lenya. You're my friend, but the truth counts for more.'

I went to the town committee immediately after my conversation with Kramarenko. Kolesov wasn't there. That was annoying. And Bulatov was running round the workshops somewhere.

I went to the chief engineer of the complex to find out if he were involved in the business with Leonid Ivanovich Kramarenko or not.

Dmitry greeted my appearance with noisy joviality. He came over to me, his dear kind eyes fixed on me through the thick lenses of his glasses and a friendly smile on his full boyish lips.

'To be frank, I didn't expect you to change your anger for kindness so soon and make my day by giving me your attention like this. It's good to see you.'

'I haven't come with an olive branch.'

'Never mind. That won't mean the end of the world for me. The lion's clawmarks on my body will do me honour.'

I didn't reply to his silly banter. I went straight to the heart of the matter. 'You know, don't you, the very best furnace worker in the complex?'

'Leonid Ivanovich? Who doesn't know him? His spark has kindled an eternal flame.'

'And did you know he's been pensioned off?'

'I did hear something of the sort.'

'And weren't you surprised?'

'Whatever for? Hundreds of people retire every month. It's a natural process.'

'But Leonid Ivanovich is as fit as a fiddle for work. He can go on for years. And his service to the complex has been enormous. He was the first person to master the foreign technology; the first one to exceed the planned capacity of the American blast furnace. He initiated the Stakhanovite movement [record-breaking plan overfulfilment of the Stalin era] in the complex. He's an old communist . . .'

Voronkov listened carefully, nodded approvingly and said, without ceasing to smile: 'I have nothing to do with this business. The director is in charge of personnel when it comes to foremen and engineering and technical workers.'

'Personnel are people, Mityay. No one is forbidden to help them when they need it. As a human being you could have helped Leonid Ivanovich.'

'Yes, I could, but . . .'

'You were afraid of a direct conflict with Bulatov?'

'I didn't know that Leonid Ivanovich had taken offence. I didn't know that someone should have intervened on his behalf . . . What's the matter?'

'The matter is that his retirement is a fig leaf. They had their revenge on him because, without even knowing it himself, he helped the town committee discover the director's secret.'

'What secret?'

'You've seen those old pits, hollows, channels and squares left by the stacks of pig iron on the area where the ladles are, haven't you? On top it's all rejects, but underneath . . . The director knew what he was doing when he created a gold fund of surplus smelted metal that didn't appear in the accounts. He was laying down his own straw matting so that in the future he could wade through the puddles. A far-sighted comrade indeed. He created the illusion of consistent rhythmical work in the blast furnaces, sent in triumphant reports to the Ministry and the province committee, and received congratulations and bonuses. The town committee put a stop to these dirty tricks. Is that news to you, Mityay?'

'Well, no . . . I was certain that the cast iron in the stacks was sub-standard, and I couldn't see anything wrong in our using it when times became hard. The clients didn't complain . . . It wasn't done just to make life easy. Metallurgical enterprises have such harsh conditions imposed over supplies of material and technology that sometimes we're all forced – some more often than others – to bend the rules a bit.'

'You mean, fiddle?'

'In a sense, yes, fiddle, but not for personal gain. In the interest of the plan.'

'In a word, you're saying anything goes as long as you achieve the sacred goal. Is that it?'

'Not altogether, but there's some truth in what you're saying. The five-year plan has given our complex the optimum target for cast iron production. Sometimes there's a discrepancy between what we have to do and what we're capable of. The state plan and our socialist obligations often hang by a thread. That's why we – and it's not only us – in order to save the plan, are forced to use cunning, to break existing norms and rules or depart from them . . .'

Aleksandr Avdeenko, *The Sweat of One's Brow* [*V pote litsa svoego*], *Novy mir*, 1978, nos 1–3

The second extract is taken from an epic work, *Brothers and Sisters*, by Fyodor Abramov, one of the more trenchant of Soviet writers, which deals with agricultural questions. Abramov (1920–83) comes from a village in the hard northern forests of Russia. He was a critic and teacher at Leningrad University in the 1950s, becoming a full-time writer in 1960. *Brothers and Sisters*, which runs to four volumes, is a product of many years' writing, the story of life in a village in Abramov's native Arkhangelsk region, centred around the Pryaslin family. The first volume is set in the war and the fourth volume, *The House*, from which the extract below is taken, in the mid-1970s. Overall it is a highly critical study of government un- scrupulousness, official callousness and falsified figures, and of an often passive or indifferent peasantry, and Abramov's writing has been severely criticised accordingly. The chief character, Mikhail Pryaslin, a teenager in the war when the story opens, is an honest, intelligent but unfulfilled man, who sticks it out in the countryside despite the lure of the bright lights that take so many of the best people from the villages. Pryaslin, however, stays because he instinc- tively seeks to keep his widowed mother and family together and is then tied down, not for any higher idealistic motives. Governmental abuse and neglect are to blame for the harsh and thankless life he and other Russian peasants lead.

In the passage which follows Mikhail berates both the younger generation and local authority for what he sees as destructive farm- ing methods, stemming from a fundamental lack of responsibility. The Party leadership can issue resolutions, such as the Non-Black Earth Zone campaign of the 1970s, referred to in the extract (a major effort to improve yields in areas such as those of Mikhail's village), but ultimately much still depends on the enthusiasm and initiative of a workforce that appears to possess neither quality in abundance.

THE HOUSE
Fyodor Abramov

[Mikhail's brother, Pyotr, and sister, Lisa, are speaking. The farm has been accorded the status of a state farm [*sovkhoz*], in theory a step forward from being a collective farm [*kolkhoz*] and likely to have brought with it more investment and greater mechanisation.]

'And what's the relationship like between him and the manager [i.e. between Mikhail Pryaslin and the farm manager, Taborsky]?'

'With that Taborsky? There's no relationship; it's just warfare.'

'Oh, I see . . .' Pyotr forced a smile. 'I thought he only fought with his sister and his brothers.'

'We brothers and sisters rub along all right, Petya. Sooner or later we'll sort things out. But him and that Taborsky, I don't know how they'll part. Taborsky's a swindler, a sly one as you've never seen the like of, and he's surrounded himself with people on the fiddle. And Mikhail — well, you know yourself what he's like. Straight as a die. So there you have the war between them.'

'Has it been going on long?'

'The war? Well, they used to have a go at each other when it was a collective farm. The time was when not a single meeting went by without their getting at each other's throat. Mind you, at least in those days the people would vote for Mikhail . . .'

'And now?'

'Now we're a state farm. There are no meetings any more. Taborsky has all the power [the appointed manager as opposed to the elected chairman of the collective].' Lisa carefully smoothed out the crease in the old oilskin tablecloth. 'And they're not so fond of Mikhail any more . . .'

'Who aren't they fond of? Mikhail?'

'Who else?'

Pyotr straightened up.

'Why?'

'On account of work. He's mad keen on it. He won't leave people in peace.'

Pyotr did not take his eyes off his sister. This was the first time in his life he had heard anything like it: people not liking someone because of work. Where? In Pekashino!

'That's the way it is, Petya! This is the third year he's done the haymaking all by himself. The time was when once the haymaking started everyone would be queueing up to work with Mikhail, there was no holding them, but now they're not so keen. Now they'll work with anyone as long as it's not Mikhail.'

'But why?' Pyotr still could not make head or tail of it all.

'Because people are different now. We don't want to break our backs like we did before; everyone's after the easy life. Remember how we grafted in the old days? Till we dropped? If your hands couldn't hold the rake, they'd tie the rake to your hands with rope. And now it's like in the town: you mess about for your seven hours and you're off home. And if you want more out of them you must pay through the nose for it. Well, everyone knows what Mikhail's like: work himself to death and won't give anyone else a break. Harvest time! Harvest day feeds the winter – they don't say that any more. Now it's "We don't want to work with Pryaslin". So he don't want to be with folk and they don't want to be with him.' Lisa fell silent for a moment, and then concluded: 'That's the way it is now . . . In the old days work made the people suffer; now people make the work suffer . . .'

Rumours of a new drought in the south started to circulate at the end of June: everything was burning at the root – wheat and grass. They drove the cattle north, and then something quite extraordinary happened: the outskirts of Moscow were on fire, and Moscow itself was gasping because of the smoke ... [This actually occurred in 1976.]

However, Pinezhye, far-off polar Pinezhye, concealed behind the mighty thousand-kilometre curtain of northern forests, did not learn of this disaster for a long time.

Hell on the Pinega began about ten days after Petrov Day [29 June, old style, a traditional saint's day holiday] with dry thunderstorms, when suddenly all over the district forest fires started to roar.

Smoke, fumes, dust ... Black clouds of gnats and midges from the taiga ... The cattle lowing for fodder – all the grazing land burnt out ... And the hot weather and sweltering heat, damn them! There was nowhere to shelter, nowhere to sit down and cool off – neither in the baking-hot wooden house, nor in the dried-up river, where the last little fish was gasping.

The devout old women whispered repentantly: 'It's because of our sins, our sins ... Because we've forgotten God ...'

But those who were a bit younger, more lettered, they reckoned it was to do with science and outer space, with man having infringed the forbidden boundaries of the universe ...

Good on yer, field! thought Mikhail, coming out of the shrubs. Asp and birch trees are closing in on you from all sides, but like a soldier surrounded by the enemy you'll stand there to the death!

But what the bloody hell's all this? Why is this field, in the middle of summer, all bare, not a single blade of grass?

He went nearer, and what from a distance had seemed improbable, wild, became obvious: the wedge of land was ploughed up. And what's more it was sown with rye: grain was scattered the whole length of the field edge. That's the way all tractor-drivers work these days – they never finish off the ends of the fields neatly.

No, it can't be! thought Mikhail, shaking his head. They can't have sown rye in dry weather like this. That's just like throwing seed into a blazing stove.

He went out on to the field and with his good hand [he had injured a hand earlier in the story] managed to turn over a clod of earth together with the clay, and then all his doubts were dispelled: the field had been sown. He counted seven little brown seeds under the clod.

Mikhail stood dumbfounded for a long time over the hole in which, orphaned and useless, the tiny seeds lay right on the surface of the earth, not even pressed into it. And then suddenly other thoughts, unconnected with the drought, started to whirl in his head.

This was a grave for the seeds, he thought. When would the grain ever grow through that? Would a seed shoot ever get through that clod of earth?

Mikhail turned over another clod, then a third, then a fourth . . . It was the same everywhere: the seed lay in the deep furrow as if in a grave, crushed by the slabs of clay.

So that's how we'd ruined the fields! We couldn't wait to get tractors and then we let them gnaw their way into the earth.

Yes, yes, yes. When they used to do the ploughing with a low-powered horse, they furrowed only the top of the ploughland, only turned up the top layer. But then the tractor came on the scene and they started turning the ground inside out. The deeper the better, they said. Oh, no, not better. The top layer of a field is alive, the soil produces, there's strength in it, whereas under the soil there's only yellow sand, dead clay. And we've dug the soil two feet into the sand and buried it under the clay like under a stone slab. Once that's done, there's no escaping.

Yes, yes, said Mikhail to himself, that's how we've killed off the fields. With deep ploughing. And the times he'd regretted he was badly educated. The times he'd felt guilty for not saddling the iron horse! All this had happened before his very eyes; before his very eyes they'd written off the fields as fallow land, unprofitable land, and he himself, when he'd been a leader of a work team, had demanded that they write off that land. What was the point of sowing seed there in vain?

And now he recalled the occasion when he had scoffed at the Siberian agronomist, Maltsev, who, he'd read in some article, had virtually given up all ploughing on his collective farm . . .

Oh, the ignorance, the ignorance of Pekashino! You should smirk, you should look down your nose at educated people!

It had started to thunder by the time Mikhail had made his way through the thickets by Popov brook.

He looked up. Was that an aeroplane breaking the sound barrier? These days aeroplanes made thunder in a clear sky in broad daylight. But the blue expanse above the birch trees was wonderfully clear – neither a white streak which a plane leaves behind nor the silver cross of the plane itself.

The thunder was coming from a caterpillar tractor. Mikhail caught sight of it on the edge of the field when he came out of the stream.

The field was not ploughed up yet, only one circuit had been completed, the tractor-driver had probably been overtaken by his lunch break: these days people worked by the clock. True, they can be late for work, too; that's considered no sin, but as far as finishing work is concerned, especially if it's not piecework, then you don't go a minute over, you stick to the time-sheet.

The tractor-driver had clambered up on to the radiator (he was cleaning the windscreen with a cloth), and Mikhail recognised him by his hair. No one other than Viktor Netesov in the village had such black hair. He had it from his mother. They always used to call her 'Blackie' or 'Darkie'.

Viktor Netesov was not a bad sort of chap. He didn't drink (maybe he was the only one of his age in Pekashino who didn't). He was always a shock worker; once he was at the wheel there was no getting him off the red board [i.e. the farm's list of honour]. And his wife was a schoolteacher. And a chap like that gets up to tricks like this!

'Vitka, what are you thinking of?' Mikhail said, flying at him. 'Has the heat dried your brains up?'

Viktor calmly finished wiping the windscreen, turned off the engine and only then jumped down on to the ground.

'I'm telling you, have you gone off your head, ploughing in this heat? Do you know what they used to call this? Sabotage!'

'I'm carrying out an instruction, so you're criticising the wrong party.'

'And is it also your instructions to bury the earth?' said Mikhail, gesturing with his good hand to Popov brook.

'Can't I make it any clearer?'

'I'll give you clearer . . .' And once again Mikhail broke into a shout. 'Are you ploughing the land or turning the field into a quarry? You've turned up half a yard of clay; a man with a crowbar couldn't get through it, let alone a shoot!'

Viktor was a man or iron and he didn't lose control of himself. 'You'll have to see the agronomist about the depth of the ploughing . . . She gave the order.' Then he pursed his lips and there was just a crease where his mouth had been, and his eyes narrowed. He just turned in on himself. There was no way of reaching him now.

'I can see there's no talking to you. Your father used to work himself to death for the common good . . .'

Viktor momentarily exploded, like a valve: 'My father used to kill himself for the common good and at the same time he killed my mother and my sister . . .'

'What do you mean, killed? Just you think what you're saying, you whippersnapper!'

'I do. For twelve years my father was making a grave for my mother and sister; well, I don't want to make a grave for my family, I want to make a life for them.'

Viktor wasn't going to waste any more time on conversations. He climbed into the cab, started the engine and a huge cloud of black dust rose over the field.

Suddenly it occurred to Mikhail: why hadn't he asked Viktor if it were he who had signed the letter that Tyuryapin had shown him?

Why not say to hell with all the fields and clear off home? No sense will come of it anyway. They'll still make you keep your trap shut: it's none of your business . . . you've no right, you're no expert.

Mikhail stopped on the top landing of the porch and, shaking his flanks like a horse in a lather – the heat still hadn't abated – he swore sharply under his breath. How come he had no right? If you see a man being killed right before your eyes, you intervene, don't you? And this wasn't a man, but the very life of Pekashino that was being killed.

Seeing him in the doorway, Taborsky jumped up from his desk and stamped his feet with joy: evidently he was fed up with the tedium of office work all on his own.

'Come in, come in, Pryaslin! What are you bringing today? An olive branch or a sword?' he chuckled, hearty and crimson. 'A sword, a sword! I can see it in your eyes. Let me tell you something: I had nothing to do with the letter the machine operators sent. I personally would have taken you to court for refusing to turn out and fight the fire; and that would have tightened the saddle girth on you. I even rang the prosecutor. The people in the district committee [*raykom*] advised against it. They said it would be too much fuss and bother: "He's a veteran collective farmer," they said . . .'

There was a time when this sort of nonsense threw Mikhail into confusion, but today it cut no ice with him. It only further confirmed his suspicions that it really was Taborsky who had put his mucky paw to the letter.

Unbuttoning the sweat-soaked collar of his shirt as he went, he went over to the desk and drank three glasses of tepid water, warmed in the sun, from the carafe.

'I've just come from a funeral.'

'A funeral?'

'Yes. I've been watching our fields being buried.'

Taborsky shook his balding head.

'I see. It's all clear: the people's inspectorate [a reference to the common Soviet practice of checking on managerial performance]. But what do you mean more specifically?'

'More specifically? More specifically, you ought to be calling for help! If they tore the skin off you, for instance, how long would you last? What are we doing to the fields? Aren't we tearing the skin off them every year?' And with that Mikhail grabbed another glass of warm water and went headlong, like a horse going downhill: he told the whole story, both what he'd just seen in the fields and what he thought about it all.

And Taborsky? What did Taborsky do? Did he rush out to the fields to stop the ploughing right away? Did he set about ringing the district committee? Sound the alarm?

Taborsky said: 'Pryaslin, I advise you not to interfere with the machine operators. At the present moment, just when the experts in the department have made some critical comments about you, do you know how this statement of yours could be construed? Think about it, think about it properly. And don't worry on account of the fields. The Party thought about it a good bit before you or I did. Have you heard about the resolution regarding the Non-Black Earth Zone? The second virgin lands, a great many milliards, have been allocated. So our turn will come eventually. When the time comes we'll clear all these fields properly.'

'And are we going to do something ourselves? Or are we just going to sit twiddling our thumbs and wait for our turn to come?'

'Pryaslin, we are going to carry out the Party's resolutions. There's the plan. And do you know what the plan is? It's the iron law of our life . . .'

'Why are you making public speeches to me?'

'Take it easy, Pryaslin, take it easy. Nerve cells don't get replaced . . .'

Mikhail wasn't listening to him any more. Taborsky wouldn't change overnight; Mikhail's only pleasure was to let him have the rough edge of his tongue.

Fyodor Abramov, *The House* [*Dom*], *Novy mir*, 1978, no. 12

Further Reading

Studies of the Soviet economy are legion. Useful introductions include A. Nove, *The Soviet Economic System* (London, 1977), and R. Campbell, *Soviet-Type Economies* (New York, 1974). Slightly more specialised are L. Schapiro and J. Godson (eds), *The Soviet Worker* (London, 1981); G. V. Osipov (ed.), *Industry and Industrial Labour in the USSR* (London, 1966); and A. McAuley, *Economic Welfare in the Soviet Union* (London, 1979).

Literary treatments include A. Solzhenitsyn's study of peasant life, 'Matryona's House', in *Stories and Prose Poems* (Harmondsworth, 1973);

and V. Aksyonov's 'Oranges from Morocco', in *The Steel Bird and Other Stories* (Ann Arbor, Mich., 1979).

Two industrial novels from earlier times, but of great interest, are V. Katayev, *Time, Forward* (Bloomington, Ind., 1976, first published in 1932), and V. Dudintsev, *Not by Bread Alone* (London, 1957).

The impact of the rural economy on a Muscovite banished to a village is graphically described in A. Amalrik's *Involuntary Journey to Siberia* (London, 1970).

6

Soviet Society

The demographic and political earthquakes which were inflicted on
Soviet Russia under Lenin and Stalin – revolution, civil war, disease
and famine, collectivisation and rapid industrialisation, German
occupation and world war – did much to shatter the structure of
society. The old Tsarist regime had presided over a society of 'estates'
– nobles, peasants and workers – that, despite its tensions, had deep
roots. The Soviet state, particularly under Stalin, presided over an
'atomised' society of uprooted individuals and fragmented groups.
Despite the much greater social and political stability of the post-
Stalin era, this 'uprootedness' is still an important phenomenon.
More than 2 million people still leave the countryside for the towns
every year; urbanisation continues apace, and many Soviet citizens
are truly *déclassé*, neither peasants nor true urbanites, and adrift
from traditional values. This phenomenon has been chronicled by
many, not least the writer Vasiliy Shukshin (1929–74), whose books
and films (in which he often starred) earned the praise in the 1970s of
Leonid Brezhnev and Aleksandr Solzhenitsyn simultaneously – a
considerable achievement.

Nevertheless, as with any society, there is a fairly clear structure of
status and power. Officially there are three main groups or 'social
levels': workers, peasants and the 'working and creative intelligentsia' (i.e. non-manual white-collar workers and professionals). Just
over 20 per cent of the labour force are on the land; 25 per cent are
members of the official intelligentsia; and just over 50 per cent are
manual workers in the industrial sector. Access to power and status
is unequal, with the intelligentsia plainly some way ahead of the
peasantry on almost any indicator. Broadly speaking, there are three
fairly clear social divisions which are related to this structure:
peasant and worker, or town versus country; manual as opposed to
non-manual labour; and the political leadership – with its privilege
and power – as opposed to the technocratic and professional groups
– whose position is based on skill and knowledge.

It may be that, as the regime itself declares, the modern era of 'developed socialism' is marked above all by a high level of social unity. Certainly there are societies with deeper class antagonisms, and capitalist states, though they may not have the same divisions, are certainly not without structural inequalities of their own. However, Soviet society is now part of a complex modern industrial country with necessarily much stratification and social differentiation. In the first two extracts which follow we seek to illustrate this point. The first passage, from the Siberian writer Valentin Rasputin, is a picture of class attitudes and social divisions, portraying what happens when a peasant boards a first ('soft') class railway carriage. The second extract, from Pavel Nilin, is a reminder that, happily, people are individuals and not always easily categorisable; that, despite growing social stability, this is still a highly complex, heterogeneous society.

Valentin Rasputin was born in 1937 in the Siberian village of Ust-Uda on the River Angara, about half way between the cities of Bratsk and Irkutsk. He later studied at the University of Irkutsk, where he now lives. In the early 1960s, after graduation, Rasputin worked as a journalist. He then started to publish short stories in Siberian journals and is today a leading exponent of the 'village prose' genre which has attracted much popular and critical acclaim throughout the Soviet Union. *Money for Maria*, from which the extract below is taken, was Rasputin's first widely successful story. Subsequent works have included *Live and Remember* (1974) and *Farewell to Matyora* (1976; there is an extract in Chapter 7). His early writing was often a romantic celebration of the Siberian forests and villages. Latterly Rasputin has been more concerned with exploring individual psychology.

Money for Maria is a Siberian tale. Maria runs the collective farm store and is faced with a thousand-rouble shortage in the accounts at inventory time. She and her husband, Kuzma, a driver, are innocent, as everyone knows, but the law must take its course and Kuzma has just five days in which to find this very considerable sum for Maria, or she will go to gaol for five years. Whether Kuzma is successful and Maria does not have to leave her four young children is never revealed; the story is that of Kuzma's efforts to raise the money, and implicitly a protest at the harshness of Soviet law. It is worth noting that in the mid-1960s the average wage income of collective farm workers was little more than thirty roubles a month, although this could be supplemented from private-plot earnings.

Kuzma's search takes him to see his brother.

MONEY FOR MARIA

Valentin Rasputin

If worst came to worst and he did not collect the money in the village he could make the long trip to the city and ask Alexei for it. He had heard that his brother was well off. Kuzma had never visited his brother. The last time they had seen each other was seven years before, at their father's funeral. That had been in the autumn, at the very peak of the harvest season, and Alexei had spent only two days in the village, going home directly after the funeral. He promised to come back for the forty day memorial feast when all the family would gather, but he did not come and the feast was held without him. Two months or so later he wrote that he had been away on a business trip.

Kuzma rarely thought about Alexei. Only when he recalled his father and mother. When he recalled them it was only natural for him to remember that he was not an only son, that he had a brother. But he and his brother had lost contact so completely that the very thought of Alexei seemed unreal to Kuzma, as if it were a thought prompted by somebody else, not the natural issue of his own mind. And again he would forget all about him. It seemed they were not permanently brothers, but only on their occasional meetings, and also far back in their childhood when they had grown up together in the village.

Three years before, Maria had gone to consult a physician in the city and had spent two nights at Alexei's. When she came back she said she would have felt better staying with strangers. That Alexei and his wife were well off she reported without surprise or envy. 'They have a TV and a washing machine and all that, and they watched me as if they were afraid I'd break something, and his wife followed me about with a rag, wiping up my tracks after me. They weren't interested in anything I said. You and me are nothing to them, Kuzma. I wouldn't go back there, not for a mountain of diamonds!'

The previous year Kuzma had given his brother's address to Mikhail Medvedev, who had studied with Alexei in the same factory school after the war. The *kolkhoz* was sending Mikhail to the city for a study course in agriculture, and he expressed a wish to see his old friend. When he came back to the farm Kuzma said:

'Well, did you go and see my brother?'

'Yes, I dropped in.'

'How is he?'

'Oh, he's all right. Healthy. Works as foreman in a factory,' was his evasive reply.

Later, when Mikhail was in his cups, he said:

'He didn't deny knowing me, but that was all. Didn't accept me as a friend. Didn't so much as offer me a drink.'

As he reflected on these things Kuzma concluded that, as far as the village was concerned, his brother was a slice severed from the loaf. Nothing would induce him to come back and see how his kinsmen and friends were getting on and so stir old feelings by roaming through scenes connected with his childhood. It would give him no pleasure to talk to the villagers, finding out from them what had become of Grandpa Fiodor, who had once switched him with nettles, or of the girls he had once seen home from a village hop. In his heart Kuzma was hurt with Alexei, but it was a mild sort of hurt. After all, Alexei answered for what he did, he was no longer a child. And the village paid him back in kind: as he forgot the village, so did the village forget him.

But surely if Kuzma came and asked for his help Alexei would not refuse it. He was his brother, his own flesh and blood. He must have some savings put by. Kuzma would explain that the loan was not for long, in a little over two months the *kolkhoz* would advance him the money and Kuzma would instantly pay him back. How was it Kuzma had not thought of applying to his brother sooner?

Happily the driver brought the bus to the station entrance and Kuzma did not have to make his way against the wind, which was still blowing unabated. Loose sheets of tin on the station roof were beating a tune, papers and cigarette ends were whirling above the ground, people were rushing about so strangely he could not tell whether the wind was sweeping them along or they were running about their business despite it. The voice announcing the arrival and departure of trains over the loudspeaker was so torn and blurred and clotted that nothing could be understood. The hoots of shunting steam engines and the piercing whistles of electric engines sounded like warnings of impending peril.

An hour before his train was due Kuzma took his place in the queue for tickets. The ticket office was not open yet and the people stood impassively, throwing belligerent looks at anyone who walked past them to the head of the queue. The minute hand on the electric clock above the ticket office jumped forward with a little click every sixty seconds, and at each click the people in the queue could not help raising their tired, strained faces to look at it.

At last the ticket office opened. The queue contracted and a hush fell upon it. The first head bent down to the tiny window. Two, three, four minutes passed without the head lifting.

'What's going on there?' called out a voice from behind. 'Haggling over the price?'

The head at fault pulled itself out of the opening in the window and the woman it belonged to turned and announced to the others: 'There's no tickets.'

'No second or third class tickets, citizens,' shouted the cashier.

The queue went into a huddle but did not disperse.

'Anything to get money out of us,' blustered a fat woman with a red face framed in a red shawl. 'Who wants their first class carriages? Why, even if you go by plane all the tickets are the same price.'

'Then take a plane,' said the cashier blandly.

'So I will,' retorted the woman. 'Play this trick once too often and you'll not have anybody using the railways. You ought to be ashamed of yourselves!'

'Fly to your heart's content. A lot we care.'

'You'll care all right when you find yourself out of a job!'

Kuzma walked away from the ticket office. The next train was in about five hours' time. Should he go first-class? The hell! Why not? There might not be second or third class tickets for that train either. Why waste five hours? Once your head's cut off, no sense in crying about your hair. An extra five roubles won't make any difference now – it's a thousand I need, why worry about a fiver?

Kuzma went back to the ticket office. The queue had dissolved; the cashier was poring over a novel.

'A ticket to the city,' said Kuzma.

'Nothing but first class tickets,' answered the girl without raising her head, as if reading the answer out of the book.

'Give me whatever you have.'

She inserted a ruler into the book to mark her place, snatched a ticket from the rack on the wall, and slipped it into the punch.

Kuzma's whole attention was now centred on hearing the announcement of his train. When it arrived he would take his place in a first class carriage and ride to town in comfort. Get there in the morning. His brother would give him the money needed to make up the thousand. Take it out of the savings bank, he supposed. They'd sit down together over a bottle in parting and then Kuzma would hurry away so as to be back before the accountant returned. After that life with Maria would resume its usual course; they'd go on living like everybody else. When this crisis was over and Maria was once more her normal self they'd go on bringing up their children, taking them to the pictures – they had a whole *kolkhoz* of their own: five men and a mother. All of them had long lives ahead. Once more when they were going to bed at night Kuzma would tease Maria, would slap her on the bottom and she would scold him sharply but not seriously because she liked him to fool with her. It didn't take a lot to make them happy.

Kuzma came to with a jolt. It was a lot. An awful lot. A thousand roubles. No, not a thousand now; he had managed to scrape together more than half the sum. God knows at what price. He had gone begging, made promises, cravenly mentioned the loan he was to be given, shamefully accepted money that burned his hands. And still it was not enough.

The train drew slowly into the station, gave one last grinding jerk and came to a halt. Kuzma was frozen but he did not climb into the carriage at once. He stood watching. A few passengers jumped out and rushed from one kiosk to another, as if the wind were whirling them about. A ray of light, fragile and transparent as a withered leaf, forced its way through the clouds, testimony to the existence of the invisible sun. It trembled precariously upon the platform and the roofs of the carriages, but presently the wind seized it and drove it away.

On the rare occasions when Kuzma took a journey he was always filled with anxiety. His feeling was that of one who has lost all his possessions and has set out on a hopeless search for replacements. This time the feeling was more acute than ever. He knew the journey must be made but he feared to make it. And then there was this wind. Obviously the wind could in no way be related to Maria's misfortune, nor to his journey; it blew as it had blown in previous years when all had been well with him and Maria. And yet he could not throw off the impression that there was some connection between these apparently unrelated things, that it was not for nothing the wind did not subside. And his being unable to buy a third class ticket also seemed to have a hidden meaning, as a warning to turn back and go home.

The loudspeaker announced that his train would leave in two minutes. Kuzma hurried to his carriage, but before getting in he cast a look at the station behind him and thought to himself: What will I come back with? Strange though it seemed, the posing of the question calmed him, as if he had murmured a prayer and entrusted his fate to someone else, thereby relieving himself of all further responsibility. He stood at the window watching the station buildings slide into one another, and it seemed incredible that he had been at home that very morning. Aeons of time seemed to have passed since then. He drew a deep breath. Soon his worry about this money would be over – for better or for worse, it would be over. In two days' time the accountant would come back and everything would be decided. Two days was not long. He felt tired, dreadfully tired, and the more dreadful for not being physically tired – he was used to physical tiredness.

'Your ticket, please,' said a voice behind him.

Kuzma turned round. A middle-aged carriage attendant, the worse for many years of travelling, was standing at his shoulder. She took his ticket and turned it in her fingers, glancing from the ticket to him and back again several times as if she thought he must have stolen or forged it, and as if she regretted that railway tickets did not carry the passenger's photograph, for nothing could be proved without a photograph. She looked down at his boots and Kuzma looked down at them too. Against the bright glass-clean carpet his mud stained, outsize, imitation leather boots looked like tractor treads in a flower garden. He felt ashamed and murmured apologetically:

'I couldn't get a second or third class ticket.'

'And ain't you glad,' she said viciously. Unable to put him out yet unwilling to continue the conversation, she made a sign that he was to follow her.

She knocked at one of the blue doors, slid it back and stood aside so that those within the compartment could get a full view of Kuzma and his boots, his sweater and army bag, then said in a voice as apologetic as the one in which Kuzma had just addressed her:

'Sorry, but here's another passenger . . .' She paused before adding in self-justification: 'He has a ticket.'

'Not really!' exclaimed a military man, shutting one eye. Later Kuzma observed that he was a colonel.

'Impossible!' said a man in a white vest that spanned a protruding belly. 'Impossible!' he repeated in feigned horror.

The carriage attendant smiled stiffly.

'Yes, he has a ticket.'

'Do you mean to say you couldn't have found us a passenger without a ticket?' chided the colonel with a shake of his head and a cluck of his tongue. 'We did ask you, you know.'

At that the man in the white vest broke into unrestrained laughter, making quick little chuffs like a motorcycle at half throttle, and the colonel, his bluff called, grinned broadly.

'You're just joking,' said the carriage attendant in obvious relief. 'I really haven't anywhere else to put him, all the compartments are full.' As she went away she herself made an attempt at levity: 'But he has a ticket all right.'

'Come in, come in,' said the colonel to Kuzma.

Kuzma stepped forward and halted in the doorway.

'That's your bunk,' said the colonel nodding towards an upper berth. 'Let it down and settle in if you want to. Don't mind us.'

'I won't.'

'Were you in the war?'

'Yes.'

'All the better. Nothing can frighten you after that.'

'As to all the compartments being full, she exaggerated, to put it mildly,' came the unexpected comment of a man stretched out on the second lower berth. 'Next door in No. 9 there are only three passengers too, but she didn't put him in there.'

'Oh, no,' replied the man in the white vest with meaningful emphasis. 'You couldn't expect her to be on such easy terms with *them*.'

'And she can be with us?'

'She's used to sizing people up, Gennady Ivanovich. She doesn't need identification papers. Take you, for instance, she saw at first glance you were nothing more than the director of some radio station.' The man in the white vest winked at the colonel.

'Not the director of a radio station but chairman of the regional committee for radio and television,' Gennady Ivanovich corrected him frostily.

'It's all the same to her, you may be sure.'

'I can't understand it,' and Gennady Ivanovich pursed his lips without specifying what he could not understand. He was lying in pyjamas, with socks pulled up over the bottom of the legs, a small man with a handsome if effeminate face, the most striking feature of which was his big cold eyes. He wore his hair long and slicked down and he turned his head slowly and with dignity. Once it was turned he adjusted it to a graceful pose.

Kuzma was still standing in the doorway. He wanted to take off his sweater but both hooks on his side of the compartment were occupied and he didn't dare hang it on top of that expensive brown coat; not that the sweater was dirty, but he'd worn it, after all. He had no trouble with his army bag; he just put it on the floor near the door.

If he let down his berth he might find a place on it for his sweater – at the foot, say – but he did not know how to let it down. He tried pulling it, but on turning round he met the scornful eyes of Gennady Ivanovich.

'Wait a minute,' said the colonel, getting up and shooting the bolt that held the berth. 'That's how you do it. The technical age, man. You're a big fellow, a few more pulls like that and you'd have this carriage apart.'

'You from the village?' asked the man in the white vest.

'Yes.'

'Your bedding must be somewhere up there,' said the colonel, pointing to the niche above the door that resembled the stove bunk in a village house. It was into this niche that Kuzma stuffed his sweater because his berth had a white cover on it that he dared not contaminate with his sweater. Thank goodness he had found a place for it. He felt easier. Now all he had to do was to find a place for himself.

'How do you suppose I guessed our friend here was from the village, Gennady Ivanovich?' asked the man in the white vest.

'The country aroma.'

'Not at all. If you observe closely you will note that the faces of countryfolk almost without exception are browned by wind and weather.'

'And I thought you had scented him out,' said Gennady Ivanovich mockingly.

The colonel moved over and Kuzma sat down, first on the edge of the berth, then, seeing that Gennady Ivanovich was aware of his awkwardness, he settled back into a more natural position. The three of them occupied one lower berth, Kuzma next to the door, the man in the white vest next to the window, the colonel between them, while Gennady Ivanovich lay with his knees drawn up on the opposite berth. Kuzma lifted his eyes to Gennady Ivanovich's face and instantly dropped them. Gennady Ivanovich was studying him intently. It seemed to Kuzma that he did not take his eyes off him, but surely that was impossible; it must be that his eyes just gave that impression. It's clear, said Kuzma to himself, he's been bossing people about for a long time and he hasn't much softness of heart; he has a puny voice, can't get very far with a voice like that, so he falls back on his eyes – strikes fear into their hearts with his eyes.

'How are things in the country? Is the harvest in?' asked the man in the white vest.

'Oh, yes.'

'A good harvest?'

'Not bad this year. In our district we never have a very big harvest but this year we took in twelve hundredweight of wheat to a hectare.'

'It's been a good year for crops in general,' said the colonel. 'The village will breathe freely this year.'

'The village always breathes freely,' said Gennady Ivanovich with emphasis. 'If the villagers need money they borrow from the state, and to pay it back they borrow again, and that's how it goes until there's nothing left for the state to do but spit on their debts and wipe them off the slate.'

'That's hardly a sign of affluence in the village,' observed the man in the white vest. 'You know that as well as I do.'

Gennady Ivanovich sniffed.

'How many workers does your factory lose every autumn when they're sent to help the farmers gather in the crops?' he asked.

'Can't be helped. Apparently there's no other way out. The farmers can't cope with the work themselves.'

'Humbug. But even if that were so, why is it that at the end of the year when you're sweating to fulfil your plan at the factory and the village folk have practically nothing to do, they don't send their people to help you as you did them? On an equal footing, like good neighbours.'

'Factory work requires special qualifications.'

'There's lots of jobs in a factory that can be done without special qualifications.'

'You talk as if you knew the work better than I do.'

'I don't, of course, but that's not the point. Once a man who had tuberculosis made an interesting confession to me. He said he could have been cured long ago if he'd wanted to be, but he didn't. Sounds crazy? I thought so too until he explained. He spends four or five months every year in hospital completely supported by the state; or in a sanatorium where the patients go fishing and take walks in the woods while the state goes on paying him his salary in full. All his medical treatment is *gratis*, his food is the best, he's the first to be given a good flat – all the blessings, all the privileges, just because he's sick. So when he comes home from a sanatorium he intentionally begins to drink and smoke, especially if he finds a great improvement in his health. Anything not to lose his privileges. He is so used to them he can't imagine how to live without them . . .'

'So what?' said the man in the white vest.

'Nothing,' replied Gennady Ivanovich with a condescending smile. 'Surely you won't deny that the villagers enjoy a rather privileged position. We sell them machines at reduced prices and buy their wheat for inflated prices. With the cunning and hard practical sense typical of country people, they have decided it is not to their advantage to do everything themselves. They could if they wanted to, but they know only too well that at harvest time the towns will send them workers and machines and the government, if necessary, will give them money.'

He seems to know more about it than all the rest of us put together, Kuzma thought to himself.

'We all eat their bread,' said the man in the white vest.

'So far as I know, your factory doesn't make machines for its own consumption either,' observed Gennady Ivanovich, and the man in the white vest conceded the point with the slightest of nods. 'You're right when you say we all eat bread, but we must demand from everybody the best they can give in the particular field entrusted to them, and be inflexible in demanding it. It's required of us, why shouldn't it be of them? But for some reason we handle the village with kid gloves, as if it weren't a part of our state at all. We make deals with it.'

'Why are you so set against the village?' asked the colonel calmly, but behind his calmness one sensed he was politely if firmly requesting that this tedious quarrel be ended.

'Set against it? I'm not. I'm only trying to get to the root of its backwardness,' said Gennady Ivanovich, loath to give in. 'It's my opinion that we ourselves are to blame. People are beginning to realise this. A few towns refused to send workers and students to help the farmers with the harvest, and the farmers, it seems, managed very well without them.'

'I dare say there are people a lot better equipped to solve this problem than you and me, Gennady Ivanovich. Why should we waste time on it?' said the colonel, narrowing his eyes good naturedly but preserving his firmness of tone. 'Let's turn to something we're more competent at – a game of preference, for instance.'

The man in the white vest instantly perked up.

'That's right. High time to stop this talk or before you know it we'll be quarrelling about God knows what. Who do you think we are, the Council of Ministers?' Turning to Kuzma: 'Do you play preference?'

'Preference?' Kuzma did not even know what it was.

'He only plays "fool",' said Gennady Ivanovich.

'I do know how to play "fool",' confessed Kuzma innocently.

There was a burst of laughter. The chuff-chuffing of the man in the white vest could be heard from one end of the carriage to the other; Gennady Ivanovich only grinned; the colonel shook all over, and when he stopped he patted Kuzma on the shoulder and said:

' "Fool" is a good game too, but we need a fourth for preference. We'll play "fool" next time.' He turned to the man in the white vest. 'You'll have to go and get that friend of yours again.'

'Aye, aye, colonel!' saluted the man, springing to his feet.

They began moving about and talking in loud voices and the compartment was suddenly very crowded. Only Gennady Ivanovich remained lying where he was undisturbed. The man in the white vest pulled on his jacket and buttoned it over his bulging belly, then, clowning, scratched his nose and cocked an eye at Gennady Ivanovich.

'How much did we check to your account yesterday, Gennady Ivanovich?'

'Not much.'

'Not enough?'

'Oh, it's enough, but . . .' Gennady Ivanovich glanced at his watch. 'The bar's closed, can't buy anything now.'

'That can be arranged.'

The man in the white vest left the compartment whistling a merry tune, and presently his voice rang out in the corridor:

'Madam! Be so good as to come to our compartment!'

The next moment the carriage attendant appeared in the doorway and fixed her tired eyes on the colonel. He gestured toward Gennady Ivanovich, who addressed her in a brusque manner, not at all as if he were asking a favour:

'One good deed deserves another, my good woman. We took in your passenger with the ticket, and now we should like to ask you to do us a favour in return.' He held out some money. 'A bottle of cognac if you have no objections. Those people in the bar are your friends; they'll do it for you.'

'Very well,' she said in a habitual tone of acquiescence.

Kuzma wondered whether he ought to get out of the way by climbing to his upper berth or by standing out in the corridor. In either case he would have to take off his boots, for the carriage attendant would scream at him for dirtying her carpet in the corridor. She puts on airs but she's no better than me, Kuzma said to himself; it's only that she has a different job. Just see what a job can do to a person!

As Kuzma pulled off his boots and folded up his linen foot wrappings he again felt the eyes of Gennady Ivanovich on him. This disconcerted him and excited mixed feelings of shame and anger. There on the floor beside him stood the colonel's polished leather boots. Kuzma hastily shoved his own under the berth and went out into the corridor in his socks. Let them find fault now if they can, he thought viciously.

Standing there at the window he could hear the voice of the carriage attendant delivering the bottle of cognac, then there was a blending of voices, among them the voice of the man who had come to make a fourth for preference. Their laughter and discussion of scores was interrupted by a brief pause during which Kuzma heard the familiar gurgling of poured liquor and a smacking of lips.

The wind had not died down. The sky was gray with dirty streaks, like the surface of a stream in flood. Little settlements of five or six houses were scattered along the railway as if the wind had broken a big station into bits. Kuzma could see the quivering and the tension of the telegraph wires and seemed to hear them humming frantically in their effort to tear themselves loose and find peace.

'Hey, friend!' called out the man in the white vest, causing Kuzma to turn round. 'What if you exchange compartments with this fellow here?' indicating the fourth for preference. 'His ticket's in the next carriage, second class; we'd like to be together.'

'If you agree I think you'll be even more comfortable there,' put in the fourth for preference.

'It's all the same to me,' said Kuzma indifferently.

The colonel looked intently at him.

'You don't have to go if you don't want to, it's not obligatory, you know. We just thought we might disturb you if we stay up late playing.'

'It's all the same to me,' repeated Kuzma.

'Splendid,' said the man in the white vest. 'I told you he'd agree. All we have to do now is tell the two attendants. You can come and visit us if you like,' he said to Kuzma. 'Right next door, in the next carriage. We'll fix you up in a jiffy.'

A minute later Kuzma was wrapping up his feet and pulling on his boots again; with a little leap he caught hold of the sleeve of his sweater and pulled it down from the niche; he picked his bag up off the floor, and there he was, ready to move. Here or there – it really was all the same to him. The only thing he cared about was getting to his destination. If he could move to a third class carriage he would be happier still. Who knew, perhaps somebody would make such a proposal.

The fourth at preference was waiting to see him to his new compartment.

'Goodbye,' said Kuzma, turning round.

'Good luck,' said the colonel.

Valentin Rasputin, *Money for Maria* [*Dengi dlya Marii*], trans. Kevin Windle and Margaret Wettlin (London: Quartet, 1981)

The second extract is taken from a story by Pavel Nilin, 'Married for the First Time', published in 1978. This story portrays the complexity of the social structure of urban Russia mentioned at the beginning of this chapter and reveals class, generation and attitude differences. The narrator is an honest, toiling mother; there is a feckless younger generation, and an influential friend whose upward progress in this 'society of connections' suggests that whom you know matters at least as much as what you are. (*Blat* is the key word here: 'connections' or 'old-boy network'.) Much of the small change of everyday life (for which there is a single, terse Russian word, *byt*) in Moscow is also depicted. There is a strong whiff of contempt for the provinces, bad housing, and bureaucratic hassles (not least the necessity for all aspiring citizens of Moscow to get official permission before they can live there). Some of the pressures to which women and the family are subject are also on display.

This is territory that has been well explored by a number of contemporary Soviet writers, including, for example, Yuriy Trifonov, whose novels of the urban middle classes, such as *The Exchange, The House on the Embankment* and *The Long Goodbye*, have achieved a considerable reputation. Natalya Baranskaya in *Novy mir* (1969, no. 11) gave eloquent expression to the lot of the Soviet housewife in 'A Week Like Any Other'. Pavel Nilin is a less celebrated writer than Trifonov, but 'Married for the First Time' is a good representative example of contemporary middlebrow Soviet fiction, and, in having for its central character a rather elderly unmarried mother, gives a fresh twist to some standard themes.

Pavel Nilin was born in 1908. Like Rasputin, he grew up in Siberia and trained as a journalist, but there the similarities end. Nilin's first published work, with the classically socialist–realist title *Man Goes Upward*, appeared in 1936. He won a State Prize in 1941, was a *Pravda* war correspondent, and has written copiously since. As is often the case, however, Nilin is not necessarily easy to categorise. In 1956 he wrote a sharp novel about ends and means, *Comrade Venka* (*Zhestokost*, literally 'cruelty', was the Russian title). Set just after the Civil War, it is a study of individual conscience versus revolutionary politics.

MARRIED FOR THE FIRST TIME
Pavel Nilin

I don't understand men who are alcoholics. What does the phrase 'I can't leave the vodka alone' mean? Take me, for instance. I used to be mad about the cinema; I couldn't tell you how much I liked it. There was a time when you could forget giving me a crust of bread, just take me to see a film. I saw some pictures two, three, four times. But as soon as Tamara was born that was the end of all that. And why? Because when you have a child to bring up, especially if you've no husband, the child always comes first. You have to consider that it needs rusks and milk and sweets and shoes. And there's no money left to spend on trifles. It's better to hang on to it in case you need it later. The child comes first and foremost.

Even so, of course, a lot of people regarded Tamara as a mistake of my youth. I had her before I was even eighteen. And naturally there was no talk of getting married. And there couldn't be, since Viktor, as the saying goes, didn't want to make himself known. He went away immediately to work on a building site on the Angara [in Siberia] and didn't even leave an address.

I was left alone with Tamara in the hostel. That is to say, not quite alone, but almost; I had two girlfriends who, like me, were cement workers – Galya Tustakova and Tina Shalashaeva.

This was more than twenty years ago, but I can still remember down to the last detail those two friends of mine bringing me home to the hostel from the maternity hospital. They had even bought some flowers and a bottle of red wine for the occasion 'to wet the baby's head'.

I remember that it was all sort of fuss and bother and, as usual, with Galya Tustakova fussing most of all.

'There's an important meeting', she said, 'taking place downstairs in the Red Corner [the hostel club and social area], about morality. Obviously you're not going. But Osetrov has told me I must speak. I'll just borrow your stockings for a minute, if you don't mind; one of mine has a ladder.'

'Of course,' I said. And then I saw Lichagin the hall warden coming in our direction.

'Well, congratulations, Antonida,' said Lichagin. And without being invited he poured himself a glass of wine from the bottle. He drank it, dried his lips on the tablecloth, sighed and said: 'But just put yourself in my shoes, Antonida. A baby, especially a girl, is a very fine thing. But, according to the rules concerning the internal good order of this hostel, it's out of the question for her to be here. As far as our organisation is concerned she is an outsider. You know yourself that after eleven o'clock at night it has to be as quiet as the grave here. And a baby in a hostel might start screaming at any time or doing whatever it likes. So what's the solution? The solution is that I have to turn you out. And as soon as possible . . .'

After hearing these words I just sat with my little daughter and felt very upset, although, of course, I had realised before that I would have to leave the hostel. Only not this very minute.

I was on the point of bursting into tears when Tina Shalashaeva, the first one back from the meeting, gave me some news. It appeared that Galya Tustakova, our best friend, had been the first one to speak in the discussions on morality and by way of an example of moral degeneration had cited none other than myself, who, she said, had had a baby when she had no husband and who had had no one even to fetch her, i.e. me, from the maternity hospital.

'What's all the fuss about?' said Galya Tustakova, even taking offence at me, when I told her what I thought of her. 'Osetrov', she said, 'asked me about two months ago to prepare for the debate and find some examples. First of all,' said Galya, 'I only intended to mention Katka Maryasina, since she has a baby that isn't anyone's, either. But seeing as she married anyway the other day, I didn't refer to her and left her out of what I said. I'd already', said Galya, 'typed my speech out beforehand in the office. True, Osetrov cut it down a lot for me. That way, he said, it would be not so much a speech as a co-report. But Osetrov left all the examples in. Nelka Zolotova and Zinka Purysheva and, of course, you. Don't lose your temper. It's all for the good of the cause, after all [a standard political cliché]. For the good of your cause, too. Morality is the most important issue today. And I had to speak as I had been told to. So what's all the fuss about? It's no secret that you used to knock around with that Vitka Kokushev. If I had the female qualities you have, I wouldn't have touched that Vitka Kokushev with a barge-pole. What has he going for him? He's just a useless metal worker who hasn't finished studying yet, and apart from that a boozer. So he wears a green hat and drainpipe trousers? Like an artist. And now because of what he's done you must leave the hostel and probably, what's more, you won't get an education. You can't', said Galya, 'bring up a baby and study at the same time, not even on a correspondence course. Well, am I right?'

It turned out that Galya was right. I had to give up my studies (and I was a good student and very interested in my subjects). And I had to leave the hostel. And I couldn't go back to my mother in the country – or, rather, I didn't want idle talk all round the village about how it had happened, where it happened, and whose it was.

True, in the course of time I managed to acquire my own room. But it's easy to say 'in the course of time'.

Tamara was seven by the time I had fought all the legal battles and acquired that room after the death of the old woman from whom I rented a corner, and I was registered once again in the hostel.

The warden Lichagin had turned me out but not taken my name off the books. I mustn't forget that it was Galya Tustakova who had helped me with this. She had really put the wind up Lichagin.

'If anything happens,' she had told him, 'I'll go straight to Osetrov and he won't just keep her registered here in the hostel; he might well have you, Lichagin, thrown out. Do you think that Soviet power has come to an end that you can throw an unmarried mother and her child on to the streets?'

So Lichagin hadn't taken me off the register. He was probably scared. And, anyway, I'd slipped him ten roubles at the time.

[The baby grows up.]

Of course, I had a few encounters of sorts after Viktor. There was even one man called Ashot, a television technician, who suggested we get married legally. But Tamara didn't like him. She thought his ears were too big and hairy, like, she said, that wolf that Little Red Riding Hood meets. Ashot actually did have hairy ears for some reason – black curly hairs. But he was a kind man, good-humoured. And that was another reason why Tamara didn't like him – he laughed too loudly. But the main thing was, Ashot was once reckless enough to kiss me when Tamara was there. And, after that, whenever she lost her temper, she would shout at me: 'Go and kiss your Ashot!'

Tamara was nearly fourteen then. She understood a great deal. And I was afraid there might be some conflict between us. Anyhow, my daughter was not just closer to me than anything else; she would, I hoped (as we all hope when we think of our children), fulfil – she must fulfil – all my desires, hopes and dreams. That is, perhaps, we think our children will accomplish what we failed one way or another to accomplish.

Tamara's ambition, when she left school, was to join a musical ensemble. I shared her ambition. But she wasn't accepted at first. They said she wasn't good enough.

And then who should turn up again but my old friend, Galya Tustakova, whom I was seeing less and less frequently at the time. Whenever we did meet, though, she always told me in great detail how she was living or, more precisely, how she was prospering. She probably found it pleasant to tell me in particular about what she once was and what she had now become.

After every one of these conversations my heart would ache a little and I'd think to myself: Perhaps if I hadn't given up studying I'd also have become someone in top management, like Galya. Though, to be frank, I would hardly have done as well as Galya. She is really bright in comparison with someone like me. But, then, why make comparisons?

That man Osetrov, who helped her and pushed her forward everywhere, either died or retired, who knows? Galya no longer remembered him. She herself now held some important post by the time I met her again, and I complained to her in passing that my Tamara just couldn't get into the ensemble.

'Ring me the day after tomorrow,' said Galya. 'I'll find out what the situation is and on whom it all depends. I'll soon sort out this problem of yours easily enough. What's all the fuss about?'

A couple of days later she said: 'Tell Tamara to go and see a man called Altukhov at two o'clock this afternoon and say that Galina Borisovna sent her.'

'And who's this Galina Borisovna?' I asked.

'What's the matter with you?' she asked in astonishment. 'Are you mental or something? I am Galina Borisovna. You're still used to the old days, calling me Galya. I've been Galina Borisovna for a long time now. So what's all the fuss about? And remember, if you need anything or you have difficulties over anything, always ring me – either at home or at work. I won't forget our old, indestructible friendship. I always have been and always will be a democrat. That's why the people around me like me.'

So what was one to think? Was Galya Tustakova a snake, as Tina Shalashaeva once put it, or wasn't she?

She also helped me to exchange my single room for two rooms, that is, a self-contained little flat. And it was all done in a matter-of-fact sort of way. She promised: 'I'll come to your housewarming, or, better still,' she laughed, 'to Tamara's wedding. I hope Tamara doesn't make the same mistake as her mum . . .'

However, Tamara married sooner than expected, and it was just as sudden for me.

She met her present husband, also Viktor, just like her father who hadn't wanted to make himself known, in the ensemble called 'The Blue Cocks', in which as yet he wasn't working but in which he proposed to get a job eventually.

He regarded himself as either an actor or a director or something else, this Viktor. To cut a long story short, he had come somewhere from the Ural mountains. And, although he wasn't settled in a job yet, he and Tamara married. And naturally they registered their place of residence as our tiny two-roomed flat, which, to repeat myself, I had managed to get with so much difficulty – even though Galya Tustakova had helped me – in exchange for the single room.

No matter how many new blocks are built the housing issue is still there. And you might say it was that which sparked off our conflict. Or not just that.

But first of all I ought to explain how Tamara's character had developed in relation to me.

Until she was seven – no, even up till she was thirteen – she rather liked the fact that I was no longer cleaning railway coaches and the whole station, but was now working as a laboratory assistant, as it was officially called. She was, as it were, even proud of me and told her girlfriends: 'My mum works as a laboratory assistant in a scientific institute.'

Then she dropped in on me at work a couple of times and saw that all I did was wash flasks, phials and test tubes, and perhaps she started to feel embarrassed that I wasn't a scientist. Once she said to me (but this was when she was about sixteen): 'You could have dedicated your life to something.'

I didn't altogether understand what it meant or what it was for, this 'dedicate'. I asked her to repeat it. But she just dismissed the whole thing.

'Oh,' she said, 'what's the point of talking to you? You'll never understand anyway . . .'

It goes without saying that Tamara brought this Viktor of hers into our flat to take up permanent residence without even asking. She just said with a smile, as she put the application form from the housing office in front of me: 'Just sign here to say you're requesting your son-in-law, your daughter's husband, to be registered in your living-space.'

'And will they register him?' I asked.

'How could they dare not to,' she laughed for some reason, 'if he's my legal husband and I'm officially registered with him? He can't sleep at the railway station every night . . .'

By that time Tamara was quite well established in the ensemble called 'The Blue Cocks'. (They've bred for all they're worth now, singing and dancing as if before some great disaster.)

But, as I realised later, Viktor was only on their books but didn't actually work anywhere. Or, more exactly, he worked at home, but what he did was impossible to discover because he firmly locked the door into one room, the biggest one, and even ordered a separate mortice lock for it.

I once asked Tamara: 'What does your husband do?'

'Don't worry. Whatever it is, he's not forging bank-notes,' she laughed.

Although there was nothing to laugh at, because she then said: 'We haven't any money. I know you have some cash in your savings book. Lend us a hundred roubles. I'm going to have a baby soon. I'll have to buy a few bits and pieces.'

And so I became a grandmother at forty. There was still six months to go before I was actually forty. But my joy knew no bounds. I loved my grandson, perhaps even more than I had once loved Tamara. I used to dash home from work as fast as I could so as to see my grandson and cuddle him all the sooner.

I wanted him to be called Nikolay, probably because my name was Antonina Nikolaevna. But Viktor thought of a name for him –

Maksim. Well, so be it, Maksim. What's the difference? He was a beautiful boy, huge, with jolly blue eyes, just a little mischievous like Viktor's, the man who had run off and whom I should have forgotten for ever, but of whom, believe me, I dreamt almost every night for many years.

I took not just a hundred roubles out of my savings, but almost all that I had, since I could see that this Viktor, Maksim's father, was only capable of thinking up babies' names, and there was a pram and all the other things to be bought somehow.

'But what does he plan to do?' I dared to ask Tamara one day regarding her husband. 'After all, you must do something . . .'

'He is doing something,' she said, 'only it's not work to your way of thinking. He's an artist, you see. And you'll really be ashamed of yourself when he's created something . . .'

At weekends, instead of gossiping with the neighbours or watching their televisions from morning till night, with almost no trouble at all, I wash down the entrance halls in two housing offices and in those two days I also go and do the housework in flats in two or three blocks. Ten, twenty or even thirty roubles extra is never out of place in any family. And in our family it's just a drop in the ocean. Though when the neighbours look at me they're sort of envious. Why are you so money-mad, Antonina, they say, going out to work even on your days off, not sparing your health and strength? But you can't explain everything to everybody, can you?

I had tried not to bring up Tamara like that. From her earliest years I'd tried to instil only one thing in her: your business, I'd say, is to study, and then, of course, everything will come your way of its own accord.

As a child, at about four years old, she became mad keen on wanting to make dolls' dresses: 'Mum, give me the needle, cotton and scissors.' But I was afraid that she would accidentally prick herself or swallow the needle. Yet she still made the odd thing. These days if she needs all but a button sewn on she takes it to the mender's. And she'll spend the very last five or ten roubles in the house – money which wouldn't be there at all if I didn't do some extra work somewhere. These days a lot of people consider it somehow shameful to take on some manual work, especially if you already have a full-time job. I don't know if we are all too proud, or if there's something else happening to us.

One day Tamara told me that they or we – I no longer knew who – were going to have Yeremeev coming on Sunday. He was a big man in the theatre world: an old acquaintance of Viktor's from their days in the Urals.

'We'll have to entertain him properly, not spare a penny, so he can see we're not beggars,' said Tamara, 'especially as Viktor's father brought some money with him. Try to do everything just right, Mum . . .'

Well, of course, with that sort of bidding I really went to town. Obviously I'd have to do a lot more than bortsch. I laid on everything that circumstances and finances allowed.

And Yeremeev really did come: a tall, rather handsome man with a very nervous, heavily lined face.

In all my born days no one had ever kissed my hand under any circumstances, and on precious few occasions had even so much as shaken it. But this Yeremeev, as soon as he came into my little flat with its low ceiling, really put on quite a show and kissed my hand, which made me wonder where to put myself. After all, I'm, you could say, a common or garden woman with no special education, although I'd recently become a member of the local trade union committee. Then all of a sudden a man like Yeremeev, whom I'd seen myself more than once on the television, is there kissing my hand, bowing and even clicking his heels. That's something I'll certainly never forget.

Yeremeev did not come alone. There were two more actors with him: 'The chorus', as he put it himself, joking. But there wasn't a word out of them the whole time; they just drank and ate. And it was only when Yeremeev himself had obviously had enough to drink and started talking about some character in a play called Ulyalaev, whom only Viktor in the whole Soviet Union could play, did the other two start noisily backing him up, saying that you could see right away that Viktor was a man of iron, who sensed the truth of life like iron, that he was a typical Ulyalaev, no two ways about it. And where did this Ulyalaev suddenly spring from? I wondered. And who was he? Maybe it wasn't Ulyalaev. Maybe I'm mixed up. But I did understand that there was a part that was very important in the theatre or the films and only our Viktor was capable of playing it.

'I'll give you an audition for the part of Ulyalaev in a few days,' promised Yeremeev, still not very drunk.

And all the time he kept saying that he mustn't drink, that he had a bad liver and that the doctors had categorically forbidden him to drink, but on rare occasions he still allowed himself to, just so as to be sociable and not spoil the atmosphere. And he said that some people said he was too big for his boots. He had such a lot of work in the theatre and in films and on the television.

I liked Yeremeev's appearance and the way he talked to you. This was a real actor.

But a year went by and he stopped coming to see us. And he forgot about Viktor, too, I suppose. We only saw Yeremeev on the television. He played a spy, and then a professor. But that meant nothing to us any more.

'Ham,' said Viktor when he saw him on television.

Tamara had a second child, a lovely little boy again and just like me, everyone said (and I wasn't even the one who'd given birth). This time they called the boy Nikolay, but not after my father, but after Viktor's, who was called Nikolay Stepanovich. And, although he didn't come to Moscow often, he still sent his money, that is, his pension, every month as he'd promised for the maintenance of his son's family.

They say that up to the age of 30 time passes slowly and not very noticeably, but after you get to 30 it's like the meter on a taxi. That's exactly the feeling I have. And I can see everything around me changing.

Some of Viktor's companions who used to visit us in due course achieved something. One of them, together with a friend, painted a picture called 'In the Fiery Furnace' and there was even something in the newspaper about it. Another one played twice in crowd scenes in films. Another one created something or other. There was a lot of work to be done. You can work for all you're worth. But you must admit not everyone, as I noticed a long time ago, not everyone by a long chalk, wants to work.

And our Viktor was always thinking something over. You couldn't say he was a loafer. He'd be reading books all day and even writing something, but it was all done at home and there was nothing to see for it afterwards. True, once or twice a week he went off to a film studio, but there was hardly ever any point in it . . .

In the mornings when I was getting ready to go to work I often watched Viktor eating his fried eggs (that was his staple diet) and reading the paper. He had to have something to read when he was eating so as to occupy or distract his thoughts, as Tamara said. And she used to do likewise – pick up a book when she was eating – but that was only so she didn't have to talk to me. Then one morning I had the devil in me and joked about it. I said:

> 'A man, a beast or a bird
> They all have jobs to do;
> An insect carries its load
> And the bee seeks honey too . . . And why?

Because', I said, 'they must all eat and drink. And everyone has a load to carry, whether you're a man or an insect . . .'

Viktor threw down the newspaper, pushed his pan of fried eggs away and shouted: 'I'm fed up with your eternal stupid remarks! Go and wash your test tubes but keep out of my affairs. I want a bit of peace and quiet in my own home!'

Well, I didn't bother to remind him whose home it was. I just went to work.

But the next morning Tamara said to me: 'Mum, why don't you go and live with Aunt Klava for a bit? This will come to no good as things are. Viktor's livid with you. He might clear off and leave me. You don't want my children to be left without a father just as I was, thanks to you?'

With these words Tamara made large round eyes almost exactly as Viktor, her nameless father, used to when he was full of astonishment or indignation at something. I remember the last time he made eyes like that was when he learnt I was pregnant. 'And what is it to do with me?' he asked, widening his beautiful blue eyes. 'Oh, what do you mean, Vitusik?' I said. 'I've only been with you, Vitusik . . .' 'Vitusik, Vitusik,' he mimicked, 'how do I know who you've been knocking around with apart from me? You get all sorts of people coming into this girls' hostel . . .' When he said that I was at a complete loss, almost exactly as I was after Tamara's words.

'Shall I have a word with Aunt Klava, if you feel awkward about it? Maybe she can take you in. Of course, you can come and visit us . . .'

I didn't say anything in reply to Tamara. I couldn't think of anything. That was a fine idea – to go to Aunt Klava. Whatever for? She had only one room, and a young husband. And she didn't owe me any favours.

The next day I stayed late at work wondering all the time what I could do. At last I asked the cleaning superintendent if I could stay in the institute overnight as we were having our flat renovated. I felt too embarrassed to say that my own daughter had practically driven me out of my own house.

'By all means,' said the superintendent. 'Stay overnight as long as you like, but not in the offices; anywhere in the laboratory or the annexes.'

My first night in the deserted institute was terrifying. The rats, which you could hardly hear during the day because they were in closed cages, made a terrible noise at night as if they were negotiating or swearing at each other before a fight, and perhaps they were fighting already because the cages kept scraping.

However, you get used to everything. The next night I wasn't afraid and I didn't get upset. I just thought: Isn't Tamara worried because her mother hasn't come home from work? Maybe she's decided that I have gone to Aunt Klava's, that is, my elder sister's, after all?

And how are my grandsons? After all, with me they may not have been better off, but they were jollier. I was the one who usually took them to the kindergarten and picked them up in the late afternoon. And I read them fairy stories after their supper before they went to sleep. Or I pretended to read, but really told them stories myself which I had heard when I was a child in the country.

Would Tamara and Viktor really find things easier without me than with me?

But about eight days went by and none of my family noticed I was gone. Didn't anyone need me?

The very hot summer was coming to an end when one day at twelve o'clock Galya Tustakova turned up in our institute.

'What are you doing here?' she said in surprise.

And she didn't ask any more questions. She probably didn't even catch what I said in reply to her. She was on her way to see the director. But afterwards she sought me out again, although I was on my way out to the yard to empty the wet shavings from the guinea pigs into the dustbins. There in the yard she told me quickly that she was now working somewhere as a senior methodologist and her husband was in the Academy of Sciences.

'What, is he a scientist, then?' I asked.

'Oh, no,' said Galya angrily, dismissing the question for some reason. 'Though in a word he's no worse than any scientist. He has everything on his plate. So what's all the fuss about? We're just going off to Sochi [the popular Black Sea holiday resort]. Incidentally, you don't want to keep house for me, do you? We can go over to my place right now. I'm free', she said, looking at her wristwatch, 'until two o'clock this afternoon.'

'But I'm working now,' I said.

'Oh, that's no problem. We'll fix that,' said Galya with a laugh. 'What's all the fuss about?'

And having had a word with our cleaning superintendent she gave me a lift in her Moskvich to her house on Lomonosovsky Prospekt.

'You realise what an awful situation it is these days?' she said to me, sitting at the wheel. 'It's impossible or very difficult to find anyone suitable to do your housework, for instance. That firm "Zarya" is only just sorting itself out. And they have staff problems.

You know, everyone wants to be a boss these days. Very few want to do manual work. I'm very glad I met you. You can help me out right now while my husband and I are away. One must take the holiday trips when they're there. Always. You must help me out . . .'

[Eventually, through Galya's good offices again, the heroine finds a man who, despite having only one leg, unexpectedly turns out to be her salvation.]

I went upstairs to Tamara on my own. Yefim Yemelyanovich [her husband-to-be] stayed in the car. It wouldn't have been very easy for him to climb up to the fourth floor when there was no lift.

'And where have you been, our dear granny?' said Tamara by way of a welcome.

Of course, I went straight in to the grandchildren first of all and kissed them in turn. I burst out crying. What else? They were my own flesh and blood. And parting is never easy, of course. Then I took my winter coat out of the wardrobe – though it was a hot day, even stuffy.

'What are you up to?' said Tamara in surprise.

'I'm going away.'

'For long?' she laughed.

'Maybe for ever,' I said. And I set about packing my three best dresses and my coat.

'How are you going to manage that bundle?'

'I have a car.'

'A car?' said Tamara in even greater surprise. 'Where from? Whose is it?'

'My husband's,' I said with sudden brazenness. And then I said firmly: 'I'm getting married, Tamara.'

'Viktor!' shouted Tamara, somehow at a loss, but still with a certain derision. 'Viktor, come here! Come here. Mum's going away. She's getting married.'

Viktor came out, said hullo and nodded at my bundle.

'What are you doing?' he said.

'You ought to introduce us to your husband or fiancé,' said Tamara with a sort of pitiful laugh. 'Where is he, then?'

'He's in the car.'

'What is he, a chauffeur or something?' asked Tamara. 'Let him pop up at least.'

At that I felt a bit awkward for some reason. In a word, I didn't want to tell Tamara and Viktor that it was difficult for Yefim Yemelyanovich to pop in.

'Next time,' I said. 'He'll come up next time. And I hope you'll come and see us. We have a very nice place. And I hope the grand-children will come later on, too. There's nice fresh air there.'

'Where is it, then?' asked Tamara, her curiosity getting the better of her.

But I pretended not to hear and set about tying up my bundle.

'I'll give you a hand,' said Viktor, picking it up.

By now Yefim Yemelyanovich was walking up and down by the car. No, you couldn't see that he had a leg missing. A tall and, as it seemed to me, very handsome man, though not particularly young, was walking up and down by the car.

The two men greeted each other politely. And then they started putting my things in the car.

'Is this a Zhiguli?' asked Viktor looking at the car.

'No, it's just an old Zaporozhets,' said Yefim Yemelyanovich. 'I'll probably get a new car shortly . . .'

Soon afterwards we really did get married and he gave me a gold ring. I was so happy to have a husband, to be married. And, I thought to myself, I don't care who knows it.

Pavel Nilin, 'Married for the First Time' ['Vpervyye zamuzhem'], *Novy mir*, 1978, no. 1

The final extract in this chapter is a slice of social life taken from an unofficial, and therefore uncensored, publication – *Metropol'* – issued by a group of writers and artists in 1979 as a challenge to the authorities. Self-publication, or samizdat, is technically legal under the Soviet Constitution, but its practitioners are usually persecuted, as have been many of the contributors to *Metropol'*. What was highly unusual about *Metropol'*, however, was that many of the contributors were widely known and officially recognised writers with considerable reputations: for example, Andrey Voznesensky, Bella Akhmadulina, Andrey Bitov, Fazil Iskander and the bard, Vladimir Vysotsky. Furthermore, the contents of *Metropol'* were markedly apolitical, with no direct criticism of the Soviet regime or attacks on government policies.

This applies to the extract which follows. *Two Notebooks* by Pyotr Kozhevnikov (b. 1953) consists of the diaries of two Leningrad teenagers. Both appear to be part of what, for want of a better description, might be termed the Soviet lower middle class. Like most Soviet students, Misha and Galya's main business is work and examinations, but they are also members of a generation widely considered to be more frivolous than their elders – understandably, for they have not endured famine, terror or war. *Two Notebooks* is therefore of some sociological interest in revealing a flourishing urban youth sub-culture. It is also a useful reminder that samizdat writing is not necessarily any more critical than or aesthetically superior to officially published work.

TWO NOTEBOOKS

Pyotr Kozhevnikov

From Galya's Diary

20th May

Yesterday Marinka was late for school and felt ill all day. She did not go to the night class and asked if she could drop in on me in the evening. Mum's working nights and I said I'd be at home. When Marinka came she told me she'd become a woman. The guy who had kissed her on the mouth had said that if she loved him then she ought to give herself to him. They were at a party. Everyone was drunk, Marinka and Sashka went off into a field and she gave in to him there in a derelict house. They didn't quite make it right away and they went to the house again the next day. Now Marinka doesn't know what to do if she gets pregnant. After all, she's not even sixteen yet and the bloke has to do his national service this autumn [compulsory for all men]. He'll be eighteen in July. He's an electrician. I feel sorry for Marinka. Mum was always scaring me with her stories of how painful it is to become a woman. I asked Marinka and she said she hardly felt any pain. I think it's different for everyone.

From Misha's Diary

20th May

Mum and I went to view a country cottage today. She wants to have an outdoor holiday. I met Pashka there. He's turned into a real man. I'm bigger than him. Pashka's in the third year of an electrical engineering course [in a technical school]. Started it after eight classes [i.e. at fifteen]. We were really glad we met. Agreed to get together in town. Remembered when we were children. After all, it had been eight years since we'd rented Veronika Yegorevna's cottage. When mother and father lived together they rented something, a temporary cottage, every summer in Shuvalov. I made friends with the owner's grandson the very first year. He was two years older than me but he didn't mind. In the mornings we used to run down to the lake to swim, after dinner we had fights in the garden with raspberry twigs, and in the evening they couldn't get us into separate beds. But there was one incident which broke off our friendship. Paskha was ten years old at the time and it was the last year that my parents lived together. The landlady's granddaughter by her first husband came. She was nineteen. She seemed like a full grown woman to us. All Veronika Yegorevna's accommodation was let out, so she put her up in the same room as Pashka. Every day there were blokes calling for Ritka and she disappeared with them till late at night. Once after dinner, without waiting for Pashka in the garden, I went into the owner's house. When I opened the door into his room there was Ritka sitting on the bed. She was wearing a pink corset and she was fastening a stocking drawn all the way up her leg to her suspender belt. The other stocking was dangling on the chair over a flowery dress. Pashka was sitting next to her. I had always seen Ritka in a dress or a swim suit before and now for the first time I saw her in her underwear. I liked her a lot. I had an urge to touch her pink bra just where it pushed out the tops of her breasts. I only wanted to touch. But Ritka started to shout, why hadn't I knocked before I came in? I asked why Pashka was allowed to sit next to her and not me? She said that Pashka was a relative of hers. I remember that I was so angry with Pashka then that I didn't play with him for the rest of the summer. Now I realise why he was sitting behind her back. Pashka was helping her to get dressed.

From Galya's Diary

27th May

Something terrible had happened. Someone's died – a bloke. I don't even know how to write about it all. In a house in the street next to ours they were having a party. They were drug addicts. The girl whom this guy loved lost her temper with him over something. He said he was sorry. She said she'd forgive him if he jumped out of the window. And the bloke went out on to the ledge and jumped. From the eighth floor. Dead. Broke every bone in his body. They say it was awful to watch. The police were called. The people at the party saw the mess on the asphalt from the window and cleared off. The girl as well. Then the blokes waited till there was nobody around in her block and broke into her flat. Smashed her head against the radiator and trampled on her. Stole a lot of gold things. The girl's from a rich family. The blokes were caught later and done for drugs and beating her up. Put them all inside. The girl wasn't charged, though. She's in hospital in a serious condition and she'll be an invalid all her life. They really damaged her inside. Everyone in our crowd is talking about it now. Of course, everyone has his own point of view. Some say that if they hadn't been on drugs nothing would have happened. The bloke was a fool for jumping, but after all he did want to prove that he was ready for anything, that he loved her so much that he was ready to die if she gave the word. She's a bitch – though, of course, it was awful that they sorted her out like they did. It's always rotten seeing a girl beaten up. When we used to go skating in winter the girls there were often fighting over the blokes. And they fight worse than the blokes. They had their skates in their hands and hit you in the face and on the head with them. Me and Marinka saw fights like that several times. We used to go there with blokes so we never had scrapes like that. But I've seen beaten up girls – and it's terrible.

From Misha's Diary

27th May

After classes yesterday Lekha and I went to Petropavlovka [a Leningrad beach]. It was too cold to swim. We sunbathed on the breakwater. We kept throwing pebbles down on the people below. The people sunbathing under the wall were angry and couldn't work out who was bothering them. They probably blamed each other. Lekha said he was thinking of packing in school. Generally he's different from us blokes. His stepfather is a sculptor and his mother's a singer. He's a clever bloke, knows a lot and is interesting to talk to. True, he's very domestic and quiet, but the lads don't hold it against him. Probably because I'm a pal of his. Even though he's skinny, Lekha looks a bit like a girl. No shape to his muscles, a big bum, fat nipples. Adolescence. He often lowers his eyes, takes offence. He looks as if he's just said his prayers, and his eyes are blue and there's often a sort of horror in them at something that the rest of us can't see, but it's really terrible. Lekha is very candid. When Potapov asked him if he'd slept with a woman he answered: 'I can't say I have.' When I'm with Lekha I almost never swear. But in general I think that people often call things names that you don't find in books. For example, sometimes I myself think in nothing but swear words. They whirl round in my head the whole time. But for some reason I don't write them down in my diary.

About seven o'clock we went off to the Kirov cinema [named after the Leningrad party leader assassinated in 1934]. They show old films there and there's something to see. We wanted to get into a horror film. But there was nothing decent on this time. Then we went to the Smolensk cemetery. I really like the cemetery. I spent all my childhood there. Whenever I come back it's like re-reading a book. Everything is so familiar, as if you're a character in the book too.

True, the cemetery's gone to pot lately. A lot of monuments broken. Workmen take the stones and railings away. You kick the bucket and they rob you. Better to be burnt. But even then some sod will nick your ashes and sprinkle them on his cabbage patch or just on his marigolds on his balcony. We crossed the cemetery to the sports court. There was a training session going on there. We watched. The court was divided off from the cemetery just by the fence, and when we were children me and my mates loved sitting on the fence and watching the dogs. Their owners always used to set them on us. We threw stones at the dogs but we should have aimed at the owners. Then I dragged Lekha off to the bay. He didn't want to come, but I tempted him with the cattails there. But there wasn't any there. It was all built up and spoilt. In the old days me and my friends used to go swimming in the bay and sunbathe in the nude and then run about in the long grass, which covered us from the neck down. Ducks flew out of the grass and gulls called above the coastline. When the grass dried out we burnt it. Now there are houses all around and it's swarming with people. We reached the scoop. We wanted to take a boat ride. There was a long queue and Lekha had to go off and do something. We climbed on a Number 7 bus and we parted at the métro station. Lekha caught the métro to Vosstaniye, and I went to the embankment. How can you kill time?

From Galya's Diary

28th May

I realised today that I've fallen in love with him. He lives in the block opposite. Also on the top floor. I can often see him through the window or from the balcony. He's six months older than me. He soon jilts all the girls he goes out with. And he has one who's three years older than him. Marinka introduced me to him today. She was with Sashka and me at his place. We bought three bottles of wine. When we'd drunk them and listened to some music we went out. On the way Sashka met two of his friends, who had girls with them. We went with them over the railway line into a field. Usually horrible things happen there. Once I was out with Marinka and we went into a ramshackle house. It was only one storey, small and no one knew what it had been used for before. There were empty bottles and dog ends all over the floor. There was a dirty, old divan bed. (It was on this that Marinka had become a woman when Sashka had brought her here.)

The first time we went there, we were scared but curious. After that, every time we went into the field we looked behind the house. Once we saw a soldier take a drunk girl in there. They came out almost an hour later. The girl was crying. Her tears made the mascara on her eyelids run and there were black streaks all down her cheeks.

We played about in the field while the sun was still shining. Then we went off to our homes. There's a lot of tests on at college at the moment – must do some work for them. At college the exams are coming up soon. I've come home and I can't do anything. Sitting, looking out of the window, but I can't see Tolya. And I really want to be with him a bit longer. I had a letter from Seva yesterday. I planned to write to him today but what can I say to him? I don't love him any more. I want to talk to Mum. Maybe Mum can suggest what I should do?

From Misha's Diary

28th May

After school I went to see Romin. He runs our ensemble. He's finishing school this year [i.e. a technical school from 15 to 18]. He's put up with it for three years and now he's realised that his vocation is music, not being a professional joiner, which he can't stand. Vadim plays the guitar really well, but his singing's not so good, no voice. On the whole he's a great guy. He may be a bit puny, but he's very independent and has a great air of dignity about him. He's really fond of taking the mickey. But when he smiles his eyes are serious. They look like melted pewter with mustard mixed in. I took Vadim a porn magazine which he wanted to reproduce a photograph from, but I wasn't too keen on looking at the picture. It's a magazine of coloured photographs, Swedish. I took it off a classmate when he was showing it round the class.

It was good at Romin's. He only has a cupboard and a campbed in his room, and by the window a stereo tape recorder. The cupboard is half full of tapes. Vadim's been very lucky with the neighbours. When I asked him if the other residents tell him off for playing loud music, he said that the neighbours sometimes shout at him to turn the volume up a bit. And in summer people dance outside his windows.

Vadim has managed to get hold of some American stereo headphones for a time. He let me use them to listen to some music and it sounded more powerful and authentic. I'm generally very fond of listening to music. Our music is the art of the future. It belongs to us because we're heading for the future. We'll take up the positions our fathers took, as they took the positions of our grandfathers . . . When you listen to music a completely different world opens up before you. Sometimes it's not very pretty, not very just, but it's always sincere. It's alien but near to us. We experience the fates of others in it. They're alien, but near. They're complicated and seem inaccessible, but you get into them and live at one with them for a few moments. And, when music becomes more elevated than anything else in the world, then my as yet undispelled love meets the music as it flows from the shores of human consciousness. And music floods in right to the depths of my soul where no one can penetrate. About which no one can guess. About which no one thinks. I don't understand the words of many of the songs, but they never deceive me. I feel them and I believe, and I follow my music wherever it takes me. Whether I live or die depends on music. It's eternal! I'm mortal! But I'm not afraid of death in the depths of my music. Maybe when I die I'll go right down to the bottom of this majesty and I'll see all its beauty to its outer limits. I'll choke on the beauty of it. Sometimes when you're listening the inner rhythm catches you, and if you're dancing your excited body gobbles up all the music. I prefer sitting still and listening. I just don't move a muscle when I'm listening. Everything is real in our music. Just like things really are. The music varies. In some I can see towering over me houses which are about to crush me and you won't even hear a crunch. They're laughing at me. I can see armed drug addicts rushing about and killing viciously in their destructive mindlessness. I can see a sadistic sex maniac torturing a girl, and a body sickening for something it's never known. I see suicide, drowning in blood, and violence laughing at its own inhumanity, and bodies burnt with napalm. I see a mushroom cloud created by insane human genius towering over the planet, over the earthlings' terrified faces, petrified in the last horrific moment. In other musical pieces I'm struck by the freshness of the flowers given to a girl for the first time, an accidentally overheard confession of love, hysterical but just like all of us, all our generation. I'm struck by the sincerity of someone's confession which my music discloses to me.

From Galya's Diary

29th May

I had a letter from Vsevolod today. He asks why I haven't written? He says he's missed me a lot. He can't wait till we meet again. He's sorry that I'm so young, otherwise we could get married.

I came to know him in the village where I visited my granny almost every year for the holidays. He used to come from Petrozavodsk [a town near Leningrad] to see his uncle, whose house was next to ours. He's just come out of the army. Although I don't love him any more I'd like to know what he's like now. He's twenty-two. I've talked to Mum about him. She said that on no account should I write to him to say I don't love him any more. Seva would kill himself if he read a letter like that. I tried to write to him the way I had done in the past, but I kept crossing out what I'd written. I rewrote it four times. I sent it off.

Last night I was at Tolya's. When I went out Mum was asleep and I'd made an arrangement with him that he would open the door for me at two o'clock. Tolya lives with his parents in a flat like ours. His father drinks a lot. His mother works in the same factory as his father. She is also a painter. Tolya took me to his room. We stayed up till five o'clock. He only put his head in my lap, but didn't try to kiss me once. He's funny! I've generally noticed that he's a very limited person. Tolya completed eight classes at school [i.e. to the age of 15]. He works for the post office. Delivers the mail on a motor scooter. He doesn't go to night school. He likes his drink. Talking to him isn't much fun. We don't usually say anything.

From Misha's Diary

29th May

It was practical today. This is the way it's done at our place; half a week – theory, half a week – practical. They've made us a workshop in the factory precinct – an experimental group.

As we were coming out of the factory they caught Molchanov at the gate. He'd put guitar strings in his pockets and some in his inside jacket pocket. They practically stuck up the nose of the old girl checking his pass. Nearly everyone in the group steals things. Mainly guitar strings; you can't buy them anywhere, but they're all over the place. They also take pick-ups for electric guitars, cases and even whole bodies of guitars (they push them under the outer gates). They swipe anything that's going. When they took Molchanov off to the Chief Security Officer he was almost crying. Molchanov is very fat, and he has a mug like a hamster's. All covered in freckles. He's a quiet bloke, domestic, steals quietly too, but now he's landed in it. He'll be punished one way or another, and he'll have to carry the can for nearly everyone in the group and all for nothing. They've nick-named him 'pickled eggs'.

From Galya's Diary

30th May

I realise I don't love Tolya. He's good looking – but I don't really like him. I think his eyes, which all the girls rave about, are hard and flat. All the girls have fallen for him but he loves only me. Tolya told me today. He tried to kiss me. I didn't let him. I can't kiss someone I don't love.

Marinka came round to see me. She's pregnant. She doesn't know what to do. They say that usually you can't have an abortion the first time. She told Sashka about it all. He's agreed to marry her. But the main thing is that now her whole life is going to be really limited by the baby. She can forget about studying.

I think she ought to get rid of the baby any way she can.

From Misha's Diary

30th May

After classes today me and Laskin were kept behind to polish the floor in the main hall. We'd been late and they always make late comers do something. We polished it quickly and went to our night class. On the way Vas'ka said that he had a rouble. We went over to the day school which is opposite the college and scrounged fifty kopecks from the kids there. We bought a bottle of wine. We went to the botanical gardens. Climbed over the fence. Settled down in a pavilion which all our group knows. The pavilion is all covered in graffiti – names of boys and girls, the word 'love', and all sorts of swear words. There are even drawings with explanatory notes. I don't know why the kids do it. And when Vas'ka took his knife out I told him not to write anything.

It's strange, though. Take Vas'ka. He has clear, simply transparent, blue eyes. Ruddy cheeks, so that he always looks as if he's running a temperature. In our group they call him 'Masha'. And there he was, wanting to write or draw something filthy. Yet the main thing was it was all there in his head already. It's sort of weird. Who would believe, looking into those clear, blue eyes, that Vas'ka steals things from the factory, that Vas'ka shoots pigeons, that he swears like a mindless drunkard.

And he's the Komsomol [Party youth] organiser in our group.

Pyotr Kozhevnikov, *Two Notebooks* [*Dve tetradi*], *Metropol'* (Ardis, 1979)

Further Reading

Good general studies of Soviet society include D. Lane, *The End of Social Inequality?* (London, 1982); M. Yanowitch, *Social and Economic Inequality in the Soviet Union* (London, 1977); and B. Kerblay, *Contemporary Soviet Society* (London, 1983). Chapter 13 of D. Barry and C. Barner-Barry, *Contemporary Soviet Politics*, 2nd edn (Englewood Cliffs, NJ, 1982), corroborates much of what Kozhevnikov has to say.

Two literary works of note are Yu. Trifonov, *The House on the Embankment* (New York, 1982), a story of urban life, and D. M. Fiene (ed.), *Snowball Berry Red and Other Stories* (Ann Arbor, Mich., 1979), an anthology of the work of V. Shukshin, one of the leading 'village prose' writers of the Brezhnev era.

7

Technology and the Environment

Of all the political and social issues that have come to the fore in public discussion during recent years, few have been as significant as the environmental debate. Popular opinion at the time that the draft of the 1977 Soviet Constitution was published for discussion was strongly in favour of tough controls on pollution and environmental misuse. The 1977 Constitution explicitly recognised this with, at least on paper, clear formal commitments about environmental protection (Articles 18 and 67). This stems in part from the fact that the Soviet record on environmental matters is certainly no better than that of Western states, no truly effective mechanism to deter the polluter having yet been established.

In addition, however, there has been a certain reaction against the 'gigantomania' tradition of the Revolution: the belief that progress is an uncomplicated matter linked to simply providing more industrialisation or more electricity. Both Solzhenitsyn in his *Letter to Soviet Leaders* and, more generally, the 'village prose' writers of the 1960s and 1970s have drawn attention to the virtues of the simple, rural life with its traditional values. Such neo-Slavophil sentiments strike a deep chord with many Soviet citizens who have been only very recently uprooted from the land.

But the 1977 Constitution also included, as a 'motherhood' type of issue commanding universal support, calls for the strengthening and development of science and technology. The Lysenko era of short cuts and pseudo-science may have passed, but the overwhelming majority of Soviet people are not sceptical about the value of science and technology and still see a real need for further exploitation of the nation's resources if a truly modern industrial society is to be built. Hence, grandiose 'hero projects' and policies to 'bring all branches of the national economy to the frontiers of science and technology' (Brezhnev, 1981) still attract much support.

In the extracts that follow we seek to illustrate these related tensions, both, as it happens, in a Siberian context. This is perhaps appropriate given that the most publicised of all Soviet environmental debates has been over the slow but steady pollution of the Siberian Lake Baykal, the world's largest expanse of fresh water.

The first extract is again by Valentin Rasputin (see the previous chapter). It is taken from his novel *Farewell to Matyora*, published in 1976, which is unabashedly critical of much that passes for progress. The story is set in Siberia by the Angara River. The island of Matyora is to be flooded to make way for the building of an electric power station and the islanders have to prepare for relocation in a newly established settlement or the city. The younger ones – lured by dreams of technical progress and convenience – look forward to their new lives. The middle generation tends to be ambivalent. But the older generation bemoans what it sees as the spiritual desolation brought on by technology. The bureaucrats are only interested in themselves and 'successfully' clear Matyora. A new state farm is located on infertile land and its monotonous flats soon deteriorate. In comparison with the dehumanised new settlement, the doomed island seems an idyllic haven. The old inhabitants of Matyora have seen the past and know that it works.

The final section of our extract introduces a small spirit, a wood demon common in Russian folklore. This rather unusual element perhaps contains more than a hint that man is not necessarily master of his environment and that rationalism and the purely scientific approach to life have their limitations.

FAREWELL TO MATYORA

Valentin Rasputin

The cemetery lay behind the village by the road to the mill, on a dry, sandy rise, amid birch and pine trees, from where the Angara and her banks looked for miles around. The first to come up was Darya, bending forward determinedly, her arms stretched out as if she were picking berries; her lips were pursed sternly, betraying her toothless mouth. Nastasya was hurrying after her with some difficulty: short-windedness slowed her down and she had to keep throwing her head back and forth to catch the air. Behind them, holding a little boy by the hand, came Sima, mincing. Having upset the whole village Bogodul now kept well back and the old women rushed to the cemetery alone.

The people Bogodul had been calling devils were just finishing off their work, dragging away the sawn off posts, the fencing and crosses, and stacking them up to be burnt on one big bonfire. A burly peasant, like a bear, wearing a green tarpaulin coat and matching trousers, was striding through the graves carrying an armful of rotten old wooden gravemarkers when Darya with a final effort tore ahead of the others and struck him a glancing blow on the arm with a stick she had picked up. It was a soft blow but the shock of it made the man drop his load on the ground and he shouted in surprise:

'What yer doing, what yer doing, woman?'

'Clear off outa it, yer demon!' shouted Darya, panting with fear and anger, and she wielded the stick once again. The man jumped out of the way.

'Now then, woman, you just . . . keep your hands to yourself. I'll tie 'em up for yer. Yer . . . you . . .' His big red eyes glared at the old woman. 'What are you doing here? Is it because of the graves?'

'Clear off, we're telling you!' said Darya, advancing on the man. He retreated, stunned by her terrifying expression, which showed she was ready for anything. 'Get yer gone right now, you heathen! Ruining the graves . . .' Darya howled. 'Did you bury them here? Are your mother and father lying here? Kiddies lying here? You never had a mother or father, you heathen. You're not a person. What kind of a person would have a mind for this!' She looked at the crosses and posts that had been collected and dumped down anyhow, and howled all the more sickeningly: 'O-o-h! Do away with him, Lord God, on the spot, don't have mercy! No-o,' she said, rounding on the man again. 'You're not going off out of it just like that. You'll answer for this. You'll answer to the whole world.'

'Oh, leave off, woman!' roared the man. 'You'll do the answering. I've been given my orders and I'm doing what I'm told. I couldn't care less about your dear departed.'

'Who ordered you? Who ordered you?' asked Sima, pitching in from the side without letting go of Kolya's little hand. Sobbing, the little boy pulled her back, away from the huge, infuriated man, and Sima, giving in to him, retreated still shouting out: 'There's no sacred spot left on the earth for you lot! Yer petty tyrants!'

Hearing the noise a second peasant came out of the bushes – he was a bit smaller, a bit younger and more neat in appearance, but not one to be pushed around either and he was also wearing green tarpaulin work clothes – he came out with an axe in his hand, stopped and squinted.

'Look at this,' said the bear to him, cheering up. 'Flew at me, they did. Waving sticks around.'

'What's the matter, citizens about to be flooded?' asked the second man importantly. 'We are the sanitation work team; we're clearing the territory. By order of the Sanitary and Epidemic Centre.'

Nastasya thought these incomprehensible words were meant to mock her.

'What Snakery pediatric Centre?' she snapped back after a moment. 'Taking the mickey out of old women! You're a snake yourself! You're both greedy snakes! There ain't punishment too much for you. And don't you try 'n' scare me with that axe. Drop it.'

'What a turn up for the books this is!' said the man and stuck his axe in a nearby pine tree.

'And don't squint. Look, he squinted his eyeballs at me like a thief. Look us straight in the eye. Wha' yer been up to then, snakes?'

'Wha' yer been up to? What yer been up to?' chimed in Darya.

The orphaned graves, picked bare, piled up into equally dumb heaps, which she looked at in her feverish torment, trying to take in what had been done and getting all the more anguished because of it, once again assaulted her with their disfigurement. Losing control of herself Darya, stick in hand, again rushed at the bear as he was the nearer, but he grabbed the stick and jerked it away. Darya fell to her knees. She did not have the strength to get up right away, but she heard Sima's heart rending cry and the boy's; and then the men shouting something as if by way of a reply, then more shouting taken up by many voices, welling up into a crescendo which finally exploded; someone took hold of her and helped her to her feet, and Darya saw that all the people from the village had come running up. There were Katerina and Tatyana, Lisa and the kids, Vera, old man Yegor, Tunguska, Bogodul and some others. There was a hell of a din. The two men were surrounded, they had no chance of snarling back. Bogodul had taken possession of the axe which had been stuck in the pine tree, and was poking the bear in the chest with a sharp stick while swinging back the axe in his hand as if in preparation. Old man Yegor was shifting his eyes silently and uncomprehendingly between the crosses and stars which had been broken off the posts and the two men whose work it all was. Vera Nosareva, a strong, unemotional woman, caught sight of her mother's photograph on one of the posts and flew at the two men with such rage that they recoiled and tried to protect themselves from her, well and truly frightened. The din welled up with even more force.

'Wha's the point o' talking – let's sort 'em out right now. This is the best place to do it.'

'So they'll learn, the pagans.'

'Why profane this place? Let's chuck 'em in the Angara.'

'And they've not been punished; their hands ain't even withered.'

'Where do they get people like this?'

'They pulled them all up like carrots . . . Just think!'

'Clear 'em off the face of the earth, and she'll say thank you.'

'Fucking bastards!'

The second man, the one a bit younger, was trying to shout above the crowd, throwing his head back like a cock and turning from side to side:

'Do you think it's us? Do you think it's us? You must understand. They gave us the instructions, brought us here. We're not here on our own account.'

'Liar,' they interrupted, 'you came here in secret.'

'Let me get a word in,' said the man with an effort. 'It wasn't in secret, an official came with us. He brought us here. And your man Vorontsov here.'

'That can't be true!'

'Take us to the village – we'll get everything sorted out there. They're there.'

'That's true, let's go back to the village.'

'There's no point in that: let 'em answer for it here, where they've done the damage.'

'They won't get away from us. Let's go.'

And they herded the men off to the village. Only too glad and relieved, they hurried; the old women were unable to keep up and slackened their pace. Bogodul hopped and skipped along as if hobbled, and would not let the tall man go, constantly prodding him in the back with his stick. The man kept turning round and bellowing – in reply Bogodul twisted his mouth into a satisfied smirk and gestured to the axe in his hand. The whole noisy, nasty, fervent procession – kids in front and kids behind, and in the middle, hemming in on all sides the two men, scruffy, indignant, old men and women bent up double and more, mincing along and shouting in wheezing unison, kicking up all the dust on the road – this crowd ran into a couple of people hurrying to meet it as it approached the village: one was Vorontsov, the chairman of the village Soviet, and now of the bigger Soviet in the new settlement, and the second was unknown to them, but he looked like an office worker and he had a straw hat and a face a bit like a gipsy's.

'What's all this? What's going on here?' demanded Vorontsov from a distance as he walked. The old women immediately kicked up a racket, waving their arms, interrupting each other and pointing to the two men, who, growing a bit bolder, had broken out of the encirclement and jostled their way through to the one who looked like a gipsy.

'We're, you know, only doing what's necessary, and they set on us,' the young one said to him by way of explanation.

'Like dogs,' chimed in the lanky one and scoured the crowd with his eyes, looking for Bogodul. 'You scarecrow, I'll . . .'

He did not finish. Vorontsov interrupted him, as did the old women, who had responded to his 'dogs' comment with a roar of indignation.

'Qui-et!' he ordered, drawing out the syllables. 'Are we going to listen to each other or have a shouting match? Are we going to try and understand the position or what? . . . They,' Vorontsov nodded to the men, 'were carrying out a sanitary clearing of the cemetery. It's been authorised to do this everywhere. Is that understood? Every-where. Authorised. This is Comrade Zhuk; he's from the department dealing with the flooding of this region. It's his job and he'll explain to you. Comrade Zhuk is an official.'

'Well, if'n he's an official person, let 'im answer to the people. We thought them there were lying, and him there, that person. Who gave the order for our cemetery to be cleared away? There's people lying there, not animals. How dare they ruin the graves? Let 'im give us an answer. The dead would like to know too.'

'These little capers don't take place for nothing.'

'Mother of God! What 'ave we lived to see. You ought to die of shame for talk like that.'

'Are we going to listen, or what?' repeated Vorontsov, in a sharper tone of voice.

Calmly, almost as if by habit, Zhuk waited for them to pipe down. He looked worn out, tired, his gipsy face was ashen. To judge by appearances his job was no cushy number, especially if you reckoned that he had to explain himself like this to the local population on more than one occasion. But he began slowly and confidently, even with a touch of condescension in his voice:

'Comrades! There seems to be some misunderstanding on your part. There's been a special resolution passed.' Zhuk knew the power of words such as 'decision, resolution, directive' even when uttered softly. 'There's a special resolution passed regarding the sanitary clearing of the whole bed of the reservoir. And also the cemeteries . . . Before letting the water flow, the area to be flooded had to be put right, the territory had to be prepared . . .'

Old Yegor could not stand any more of this:

'Don't you start pulling the wool . . . You just tell us why he had to chop down the crosses?'

'And I will,' snapped Zhuk and, taking offence, started to speak faster: 'You all know the sea is going to come pouring over this place, there'll be great steam ships sailing, people coming . . . Tourists, and foreign tourists. And your crosses will be floating about. They'll be flushed out and washed away, they won't stay under the water over the graves as they ought to. You have to consider that . . .'

'And have you considered us?' shouted Vera Nosareva. 'We're living people, this is still where we live. You consider the tourist in your own good time. I've just picked up my mother's photograph that these pigs of yours left lying on the ground. How's it to be? Where am I going to start looking for her grave, who's going to show me? The steam ships will come, and how's it going to be for me here now? You can stick your tourists up . . .' Vera gasped for breath. 'As long as I live here and there's ground under my feet you're going to respect her. In the end you can get your clearing done, as long as we don't have to see it . . .'

'When is "the end"? We have seventy points designated for re-settlement, and there are cemeteries everywhere. You don't know the circumstances and you're in no position to talk.' Zhuk's voice had hardened perceptibly. 'There are eight cemeteries to be shifted altogether. That's "the end". It can't be put off any more. I have no time to spare either.'

'Don't give us that claptrap.' It was a well known fact in the village: it was difficult to stir old Yegor but, once you did, you'd better hang on tight, for nothing would stop him. And that's just the way it was now, as the old man became more and more heated. 'Git right back to where you come from,' he exclaimed. 'Don't lay another finger on that cemetery, or I'll get my gun. I don't see no "person" in you. An [official] person has to have a bit of respect for people, not just a hat on his head. Look, he applied for a job, they found him one. In the old days for work like that they . . .'

'What are they on about?' said Zhuk, turning pale and looking to Vorontsov for help. 'They don't seem to understand. They don't want to understand . . . Aren't they aware of what's going to happen here?'

'Fucking bastard!' said Bogodul, emerging from the crowd.

Vorontsov stuck out his chest and shouted:

'Why have you kicked up all this racket? What for? This isn't a menagerie!'

'And you, Vorontsov, don't you raise your voice to us,' old Yegor cut him short, coming up closer. 'You ain't been living here five minutes yerself. You're a tourist yourself . . . only you turned up before the sea. You don't give a fuck where you live, whether it's in our village or somewhere else. But I was born in Matyora. And my father was born in Matyora. And my grandfather. I'm the boss round here. And as long as I'm a local round here you ain't gonna boss me about.' Old Yegor stuck his black, gnarled finger right under

Vorontsov's nose, menacingly. 'And don't shame me. Let me live out my life without disgrace.'

'Don't you get the people all worked up, Karpov. We're going to do what must be done. We won't ask you.'

'Clear off!' urged old Yegor, pushing Vorontsov away.

'This is something else again,' agreed Vorontsov. 'We won't forget this.'

'You remember. You don't scare me.'

'He's found someone to stick up for him.'

'There's a lot like you!'

'Make yourself scarce before there's any trouble.'

Once again the old women's tempers boiled over and they started shouting, squeezing Vorontzov, Zhuk and the two men tighter into a circle. Vera kept thrusting the photograph of her mother under Zhuk's nose – he kept backing away and frowning uncomfortably; Darya and Nastasya were pressing him from the other side. Zhuk's hat was knocked sideways revealing his pitch black, curly hair, so that the resemblance to a gipsy became even greater – it looked as if at any moment he would come to the end of his tether and would jump up whooping like a gipsy and start lashing out right and left in his own fashion, breaking free from them all. Old Katerina took Vorontsov to task, rounding on him and saying over and over: 'You ain't no right, you ain't no right.' When Vorontsov tried to get away Tunguska loomed up in front of him, still silently puffing away at her pipe, wordlessly indicating to him that he should listen to Katerina. Old Yegor's deep bass kept booming out as the main, dominant voice. And to the accompaniment of all this hubbub, which was getting more and more heated, Vorontsov and Zhuk, scarcely able to get a word in edgeways, extricated themselves with some difficulty from the crowd and set off back to the village. The lanky one tried to take the axe from Bogodul, but Bogodul snarled and brandished it. Old Yegor, who happened to be next to the lanky one, advised:

'Take it easy with 'im, laddy. He was exiled out here to us. He's already sorted out one man . . .'

'What, he's a criminal, you mean?' said the tall man, his curiosity excited.

'Yeah.'

'Go on. Then I am too.'

'Okay then, just try it. We'll watch.'

But the lanky man hesitated, looked again askance at Bogodul, who was winking at him with his intimidating, almost burning red eye, and ran off to catch up the others. An hour later all four of them had sailed away from Matyora.

. . . And late into the night the old women were crawling around the cemetery, sticking the crosses back in place and setting up the posts again.

And when night came and Matyora fell asleep, from under the banks of the mill stream a little creature, hardly bigger than a cat and unlike any other animal, popped out – Master of the island. If there are brownies haunting the peasant huts, then there has to be a Master for the island as well. No one ever saw him, or met him, yet he knew everyone here and knew all that had ever gone on from one end to the other of this isolated piece of land surrounded by water and rising out of the water. That's why he was the Master, so that he might see all, know all and never interfere. That was the only way it was possible to remain Master – so that no one ever met him, no one ever even suspected his existence.

Even earlier, peeping out of his burrow, his long standing refuge on the mill stream bank, he saw the evening stars appearing and then fade. Maybe they were still now to be found somewhere, because a gray twilight was flowing down from on high and it must have been coming from somewhere, but even his sharp eyes could not make them out. Anyway, he did not like looking up at the sky; it caused him some ill defined, groundless disquiet and frightened him with its awe inspiring infinity. Let people look up there and find comfort, but what they consider aspirations amount only to memories; even in their furthermost and sweetest painted thoughts, they're only memories. No one is given the chance to dream.

It was a warm and quiet night and certainly elsewhere it was dark, but here, beneath the huge sky above the river, it was clear and transparent. It was quiet, but in this sleepy and living silence, teeming like the river, you could easily make out the babbling of the water on the upper, nearby promontory and the remote, hollow, uncertain sound of the shallows, like wind in the trees, far off on the left bank, foreign territory, and the occasional momentary splash of a fish lingering late in his play. These were the upper surface sounds discernible to the ear, the sounds of the Angara; once they were heard and identified, you could hear the sounds of the island too: the plaintive, strained swishing of the old larch tree in the cattle yard as well as the dull stamping of the grazing cows there, the juicy sounds of chewing the cud all merging into one sound, and in the village there was the constant bustle of everything alive outside – the chickens, dogs and cattle. But even these sounds were loud and coarse to the Master's ear, for with particular pleasure and special zest he was listening closely to what was going on both in the ground and close to the ground: the rustling of a mouse setting out on a hunt, the lurking flurry of a birdie, roosting in its nest, the weak, fading creaks of a waving twig, which seemed to disturb the night bird, and the breathing of the grass as it grew.

Jumping out of his burrow and pricking up his ears, identifying as usual all that was going on around, with his same customary unhurriedness and care the Master travelled his course over the island. He did not stick to one road; today he might run off to the left and tomorrow to the right, half way across his territory from somewhere around the pine grove he might turn back, or he might run right to the end or even get over on to Podmoga and stay there a few hours, checking on the life there, but he never missed out the village. It was here that all sorts of changes occurred most often. And, though the Master had a foreboding that soon everything would change in one fell swoop, to such an extent that he would no longer be Master, no longer be anything, he had come to terms with it. What will be will be. He had also come to terms with it because after he was gone there would be no other Master; there would be nothing left to be master of. He was the last. But, as long as the island remained, he was its Master.

He ran up the hill by the place where old Darya sat in the afternoons, and lifting his head he looked around. Matyora lay tranquil and motionless: the woods were growing dark, the young grass over the ground was silver with dew, the village looked black with great dim patches, where there was no knocking or rattling but it seemed as if somehow people were making ready to bang and clatter. The warmth of the day had gone and cool vapours with a bitterish tang wafted up from the ground. From somewhere the feeble, heavy sigh of the wind came through, gasped and died away – like a wave breaking on the sand. But it was the old larch which rustled longer and more alarmed; and, for no reason, as if half asleep, a cow groaned blindly, almost wailing like a cat. Far away in the undergrowth on the river bank a blackberry bush, forced down to the ground by another bush, finally broke free and sprang up to its full height, waving. The water swished – or a bubble that had floated all evening finally burst, or a fish gave a final shudder as it died: unfamiliar ripples ran over the grass and went away in narrow stripes, and only now the last of last year's leaves fell from the birch tree that stood next to the larch in the cattle yard.

The master headed for the village.

Valentin Rasputin, *Farewell to Matyora* [*Proshchaniye s Matyoroy*], *Nash sovremennik*, 1976, nos 10–11

The second extract, by contrast, consists of two poems dedicated to the building of the Baykal–Amur Railway (BAM), and symbolic of the continuing Soviet belief in 'hero projects'. BAM, under construction since the 1950s, and still uncompleted, is of major economic and strategic importance. Eventually it will run to 2,000 miles, connecting the trans-Baykal region with the Soviet Far East, enabling easier exploitation of Siberia's natural resources and offering an alternative to the existing exposed Trans-Siberian line close to the Chinese border. Although it is not without its environmental critics, BAM is one of the most celebrated hero projects of the present time, on a par with Khrushchev's Virgin Lands programme of the 1950s or the Stakhanovite movement of the Stalin years as a device for galvanising Soviet pride and enthusiasm.

Poetry plays a more important role in everyday life in the Soviet Union than in the West. Certainly in the 1960s public readings were attended with the same enthusiasm as BBC Promenade Concerts are in London. Russia has produced some of the finest poets in the world. Yet a certain amount of dross also rolls off the presses. There are special problems attaching to the translation of verse, but we hope that not too much damage has been done to the two examples we include below. They are taken from a much reprinted anthology of reportage, fiction and poetry devoted to BAM.

TO THE CHILDREN OF BAM

D. Bunin

Prettier than all the world's flowers
Fiery little eyes a-burning.
Our children, children of BAM,
Hurrying to school in the morning.
Improve your knowledge, O dear ones,
We'll give you the best we can.
There are other great projects ahead –
Together we'll build more than one BAM!

FORWARD

Stepan Grishaenkov

We know how to build roads
Winged is our homeland's ascent
Not sparing our strength in our work
We'll go forward and never relent.

Up steep slopes and over the swamp
We go through Taiga forest remote.
To ardent, exciting work
Our whole hearts we devote.

From Tynda on to grey Baykal
We'll lay trains' iron roads.
Before the BAM construction scheme,
Building history knew nothing so grandiose.

And these, the people's creations
We undertake, as October insists.
Under the Leninist sun of freedom,
We live in peace, as Leninists!

BAM – the Construction of the Century [*BAM – stroyka veka*],
Sovremennik, 6th edn (Moscow, 1980)

Further Reading

There are several studies of environmental issues in Soviet politics, including
T. Gustafson, *Reform in Soviet Politics* (Cambridge, 1981); M. Goldman,
The Spoils of Progress (Cambridge, Mass., 1972); F. Singleton (ed.),
Environmental Misuse in the Soviet Union (New York, 1976); and B.
Komarov, *The Destruction of Nature in the Soviet Union* (London, n.d.
[1980]).

Among literary treatments are the novel by F. Iskander, *The Goatibex
Constellation* (Ann Arbor, Mich., 1975), a satire on Lysenkoist-inspired
scientific experimentation, and other works by V. Rasputin, notably *Live
and Remember* (New York, 1978) and *Money for Maria and Borrowed
Time* (London, 1981). The full text of *Farewell to Matyora* has also been
translated by A. Bouis (New York, 1979).

A Soviet writer's documentary account of environmental loss is to be
found in V. Soloukhin, *A Walk in Rural Russia* (London, 1966).

8
Nationality and Religion

As befits such a vast country, the Soviet Union embraces a multi-plicity of nationalities and religious groups, many of which were inherited from a Russian Empire that had conquered diverse peoples. Nationality and religious problems were supposed to be eliminated by the Revolution. The proletarian movement would develop an international consciousness, overcoming national differences and antagonisms. Religion, an 'opiate', would also disappear once exploitation and class struggle ceased. In fact, neither has happened; both nationality consciousness and religious observance are, if anything, on the increase.

Of the two, the nationality question is undoubtedly the more serious, for it has many ramifications and is potentially explosive politically. Only just over half the population now consists of Great Russians; more than twenty other national groupings have at least 1 million people, including some 40 million Ukrainians and nearly 45 million Muslims – the latter having more than doubled in the past twenty years, and likely to double again by the end of the century. Yet the Soviet Union is culturally and politically dominated by Great Russians, and the tensions that this sets up in language, cultural identity and economic development are real and unlikely to diminish.

Equally the Soviet achievement in holding together such a diverse empire ought not to be underestimated. Living standards among many of the national minorities are higher than in central Russia itself, native elites have, so far, been relatively well satisfied, and such tensions as do exist are often to be found in relations between the national minorities themselves rather than between them and Moscow. Also, to some extent the Soviet regime derives strength not weakness from perhaps the most significant rise in national consciousness in recent years – that of the Great Russians themselves, for it is a nationalism that the regime has been able to harness fairly successfully.

The religious question is one on which the state's attitude has varied over time from one of extreme hostility to reluctant toleration. Neither approach appears to have had much impact on popular belief. There are reputedly 30–50 million regular attenders at Orthodox church services, and tenacious minority groups of Catholics – mostly in Lithuania – Baptists, Pentecostalists, Jews and others. Half the marriages that take place are in church, and some 60 per cent or more of babies are baptised. The prevalence of religious worship is not in itself a threat to regime stability; but it complicates the nationalities question and reinforces the fact that the making of 'new Soviet man' is an uphill task.

The extract which follows gives a taste of the way in which the Party actively campaigns against such 'unprogressive' social phenomena as religious belief. It is taken from a novel by Vladimir Tendryakov (b. 1923), *On Apostolic Business*, and the somewhat crude tactics employed perhaps give some indication as to why the regime has been relatively so unsuccessful in this area.

Tendryakov was one of the most notable writers of the post-Stalin era, stories such as *Three, Seven, Ace,* about the corruptibility of ordinary Soviet workers attracting much attention. Once in the vanguard of the attack on Stalinist socialist realism, Tendryakov, who is a productive writer, is today perhaps the most prominent 'thaw' figure still being published in the Soviet Union. His work has become more doubting and ambiguous than it was, however. Tendryakov appears to be less than sure about who are the positive heroes and what truly constitutes progress.

The theme of *On Apostolic Business* is the failure of materialist philosophies to satisfy man's inner aspirations and the need to recognise this – a point echoed by Nadezhda Mandelshtam in her memoirs: 'When I was young the question of the meaning of life had been superseded by the search for an aim. People are so used to this that even now they fail to see the difference between the two.'

Tendryakov's hero, Yuri Rylnikov, is a journalist in his mid-thirties, happily married and affluent, who goes through a crisis of this kind. He drops out and retreats to the supposedly more honest and holy countryside, only to find that scepticism about science and lack of material possessions do not make for better people. The Christians he meets are bigoted and often illiterate. Those who take his problems seriously are hostile to him. The local Party secretary is suspicious and nearly has him arrested. It is worth noting that contrary to normal Soviet practice Tendryakov's hero writes 'He' not 'he' etc. when referring to Christ.

ON APOSTOLIC BUSINESS

Vladimir Tendryakov

I bought myself a copy of the Bible through a bookseller I knew. [Because Bibles are not readily available in the Soviet Union.]

I did not expect to find God in it. After all, I had graduated from an institute and considered myself a relatively educated man, the spirit of the twentieth century was alive within me, and it was hardly likely that I would find something ready made among those husks of old; rather, I would create my own God, a more authentic one than the Bible's.

'What are you reading, Daddy?'

Little Tanya was squatting in front of the divan where I was lying reading the Bible, her head tucked between her little knees all covered in scratches, her bright little eyes shining up at me, the encroaching tender colouration of her fair locks and pink skin, and her taut cheeks puckered up in a smile.

'What are you reading?'

'Old fairy tales, Tanyushenka.'

'About Baba Yaga and her bony leg [the traditional Russian fairy-tale witch]?'

'No, not about her.'

'Read it to me . . . Or tell me.'

I could have told her the fairy story of a son being born of a carpenter's family, how grey-haired magicians came to the mother and told her that they had seen a star by which they could tell that a new king had been born. In all the other fairy stories magicians are never wrong, but in this one they were – the little boy grew up and became a pauper not a king, and he travelled from town to town teaching people how to be good. For this the pauper was seized and nailed to a cross.

I could have told her but I was afraid. The fairy story of the good pauper had created evil in history more than once. I was afraid that it would bring my daughter misfortune, too. Better not let her know this story for the time being; perhaps I would tell her it when she grew up, perhaps she would come across it herself.

I told her the usual story about Baba Yaga, who lived in a hut which had chicken's legs: 'Hut, hut, face me, with your back to the forest!' It was a harmless story . . .

I shielded my daughter from fairy tales, yet comforted myself with them . . . Most often with the story of Jesus Christ.

A defenceless pauper, He wandered through the world. The weak came to Him. In a world awash with blood there are more weak people than strong. The weak can become a force!

And the old gods trembled in fear. Their power over people was still great, great was people's fear of them, great the desire to appease them.

Barefoot and naked He wandered the earth preaching love, and hate was kindled around Him. He was against the usual, fearsome gods! He, who had been born in a stable, was not strong or fearsome . . .

Both the strong and the weak, both the evil by nature and the good equally continued to believe in the might of violence and the futility of love. The strong, the weak, the evil, the good, the offenders and the offended against, they all took up arms against Him.

But He did not go into hiding and issue weapons to His pupils. He did not prepare to defend Himself. He knew He was doomed.

A rebel against the gods! Ha-ha! How easy it was to deal with Him! . . .

Rome, the ruler of the world, loved order and adhered strictly to it: to each his own. Even death was dealt out strictly according to rank. Everyone from the Caesar to the pleb could be done to death, but none like the slave. The slave was executed in a slave's way – he was nailed to a cross. There is no death more humiliating.

He was born in a stable and died like a slave. He was restored to life a god, death defied by death!

The old fearsome gods died like gods – they simply disappeared from human memory. He, the weak one, became the victor, 'death defied by death'.

A fairy story that had lived for two thousand years! I comforted myself with it. But I told it to no one. Neither my daughter nor my wife . . .

[Yuri Rylnikov forsakes his family and takes up manual work on a collective farm. His beliefs soon land him in trouble with the local Party secretary, who arranges a public self-criticism session for him – a not uncommon way of dealing with people who fail to conform.]

On the wall of the club, a challengingly cumbersome building with a frivolous little porch and a sign saying 'Welcome', there was a large poster:

LECTURE

'Religious beliefs and contemporary science'

by
A. K. Lebedko,

Lecturer from the regional society, 'Knowlc lge'

8.0 p.m.
After the lecture there will be dancing.

That was curious. No, not the lecture itself. Very curious. Was this a fortuitous measure or was it somehow connected with my person? Five days before Ushatkov [chairman of the village Soviet] had taken an interest in me; to get a lecturer in five days, and not a local district one but someone special from the province, was the height of operational efficiency. Lecturers are not like the fire brigade; they don't come rushing when the alarm goes. Was it chance? . . . But, then, it was somehow too lucky for Ushatkov. And that warning visit from Teplyakov, the local policeman: 'Just leave here nice and quiet like for your own good.' Teplyakov had not disclosed that Ushatkov was up to something and that I had something to fear from him. What could it all mean?

I walked away from the poster with uneasy forebodings.

There was a rapping on the window.

'Hey, Rylnikov.'

There was a bunch of lads outside my window led by Grisha Postnov.

'Come outside.'

I went out on to the porch.

Grisha Postnov looked as though he was going to his wedding – a striped tie tied in a large knot, a nice new jacket tight at the shoulders, his round, stern face exuding the perspiration of the bathtub because of the warmth of the cloth, his golden forelock combed down to his brows, while his narrow shoes buffed up to an immaculate shine stamped the littered ground awkwardly. There were about five men standing behind Grisha, their hands in their pockets, shoulders squared, feet apart. Among them was the one whom I'd seen acquiring the new clothes in the shop that afternoon, the blue cap now pushed back on his head, the white label removed.

'What do you want?'

Grisha Postnov put his hands on his hips and said: 'We've come to take you to the lecture.'

'H'm . . .'

'Don't "h'm" us. Let's go.'

'Thanks for your concern, but I don't want to go.'

'Too bad. Other people want you to be there.'

'Which others?'

'Well, us if you like.'

'And why do you need me to be at the lecture so much?'

'We do, that's all there is to it, so don't play about. Go and get your coat on or we'll drag you there.'

'What a nice invitation!'

'Never you mind. We're not here on our own behalf; we're a sort of part-time police helpers [*druzhinniki*: volunteers, use of whom is widespread] – carrying out a task.'

'Whose task?'

'That's none of your business.'

If I refused, there would be an unedifying brawl. There were six of them and one of me; they would smash the hut up.

'Very well, then. Let's assume that I've suddenly conceived a burning desire to hear an anti-religious lecture by Comrade Lebedko.'

'OK, that's better . . . Only watch out, mate, that there's no tricks.'

I went in front and, one step away from me, carefully observing the distance, came the group, bunched together and serious-minded, full of determination, so that it was obvious to everyone we met that they were taking me!

On the club porch there was a bouquet of flowers, the village beauties in their flashy dresses, nylon stockings and high-heeled shoes, and all wearing the same fashionably coloured head scarves round their shoulders bearing the legend 'Let there always be sunshine, let there always be Mummy!' [a popular Soviet children's song]. Probably a large consignment of these scarves had recently come into the shop – just like the dark-blue caps.

'Make way, make way! Don't block the entrance!' Grisha Postnov kept shouting.

They stepped back, looked me over curiously, and started whispering.

The gloomy hall wasn't yet full, only the seats right at the back were taken, those in the corners and along the wall, furthest from the stage. The lads stood around in groups talking to each other and laughing; the girls stood around rather shyly in groups; there were a lot of fidgety kids of various school and pre-school ages. Of course the problem of religion and science which the well-versed lecturer from the big city, Comrade Lebedko, promised to present was of

particular concern to them. And there wasn't a single adult there.
Yes, there was; right in the middle of the hall in sedate isolation and
with exemplary patience shone the familiar bald head of none other
than Mikhey Karpovich 'Rudder' himself, sporting a clean shirt. It
was somehow strange to see him without his two fine sons either side
of him. When he noticed me, Mikhey Karpovich stirred, rose and
tried to shout something; he must have wanted to call me over, but
when he saw my entourage he felt embarrassed and sat down diffi-
dently.

They led me right up to the front row. 'You sit here.'

One of those accompanying me pushed a chair up for me and,
blushing with embarrassment at his own solicitude, turned away
under Grisha Postnov's threatening look.

I had the seat right in the middle with Grisha Postnov at my right
shoulder and the imposing figure of the lad with the blue cap on my
left – the thread from the torn-off label hung over his ear, he was
serene and serious; it was terrifying!

The stage was bathed in light for a gala performance by two
powerful lamps hanging from the ceiling. The stage was set with
Spartan simplicity: a perilously shaky rostrum decorated in ochre, a
table covered in faded red calico, and a jug of water on the table.
Everything was ready for the ceremonial rites, only the priests hadn't
yet arrived.

I felt somewhat offended – no, not at Grisha Postnov, what could
you expect of him? – but at Mikhey Rudder. He had become
embarrassed and turned aside, and yet if there were anyone who
sympathised with me, then it was him. Out of the whole village of
Krasnoglinka he was the only one, with the possible exception of
Auntie Dusya. Mikhey Rudder was Saint Peter. But, anyway, who
was I to condemn Rudder if the real Peter, Peter the Rock, had denied
Christ three times?

The stage was empty, the priests had been delayed. On my right
hand was Grisha Postnov, his lips pressed tightly together; on my
left, puffing quietly, the lad with the blue cap. And I was all on my
own. My Peter had renounced me and I had no sympathisers.

Just to amuse myself I started a conversation with Grisha Postnov.
I didn't dare talk to the one on my left – his profile was too severe.

'I'm completely baffled. Has the eminent guest deigned to come
here all on my account?'

'A great honour,' growled Grisha.

'I must confess, I'm flattered. The province has sent out a responsible warrior to do battle with me.'

'Don't kid yourself. He's been travelling round our district for a long time now. Just doing his job. We asked him to come, a long time ago.'

'I see. And, fool that I am, I was bursting with pride. I thought: He's a special one, an extraordinary one, just for me personally!'

'Someone like this doesn't concern himself with only one person in particular. He's an educated man, gives lectures on science and on the international situation.'

'A jack of all trades, then?'

Grisha realised that he would do better to keep quiet.

The first signs of the lecture starting came not from the stage but from the street outside. A 'commanding' voice rang out outside the doors of the auditorium: 'Come on, come on, move yourselves! They've come to swap sweet nothings! Go in, quick now!'

Behind my back there was the sound of people pouring into the hall – chit-chat, girls laughing, benches rattling.

And then at last from the side somewhere, from the peace and quiet of the wings, there appeared the chairman of the village Soviet, Ushatkov, and behind him, without any grandeur, even with a sort of unimpressive restiveness – where should he put his briefcase? – sidled the man himself!

None the less, Grisha Postnov flashed a look of triumph and pride at me as if to say, 'Now you're in for it!'

Ushatkov, out of some professional habit, touched the jug with his pencil with an air of austere insistence, took in the hall with a frosty stare, waited for the noise to abate and looked coolly at me paraded ostentatiously in the first row.

'Comrades! Here to our village of Krasnoglinka has come a representative ... H'm ... From an organisation ... From the regional society for the dissemination of useful scientific knowledge ... Comrade Anatoliy Kostantinovich Lebedko! Let us welcome him, comrades.'

He was greeted with applause, albeit scant. 'I don't want to jump the gun, anticipate events, so to speak. I will just say one thing – it's no coincidence that a lecturer has come to us, no coincidence that he is addressing us on a necessary, so to speak, most topical subject. And now, without further ado, let me hand you over to Comrade Anatoliy Kostantinovich Lebedko. Let us welcome him once again.'

And once again he was greeted with scant, polite applause. Well, why not? No skin off anyone's nose.

I was expecting Ushatkov to bring up my name right away and signal the target.

No, Lebedko didn't possess the happy appearance of a people's tribune, magnetic and quelling. He was short, he wore a reasonably well-worn suit – all right for travelling in and something he wouldn't be ashamed of wearing in front of an audience – held himself at an angle, one shoulder hunched up, the other drooping, a sad, soft, polite face, a face suggesting the meekness of an educated man. No, he was no bare-knuckle fighter, a tribune, not all-consuming, not inflaming. He was probably a bookish man, knew things pretty well, did not resort to the hackneyed ploys of town lecturers, did not mention the mistakes in the Bible that set your teeth on edge, such as God creating the earth before the sun, but he did talk about the Dead Sea Scrolls, the Essenes, the Gilgamesh Epic, and he even spoke of things which I, a former employee on a journal keen on scientific sensations, did not know – the latest information concerning the location of what the Bible called the Garden of Eden . . .

Certainly you couldn't have said that the lecture lacked substance.

'What entices the idealists, comrades . . .' He had a quiet clear voice and a gold filling glittered comfortably in his mouth. 'What entices the idealists, comrades, is the study of the immortality of the soul. Religion considers that only the body dies and the soul, having departed, continues to live. As you know, the soul of just people goes to heaven where eternal bliss awaits them. The souls of the unjust go down to hell where boiling pitch, burning pans and other terrifying instruments of torture are prepared for them. Now, we materialists, in answer to this sweet and innocent lie, honestly declare that man is mortal! There is nothing waiting for us beyond the grave. Honestly! To dream about the immortality of the soul is as unnatural and absurd as to hope that time will flow backwards, that old men will become youths, and youths babies. There are unshakeable laws, comrades, the laws of nature, you can't refuse to recognise them, it is stupid to turn your back on them. A mathematician cannot assume that the sum of the angles in a triangle be, let's say, more or less $180°$. The physicist cannot help but reckon with the laws of energy conservation. It is just as nonsensical to lull yourself to sleep with some incorporeal immortality – the immortality of the soul.'

He finished speaking and he was clapped politely once more.

Ushatkov stood up from his chair, a thin man with a transparent face, impassive.

'Don't leave yet, comrades! The lecture is, so to speak, only half of our programme this evening . . .'

No one had any doubts about that; they had all come to the club not for the lecture but for the dance afterwards. But Ushatkov had prepared something else.

'We have just heard a lecture, comrades. From it we have learnt how science views religion. To put it bluntly, it views it with hostility! And can you imagine, comrades, an intelligent, educated man banging his head on the ground in front of the icons in the company of some illiterate old woman, saying forgive me, Lord, and have mercy? Somewhere in some rotten places abroad you might see such extraordinary things going on but not here in our country! No? . . . No? . . . Out of the blue to our village of Krasnoglinka from Moscow itself has come a man just like that . . . Quiet, comrades, quiet! No need to start looking at each other. You'll see enough of him. We'll show him to you! . . . So he's come here. Who is he? . . . Comrades, he graduated from an institute in the capital, he gained knowledge from great professors and mastered his discipline, to be honest, an honourable one – he's a physicist, comrades, a physicist! He even used to write articles about his physics in journals, apparently a literate man with a good scientific background . . . And suddenly, quite openly – I might say, defiantly – this physicist confesses: "I believe in God and I'm proud of it!" They gave him his scientific spurs and look at him, falling off his horse. Obviously it's no feather bed for ideological cripples like that in Moscow, so let him come to us in Krasnoglinka. They're all clodhoppers out here, he thought, I'll make out nicely with them. But, comrades, are we such simple folk that we can't tell a rotten mushroom from a healthy one just by looking at it? And you can't scare us with your alien propaganda; we'll hear you out and won't get poisoned. And now, comrades, it's up to us to ask this guest from the capital to come out and show himself. We'll look and we'll listen . . .'

'We-will-listen!'

'Come-on-out!'

'Come on, then, Rylnikov, come out and show us what goes on inside you, so to speak.'

'Hey, you! Show yourself! Don't hide!'

There was shouting all over the hall. And next to me Grisha Postnov squealed as if stung: 'Out into the light with the obscurantist! In front of the people! Knock the Lord God out of him!

'We demand it!' roared my neighbour in the blue cap.

'Comrades!' said Ushatkov raising his thin, bony arm. 'Quiet, please, no panic! Rylnikov, the people demand. Come on out and look the people of Krasnoglinka in the eye and tell them straight, no whispering behind closed doors somewhere . . .'

'Go on, or it'll be the worse for you!' chimed in Grisha Postnov with all the presence he could muster, his eyes burning and cheeks blazing, all but grabbing me by the lapels.

There was Ushatkov with his pointed shoulders staring down at me from the chair; the lecturer wincing and embarrassed at such a sharp turn of events trying to look past me; and Grisha Postnov and his pals; and the hostile threatening rumble of people's voices at my back . . . I had to go or it would be worse for me.

I stood up and made my way towards the steps that led on to the stage. The hall was silent, silent, only the people's breathing could be heard.

I stumbled on the top step and someone in the audience laughed. As if I weren't enough of a laughing-stock already. And the laughter brought out the malice in me. I went over to the rostrum, trying to make my steps as firm as possible.

For some reason I expected the hall to be packed out and the people I was now facing to present one monolithic whole, but the hall was half-empty, with open spaces here and there, and of course the people sitting there were not so much interested in religion as in the dancing afterwards. Be that as it may, those faces, devoid of features and expression from where I was, frightened me. Faces, faces, and those bright headscarves the girls wore round their shoulders dotted throughout the hall, with 'Let there always be Mummy!' written on them.

I probably stood there for a long time, for the silence began to be suffused with malicious murmurs and whispering. It was time to start.

'Well, have you had a good look?' I asked. 'Go on, look, this is what an obscurantist looks like. Probably roughly the same as a heretic used to look in the old days – with horns on his head and hoofs for feet.'

The audience laughed. Ushatkov tapped the water-jug angrily. 'No joking, no joking! Be serious!'

'But I'm being quite serious, Comrade Ushatkov. Quite serious and quite prepared, as you see. You suggest that I show you my obscurantist insides. Very well! I'm quite prepared to. I'll do it if you can tell me how it's done.'

As the serious lecture had gone on the audience had become lulled and then tired out, having expected some entertainment. That was why it had howled furiously: 'Drag him out!' It was prepared to be cruel for the sake of some entertainment. But now I was proposing some entertainment and the audience agreed with me – and why shouldn't it? There were titters and shuffling in the hall. Ushatkov tapped the jug.

'Tell us, to start with,' he said, 'do you agree with the lecture?'

'No, not with a great deal of it.'

The laughter and shuffling suddenly stopped.

'I see! Could you inform us with what exactly?'

'Well, for instance, that there's no such thing as the immortality of the soul. I consider that there is!'

Someone at the back of the hall emitted a mockingly resonant 'Ooh-ooh!'

Lebedko looked at me with ironic disgust. To the rescue then, Bekhterev [famous Russian neuropathologist, 1857–1927]!

> 'Even if you shower him with stars
> An ass is an ass just the same,
> He'll just twitch his ears
> When you have to use your brain,'

I recited.

'What's that?!'

'That, Comrade Ushatkov, is a particle of the soul of a man who died one hundred and fifty years ago.'

'And who are those words about?'

'Not about you, I hope. You didn't even exist a hundred and fifty years ago. Comrade lecturer, help me to convince Comrade Ushatkov that poetry is a spiritual manifestation of man, an expression of his soul, so to speak . . .'

The lecturer did not reply to me; he leant back in his chair and turned an angry pink. Apparently, like Ushatkov, he had taken the poem to be addressed to him.

'The famous Russian scholar, Bekhterev,' I went on, 'wrote a work called "The immortality of the human personality from the scientific point of view". I ask you all, the esteemed lecturer and all those present, to note the words "Immortality of personality", and not simply that but from "the scientific point of view". The famous scholar asserts that the spiritual side of man never disappears without trace but lives on in one's ancestors. So more than a hundred and fifty years ago a certain man, Gavrila Romanovich Derzhavin [classical Russian poet, 1743–1816], spent his spiritual energy and wrote that poem. He himself died, but the spiritual in him, that particle of his soul, continues to live and is among us today. Now, I could have said whose soul it was, but in most cases the spiritual continues to live anonymously. You, Comrade Ushatkov, are sitting at this table, but someone expended spiritual energy on the riddle of how to stand the table-top on four legs. We don't know how many thousands of years ago that man died, his name has been forgotten, his bones have rotted away, but the spiritual in him, the expressed part of his soul, lives among us people today in the form of material tables, at which we eat, drink, work, hold meetings. And, whatever we take, whatever we concern ourselves with, we'll always run into the living souls of people long since dead. That jug of water, which you're tapping with your pencil now, Comrade Ushatkov, the pencil itself, the jacket on your back, the piece of bread you ate with your dinner – all these things consist not just of palpable material, but also of the spiritual manifestation of people who died long, long ago. Without being aware of it ourselves we are living among atomised immortal souls. And these immortal souls aren't vegetating in paradise, they are among us and they will die when the whole of mankind dies . . .'

But Ushatkov had been tapping on the jug for a long time by now. He stood up, waving a hand at me carelessly.

'Sit down! . . .'

'But I wanted to say a bit more about the immortality of the soul.'

'We've had enough. We've heard more than we want to.'

'Maybe you have, but others haven't.'

'Sit down!'

No one from the audience supported me and, with a shrug of my shoulders, I left the stage and went back to my place, sensing with every cell of my body people's eyes turned on me.

Vladimir Tendryakov, *On Apostolic Business* [*Apostolskaya komandirovka*], *Nauka i religiya*, 1969, nos 8–10

The second extract is taken from a work by one of the Soviet Union's most successful non-Russian writers, the Kirghizian Chingiz Aytmatov (b. 1928). Aytmatov comes from a remote and relatively unlettered national minority and was born in a small settlement in the foothills of the Tien Shan mountains, close to a vast desert-like area called the Hungry Steppe. Three hundred miles west, amidst some of the highest mountains in the Soviet Union, lies the Issik-Kul, a vast lake. The area as a whole lies almost 2,000 miles south-east of Moscow at the far edge of Soviet Central Asia, close to the Chinese border. Of the million-odd Kirghizians, most are descendants of nomadic tribes and many now raise sheep and horses on collective farms.

Aytmatov has risen from this background to become a major Soviet literary and establishment figure, yet he is still keen to parade rather than conceal his national culture and traditions. His reputation in the West is also substantial, for he is a genuinely fine writer tackling important themes, often with some ambiguity. His *Farewell,*

Gul'sary! (1966), for example, outwardly the tale of a Kirghiz peasant and his horse, contains much implied criticism of collectivisation and Party methods. *The White Steamship* (1970) is a haunting tale of a seven-year-old boy and his grandfather, set in the mountains above Issik-Kul. The grandfather feeds the boy's imagination with the folklore of Kirghizia. On the surface the work's principal theme is the need to preserve harmony between man and nature, 'to preserve the wealth and beauty of the world around us'. It is possible to read much more into the tale, however; the patterns of domination and dependence in the boy's family, the corruption in modern life, the prevalence of drunkenness and violence, and the final disappearance and possible suicide of the innocent boy in a worryingly 'negative' ending have all bothered Soviet critics. However, *The White Steamship* is included here not to emphasise such points, but simply as an example of skilful and effective writing by a non-Russian, and a reminder of the very real national complexities of the Soviet Union.

THE WHITE STEAMSHIP

Chingiz Aytmatov

[From a mountain top near his grandfather's home, where he lives, the boy daydreams about his parents.]

The lad looked around in all directions. Everywhere were mountains, cliffs, rocks and forests. Glittering streams flew down silently from glaciers above. Only here, down below, did the water seem to acquire a voice – to produce its incessant, eternal sounds in the river. The mountains were vast and limitless. At this moment, the boy felt very small, entirely alone and wholly lost. Alone with the mountains, everywhere the great mountains.

The sun was already starting its descent towards the lake. The heat was becoming less powerful. The first short shadows were appearing on the eastern slopes. Now the sun would sink lower and lower, and the shadows would creep down to the foot of the mountains. At this time of day, the white steamship usually appeared on the Issik-Kul.

The lad directed the binoculars to the farthest visible point and held his breath. There it was! Everything was immediately forgotten: there, in the distance, on the bluest of blue edge of the Issik-Kul, the white steamship appeared. It was underway. There it was! Long, powerful and beautiful, with its funnels all in a row. It travelled straight and smooth, as if on a string. The lad hurriedly wiped the lenses with his shirt tail and again adjusted the oculars. The ship's outlines became even clearer. Now you could see it rolling gently on the waves, and how its stern left a light trail of foam. Motionless, the lad watched the white steamship in rapture. Had it been in his power, he would have begged the white steamship to come closer, so that he could see the people on board. But the steamship knew nothing of this. It moved along its own course slowly and majestically, from an unknown origin to an unknown destination.

For a long time, the ship could be seen steaming on; for a long time, the lad thought about how he'd turn into a fish and swim down the river to join it, the white steamship.

When he first saw the white steamship one day on Guard Mountain, saw it there on the blue Issik-Kul, his heart chimed so from its dazzling beauty that he decided at once. His father – an Issik-Kul sailor – had to work precisely there, on the white steamship. And the lad believed this, because he very much wanted to.

He remembered neither his father nor his mother. He'd never seen them, even once. Neither of them visited him even a single time. But the lad knew: his father was a sailor on the Issik-Kul and his mother, after the divorce from his father, had left her son with his grandfather and moved to the city. She moved – meaning vanished. Moved to a distant city beyond the mounains, the lake, and yet more mountains.

[Grandfather Momun, the only person to show the lad any kindness, tells him the old Kirghiz legend of the Horned Deer-Mother, a Siberian maral deer, who saves the Kirghiz people from extinction by suckling two children, the only survivors of a brutal massacre, and leading them safely from their ancient homeland in Siberia to their mountain paradise.]

At last Horned Deer-Mother delivered her children to the Issik-Kul. They stood on the mountain and marvelled. Snowy crests towered everywhere around them and, amidst the mountains covered with green forests as far as the eye could see, splashed and sparkled the great sea. White waves moved across the blue water; the wind whipped them from far behind and drove them far away. No one could tell where the Issik-Kul began and where it ended. The sun rose at one end while at the other it was still night. Mountains beyond count soared around the Issik-Kul, nor could one guess how many of the same snowy peaks stood beyond these mountains.

'This is your new homeland,' said Horned Deer-Mother. 'You will live here – will farm the earth, catch fish and raise cattle. You will live here in peace for a thousand years. Your kin will endure and multiply. And your descendants will not forget the tongue which you have brought here; let them take delight in talking and singing in their own language. Live as human beings should live. And I shall be with you and your children from now and forever . . .'

This is how the boy and girl, the last of the Kirghiz tribe, found a new homeland on the blessed and eternal Issik-Kul.

Time passed quickly. The boy became a strong man and the girl a mature woman. Then they were married and became man and wife. Horned Deer-Mother did not leave the Issik-Kul but lived in the neighbouring forests.

One day at dawn, the Issik-Kul suddenly ran high and made a great clamour. Labour had come to the woman; she was in pain. The man was frightened. He ran atop a cliff and began calling loudly:

'Where are you, Horned Deer-Mother? Do you hear the clamour the Issik-Kul is making? Your daughter is giving birth. Come quickly, Horned Deer-Mother – help us . . .'

Then a lilting peal was heard from afar, like the tinkling of a caravan bell. The pealing came closer and closer; finally Horned Deer-Mother ran into sight. She carried a child's cradle on her horns, hooked under its arch – a *beshik*. The *beshik* was made of white birchwood, and a silver bell jingled on its arch. To this day, that bell jingles on Issik-Kul *beshiks*. Mothers rock their cradles and the silver bell tinkles, as if Horned Deer-Mother is running up from afar, hastening to bring a birch cradle on her horns . . .

The moment Horned Deer-Mother appeared to answer the call for her the woman gave birth.

'This *beshik* is for your first-born,' said Horned Deer-Mother. 'You will have many children – seven sons and seven daughters.'

The mother and father rejoiced. They named their first-born in honour of Horned Deer-Mother – Bugubai. Bugubai grew up, took a beauty from the Kipchak tribe as his bride, and the Bugu clan – the clan of Horned Deer-Mother – began to multiply. The Bugu clan became great and strong on the Issik-Kul. The Buguans revered Horned Deer-Mother as their goddess. An emblem was embroidered at the entrance to Buguan *yurts*: maral horns, so that it would be seen from afar that the *yurt* belonged to the Bugu clan. When the Buguans repulsed enemy raids and competed in games on horseback, the war cry 'To Bugu' resounded – and they emerged victorious. In those days, white, horned marals roamed the Issik-Kul forests, and the stars in the sky envied their beauty. They were Horned Deer-Mother's offspring. No one disturbed them; no one allowed them to be hurt. At the sight of a maral, the Buguans dismounted and made way for her. They compared the beauty of their favourite young girls with the white marals' beauty . . .

This was how life went on until the death of a very rich, very famous Buguan – he had had a thousand thousand sheep and a thousand thousand horses, and everyone near by had served as his shepherd. His sons organised a great funeral feast for him, inviting the most celebrated people from all corners of the earth to his feast. They set up a thousand and one hundred *yurts* for the guests on the shore of the Issik-Kul. No one could count how many cattle were slaughtered, how much mare's milk was drunk, how many kashgar sweets [named after the Chinese city of Kashgar, this is one of the 'eastern sweets' popular in Central Asia] were served. The sons of the rich man carried themselves with an air of great importance: people should know what rich and generous heirs survived the dead man, how they respected him and cherished his memory . . . ('Beware, my son, it's a bad sign when people make a display not of wisdom but of wealth!')

The bards, riding about on thoroughbred horses that the sons of the deceased had given them and showing off in sable hats and silk gowns, also provided for them, vied with each other to praise the deceased and his heirs.

'Where else under the sun can you see such a happy life, such a luxurious feast?' sang one.

'From the day of the earth's creation, nothing like this has taken place!' sang a second.

'No one else but we revere our parents, render homage to our parents' honour and glory, cherish their sacred names,' sang a third.

'Hey, you gas bags, what are you chirping about here? Do you really think that words worthy of these bounties exist? Are there any words equal to the deceased's glory?' sang a fourth . . .

Thus they competed day and night. ('Beware, my son, it's a bad sign when bards compete in this kind of eulogising. Singers turn into enemies of song.')

The memorable funeral feast was celebrated for many days, each like a holiday. The rich man's conceited sons wanted dearly to outshine all others and surpass everyone else on earth, so that word of them would spread through the entire world. And they thought to mount a maral's horns on the tomb of their father, so that everyone would know that this was the final resting place of their renowned ancestor of the clan of Horned Deer-Mother. ('Beware, my son: as long ago as ancient times people said that wealth breeds arrogance – and arrogance, recklessness.')

Once the sons of the plutocrat felt the wish to bestow this unheard-of honour upon their father's memory, nothing held them back. It was no sooner said than done. They dispatched hunters, and the hunters slew a maral and felled her horns. The horns were magnificent, like the wings of an eagle taking flight. The sons were duly pleased with the maral's horns, each of which had eighteen shoots – meaning the deer had lived eighteen years. Fine work! They ordered craftsmen to mount the horns on the tomb.

Old men at the feast were indignant.

'By what right did they kill a maral? Who dared raise his hand to the offspring of Horned Deer-Mother?'

The heirs of the rich man answered:

'The maral was killed on our territory. And everything that walks, crawls and flies in our domain, from flies to camels, is ours. We know how to deal with our own possessions. Be off with you.'

Servants beat the old men with lashes, mounted them backwards on horses and banished them in disgrace.

It all began with this. Great misfortune befell the progeny of Horned Deer-Mother. Almost everyone began hunting white marals in the forests. Every Buguan considered it his duty to mount maral horns on the graves of his ancestors. Now this practice was regarded as something virtuous, as a token of special respect to the memory of the dead. Those who couldn't lay hands on horns were now considered unworthy. A trade in maral horns sprang up, and they were laid in store. People emerged from the clan of Horned Deer-Mother who made their craft acquiring maral horns and selling them for money. ('Beware, my son, where money rules, there is no place for a kind word, no place for beauty.')

Dark days befell the marals of the Issik-Kul forests. They were shown no mercy. The marals took refuge in inaccessible cliffs, but were hunted down even there. Packs of hound dogs were let loose upon them, driving the marals into the ambush of hunters, who felled them with rarely a miss. Marals were killed in entire herds; they were flushed out in whole stands. Bets were laid as to who would get the horns with the most shoots.

Finally, no marals remained. The mountains had been emptied. Not at midnight nor at dawn could a maral be heard. Not in forest nor glade could one be seen grazing, galloping, tossing his horns on his back or leaping over a crevasse, like a bird in flight. People were born who would never see a maral during their entire lives. They only heard fairy tales about them – yes, and saw horns on tombs.

And what happened to Horned Deer-Mother?

She was deeply hurt and took grave offence against people. It was said that when bullets and hound dogs had made life impossible for the marals, when maral had become so few that you could easily count them on your fingers, Horned Deer-Mother mounted the very highest mountain peak, bade farewell to the Issik-Kul and led her last children across a great pass, to another land and other mountains.

These are the kind of things that can happen on earth. This is the full tale – believe it if you want to; if not, don't.

When Horned Deer-Mother left, she said that it was never to return . . .

[But the maral deer return; the boy and his grandfather and the boy's cruel and violent Uncle Orozkul sight some in the forest. The legend comes more than ever alive to the boy. He tells some visiting soldiers all about it.]

The lad calmed down somewhat and, in general, felt a bit better. The ache in his head was less severe. He even considered whether he should get up and have a look at the lorry. What kind was it, a four or six wheeler? New or old? And what kind of trailer did it have? Once last spring a real army lorry visited them on the cordon – it had tall wheels and a snub nose, as if somebody had cut off its snout. Its young driver, a soldier, let the lad sit in the cab – that was wonderful! And an officer with golden shoulder straps went into the forest with Orozkul. What was it all about? Nothing like that had ever happened before.

'What's this about – are you chasing down a spy?' the lad asked the soldier. He grinned.

'Yeah, we're hunting a spy.'

'We haven't had a single spy come our way so far,' the lad breathed sadly.

The soldier burst out laughing.

'What do you need a spy for?'

'I'd chase after him and catch him.'

'My, my, you're a nimble little fellow. But you're still small, you'd better grow up first.'

While the officer with the golden shoulder straps tramped in the forest with Orozkul, the lad and the driver warmed to their conversation.

'I love all lorries and all drivers,' said the lad.

'And why is that?' the soldier asked.

'Lorries are good – strong and fast. Then they smell good, of petrol. And drivers: they're all young and all children of Horned Deer-Mother.'

'What? What's that?' The soldier did not understand. 'Who's that horned mother?'

'You really don't know?'

'No. I never heard of such a marvel.'

'Then where do you come from?'

'I'm from Karaganda – a Cossack. I studied in a mining school.'

'No, I mean whose son are you?'

'My father's. And mother's.'

'And whose are they?'

'Also their fathers' and mothers'.'

'And they?'

'Listen, you can keep on asking that forever.'

'I'm the son of Horned Deer-Mother's sons.'

'Who told you that?'

'Grandfather.'

'Something's a bit funny somewhere,' said the soldier shaking his head doubtfully.

He was intrigued by this large headed boy with the protruding ears, the son of Horned Deer-Mother's sons. However, the soldier was somewhat embarrassed when it was revealed that he not only didn't know where his clan had begun, but didn't even know the obligatory seven generations in his family tree. The soldier knew only his father, grandfather and great-grandfather. And beyond that?

'Didn't they teach you to remember the names of your seven ancestors?' the boy asked.

'No, they didn't. And what for? So I don't know – nothing's come of it. I've managed to live without it.'

'Grandfather said that, if people don't remember their fathers, they'll turn bad.'

'Who'll turn bad? People?'

'Yes.'

'Why?'

'Grandfather says that if this happens nobody will be ashamed of the bad things they do. Because their children and their children's children won't remember him. And nobody will do good things. Because all the same, his children won't know about them.'

'That's some grandfather you have,' said the soldier with genuine wonder. 'A very interesting grandfather. Only he stuffs your head with all kinds of rubbish. You're a big headed fellow, after all – and you have ears on you like our radar on the firing range. Don't you listen to him. We're marching to Communism, we're flying in space – and what's he teaching you? He ought to sit in on our political instruction sessions, we'd wisen him up in a wink. And you, you'll grow up some day, learn how things are – and see that you clear away from your grandfather. He's an ignorant one, backward.'

'No, I'll never leave grandfather,' the boy objected. 'He's a good man.'

'Okay, that's all right for now. You'll understand later.'

Now, straining to hear the voices, the lad remembered the army lorry and how he wasn't able to make the soldier understand why local drivers, at least the ones he knew, were considered sons of Horned Deer-Mother.

[Orozkul and some hunters from the town, even grandfather Momun, slaughter and eat a sacred maral. An orgy of alcohol and eating follows. The boy, delirious with despair, leaves.]

Behind the windows of Orozkul's house, drunken voices roared and shouted. The boorish haw-hawing deafened the boy and brought him unbearable pain and torment. It seemed to him that it was this appalling laughter that made him ill. Recovering his breath, he walked across the yard. It was deserted. Near the dying fire, the lad came upon grandfather Momun, deathly drunk. The old man was lying in the dust near Horned Deer-Mother's severed horns. The dog was chewing at the stump of the maral's head.

The lad roved farther. He went down to the river. And stepped directly into the water. Hurrying, slipping and falling, he ran across the shallows, shivering from the icy spray – and when he reached the rapids the current knocked him off his feet. Floundering in the turbulent torrent, he swam, choking and freezing.

The lad swam down the river, at times face up, other times face down; sometimes being held back near piles of stones, other times rushing towards the waterfalls . . .

No one yet knew that the lad was swimming as a fish down the river. The drunken song sounded in the yard.

> From the hunch-backed, hunch-backed mountains,
> I arrived on a hunch-backed camel,
> Hey, hunch-backed dealer, open the door
> We'll drink some bitter wine . . .

This song you no longer heard. You were swimming, my lad, into your tale. Did you know that you would never turn into a fish, not reach the Issik-Kul, not see the white steamship and say to it, 'Hullo, white steamship, it's me!'

You swam.

I can only say one thing now: you rejected what your child's heart could not reconcile itself to. And that's my consolation. You lived like a bolt of lightning which once – and only once – flashed and expired. But lightning strikes from the sky. And the sky is eternal. This too is my consolation. And that a child's conscience in a person is like an embryo in a particle of grain: the grain won't grow without the embryo. That whatever awaits us on earth, truth will endure forever, as long as people are born and die.

Taking leave of you, my lad, I repeat your own words: 'Hullo, white steamship, it's me.'

Chingiz Aytmatov, *The White Steamship* [*Bely parakhod*], trans. Tatyana and George Feifer (London: Hodder & Stoughton, 1972)

Further Reading

Useful general studies of the nationalities and religion are: J. Azrael (ed.), *Soviet Nationality Policies and Practice* (New York, 1978), and H. Carrère d'Encausse, *Decline of the Empire* (New York, 1979); A. Bennigsen and C. Lemercier-Quelquejay, *Islam in the Soviet Union* (New York, 1967), and B. Bociurkiw and J. Strong, *Religion and Atheism in the USSR and Eastern Europe* (Toronto, 1975). See also G. Luckyi (ed.), *Discordant Voices: The Non-Russian Soviet Literatures* (Ontario, 1975).

Works of Aytmatov in translation, including *Farewell, Gul'sary*, are to be found in *Tales of the Mountains and Steppes* (Moscow, 1973). His most recent novel, which has received much critical acclaim, *The Day Lasts More Than a Hundred Years* (London, 1983) is an intriguing blend of science-fiction, social criticism and national awareness. Similarly some Tendryakov is available, including *Three Seven Ace and Other Stories* (London, 1973) and *A Topsy Turvy Spring* (Moscow, 1978). V. Maksimov, *Seven Days of Creation* (Harmondsworth, 1977), is an epic set in the Stalin and post-Stalin years, with a Christian theme of redemption; and A. Rybakov, *Heavy Sand* (Harmondsworth, 1981), tells of the Jewish experience during and after the Revolution and up to the German occupation.

9
Academic Life

The final extract is taken from a novel by one of the more idiosyncratic of contemporary Soviet writers, Irina Grekova. Grekova is the pen name of Irina Ventzel, born in Tallinn, Estonia, in 1907. She is a mathematician, for more than thirty years a professor at the Moscow Air Force Academy, for whom writing is a sideline developed only since the early 1960s. Grekova's voice is a distinctive one, that of a middle-aged or elderly widow and mother, a practical sort with pride in her life and her hard times but with a humorous outlook on life. She writes with some flair, and has been criticised in the Soviet press for being 'neutral' or uncommitted.

Grekova's best-known story is 'Ladies' Hairdresser' (1963), a clever parody of several elements in Soviet culture. The hairdresser, Vitaly, is a complex perfectionist whose ambition is to become an expert in dialectical materialism, in the naïve belief that this will ensure his success in Soviet society. The victim of semi-digested or poorly integrated official dogma, Vitaly unconsciously parodies the clichés of officialdom. He is a highly plausible grotesque figure, and indicative of Grekova's skill at characterisation and dialogue.

Some of Grekova's stories are plainly autobiographical, at least to the extent that their setting is a scientific institute in Moscow. This is so of her novel *The Department*, published in 1980. It is set in a department of mathematics and revolves around the death of the old professor and the appointment of his successor. A martinet with a passion for punctuality and administration, he meets resistance and eventually resigns, but *en route* Grekova has much to say about the Soviet higher education system.

It is a system which, quantitatively, is impressive. Over 5 million students, 60 per cent of them full-time, study in either universities or specialised institutes. Competition can be quite fierce, despite the fact that courses last for five years, grants are very low and new graduates are expected to work for two years in any job assigned to them, for the long-term rewards can often be considerable. Qualitatively, however, Soviet education does raise questions, most particularly the central dilemma of mass societies – how to reconcile the goals of education for all to a high level with education for the best to the highest level. There may be none of the discipline problems or radical questioning of authority that have become part of the Western educational pattern but, as in the West, there seems to be a marked conflict between the interests of the individual on the one hand and the rigidity of examinations and rote learning on the other.

In the extract which follows, the old professor, Zavalashin suggests improvements and reforms as he worries about the future of higher education. Zavalashin argues for quality rather than quantity and, like many in the department, appears to resent being made a creature of the central plan, which requires a certain *number* of graduates above all else. In this respect, Grekova mirrors some of the concerns that are to be found in other writers in this volume: Avdeenko and Abramov, for example, both comment wryly on plan tyranny; Rasputin and Granin both contribute to the debate about quality rather than quantity, as, in different ways, do Tendryakov and Aytmatov. After several generations of rapid leaps forward, there is plainly a more questioning and uncertain air abroad which is reflected in the work of such writers.

It is worth noting that Grekova's department is a typical Soviet institution. Such establishments, which take in the majority of students, are primarily teaching not research centres; almost all postgraduate work and research is concentrated in the more prestigious universities proper. The hours are extraordinarily long. The new director announces that he is going to demand a ten-hour working day. The pressures from above, notably the Dean's office, are typically Soviet plan-oriented.

Yet, despite all this, Grekova's account of an academic departmental meeting, while hardly in the same vein as the celebrated passage in Malcolm Bradbury's *The History Man*, ought to be very recognisable to Western readers. It need scarcely be added that the same applies to a number of the issues that this book has considered, for many Soviet problems have their Western counterparts.

THE DEPARTMENT
Irina Grekova

[The setting is a department of mathematics in a Moscow institute. It is an old pre-revolutionary building in a poor state of repair. The department has been promised new accommodation, but a move is not imminent. A departmental staff meeting is taking place. Participation is varied. Some lecturers are using the occasion to read novels; the Professor is apparently asleep.]

The short winter's day was coming to an end, gilded in sunshine. The spider's web it had hung by was just about to break. Outside the window in the institute's garden the wind was stirring the frozen branches of the trees. The odd leaf that had survived was hanging on them here and there . . .

The subject was fail marks (twos). [Soviet students are graded from one to five, five being the top mark.] The winter harvest had just arrived – that is, the examination season – and there were supplementary exams [for those who had not taken them when they should have] and resits. 'Not all the rye was yet taken away, but it was reaped. Things were easier now for them,' said Markin [a greying, dishevelled ironic man], quoting Nekrasov's words [famous nineteenth-century poet]. He was stuffed full of quotations, and threw them into the conversation every minute, sometimes even aptly. A terrific memory. 'Unsingleminded', Kravtsov called it. [Kravtsov, an ambitious young man, is the Professor's deputy. His doctorate is a fashionable piece on 'Methods of systems technology in the theory of self-adjusting systems'.]

According to the plan of departmental meetings the exam results were under discussion. Nina Astashova was speaking loudly in her best lecturing voice, as if addressing a huge audience, with clear diction, carefully enunciating the ends of the words; you could have taken notes from it if you had wanted to. Experienced lecturers often talk like this – loudly, urgently, authoritatively, giving an impression of haughtiness. It's artificial. It is professional training. [Nina Astashova is eventually the chief opponent of the new director.]

That is the scene. Someone is making a report.

'The question of fail marks isn't new. We discuss it every exam season. It's a waste of time talking about it. There's no solution to it. "You can't harness a horse and a frightened fallow deer to the same cart." What does the Dean's office want? Bureaucratic tidiness. It wants the percentage of good and excellent marks to keep rising steadily from exam season to exam season and the percentage of failure marks to fall. And, sure enough, one rises and the other falls! Twice a year we participate in a humiliating procedure – we hear a report on the progress of the struggle for success. Percentages are counted up, fractions of a per cent, diagrams are drawn. Isn't it a disgrace to take up busy people's time with such nonsense?'

'That's right!' boomed Semyon Spivak [a large, bushy-bearded, aggressive-looking man with a reputation for failing students] in approval.

'You'll have a chance to speak,' said Kravtsov. (NN [the Professor] was silent and enigmatic behind his glasses.) 'Please go on, Nina Ignatyevna.'

'I shall. The ambition of the Dean's office is that all the students should be outstanding. This is a clear absurdity, since the very word "outstanding" means standing out from others. A "five" [i.e. a first-class grade] is unthinkable without a background to stand out from. It's not the standard metre kept at the weights and measures office. When an examiner gives a mark, he's measuring the student's knowledge on a relative not an absolute scale.'

'Oh, come on!' said Spivak in anguish. 'We're not talking about "fives" but "twos".'

Kravtsov banged on the table with his pencil.

'May I ask the speaker to go on with her report and the rest of you to refrain from commenting.'

'Thank you. On one side of the fence we have the Dean's office, on the other there's us. They want things to look satisfactory in a formal sense; we want knowledge regardless of form. Of course, the easiest thing would be for us to comply: not give any twos, only a minimum number of threes, and fours and fives as required. That would make life easier for us; no one would reproach us, except our consciences . . .'

' "The clawed beast, tearing at the heart, conscience," ' remarked Markin obligingly [a quotation from Pushkin's *The Miserly Knight*].

'Yes, conscience,' said Astashova emphatically, her face darkening. 'And life teaches us that that's a fragile thing to rely on. It's objective conditions and not conscience that dictate a person's behaviour. These conditions, whether we like it or not, are pushing us into the world of fiction. Fictitious marks, fictitious achievements, fictitious book-keeping . . .'

'Aren't you getting off the subject, Nina Ignatyevna?' asked Kravtsov cautiously.

'On the contrary, this is very much to the point. I'm talking about our institute's affairs. How is our work being assessed? According to the average, the percentage of twos. It's quite ridiculous! Who but we ourselves give these marks? Let's make a comparison with other areas of production. Where have you ever heard of the work of a plant or factory or workshop being evaluated according to marks they award themselves? Yet that's just what's happening here! Formal criteria unsupported by objective monitoring inevitably lead to whitewashing.'

On hearing the word 'whitewashing' Kravtsov pricked up his ears and said: 'I object. That's an unsubstantiated charge.'

'No, it isn't. Let's be honest. Let everyone ask himself how many twos he would give if there weren't any pressure from above.'

'Me? I would give as many as I do now,' said Spivak.

'I believe you, but you're an exception. We all know what the rule is, though: we'll put down a three, though it should be only two.'

'I disagree,' said Kravtsov. 'I give the marks I do without being pressurised.'

'You're also an exception,' answered Astashova tetchily, her crooked tooth showing.

'Nina is right,' said Ternovsky [one of the oldest members of the department, a white-haired man with Chekhovian pince-nez and an immaculate black suit]. 'One thinks twice before one gives a two. If you do give one, it's bad all round: for the student, for you yourself, the department, the faculty . . . And where's the sense in it? Give him a two and he'll be back for a resit like a boomerang. And you don't anticipate time spent on resits in your workload, and so you're overburdened right away. All right, then, we don't want to make a habit of being overworked. But the point is that he comes back, often as not knowing less than he did before. You give him another two. And the Dean's office sends him back again. And again. According to the rules in force you can't resit more than twice – a third time and it's a question of withdrawing from the course. Yet, as we know, the Dean's office is afraid of a student's failing. And so they send him back to you time and time again "by way of an exception". Water will eventually wear away a stone. You weigh it all up, give it a bit of thought, and give him a three. That's the way it will end all the same.'

'No, not all the same!' roared Spivak. 'If anyone here thinks it's all the same, he can clear out of this institute!'

'Excuse me, comrades. We seem to have moved on to a discussion without having heard all of the report,' interrupted Kravtsov. 'Nina Ignatyevna, we've heard your criticisms. But criticism without constructive proposals is fruitless. What do you suggest at the end of the day?'

'Isn't it obvious? I suggest that we stop the practice of assessing the work of the lecturers, of the departments and of the institute as a whole by the success rate of the students. Do away with these empty reports on the progress of the struggle for success. Rid ourselves of the petty tutelage of the Dean's office . . .'

'Well, that's impossible,' said Kravtsov firmly, 'in our society . . .'

'In *our* society it *is* possible. In particular, in this institute. Let them assess our work by the output, the quality of the work of our graduates.'

'That's Utopian. Any other suggestions?'

'Only of the most general kind. We should select students more carefully, trust them more, check up on them less. And, above all, the checking must be done skilfully.'

There was a general hubbub. Kravtsov rapped his knuckles on the desk.

'Comrades, comrades, you're preventing the speaker from finishing her report.'

'Well, I think that's all I have to say. Some of you already know my view, some of you will find it unpleasant, and some will simply find it boring. It's no wonder Professor Zavalashin is asleep.'

Everyone looked at NN: he really was sleeping. This was a peculiarity of his: diatribes overwhelmed him. Something descended on him, smothered him gently, and he sank into a sleep, as into a duvet as huge as the world. True, he did not sleep on unrelenting; he always retained some contact with what was going on around him, remotely comprehending what was being said. As soon as his name was mentioned he started to wake up. He lifted his head, opened his eyes, and, after two jerks of his cheek and two false starts, said: 'I'm not asleep. I'm listening to everything.'

'That's not the way it looked to me. Your eyes were closed.'

'Heavy eyelids,' said NN, closed his eyes again and lowered his head.

'The Viy [a monster with enormous eyelids in Gogol's story of that name],' whispered Ella [Denisova, a stunning blonde nicknamed 'Miss Cybernetics'].

'It's a good job he's asleep,' responded Stella [Polyakova, her friend]. 'For Christ's sake, don't let him wake up and start talking. . . Don't wake her at dawn [the words of an old popular song].'

'Would anyone like to ask the speaker anything?' asked Kravtsov, trying to get the meeting back on course.

Markin raised his hand. 'I have a question. Two characters were mentioned: a horse and a fallow deer. How is one to understand this?'

'The Dean's office and us,' explained Spivak.

'Who's the horse and who's the deer?'

'The horse is the Dean's office, and the frightened deer is us.'

'It's the other way round,' said Astashova, her eyes flashing. 'The frightened deer is the Dean's office. They're afraid, not us. If we were, there wouldn't have been any fail marks for ages.'

'Can't we', said Markin, unabated, 'regard this conflict situation [*sic*, translator] as a stalemate?'

'That's silly,' replied Nina.

'Comrades, comrades, let's not insult each other,' interrupted

Kravtsov. 'We've still to debate the report. Who would like to say something?'

Spivak stood up, squared his shoulders and stuck his chest out. His trousers rippled, and did not so much droop as drop.

'This is all bloody nonsense, hot air: "absolute scale, relative scale". A two is a two; I just have a feeling for it. I used to get them myself. Someone who gets twos is a lover of life, a Sybarite. If you don't dish him out a two in time, then he'll skive. I know from my own example. If it hadn't been for the professors of our university generously giving me twos, I'd still be skiving today. My humble thanks to them for those twos. Of course, things were different then; no one was afraid of giving twos. If I were a student in our institute now, I'd never be transformed into a human being.'

'The role of work is the process of turning monkey into man,' chipped in Stella, stretching out her leg.

'Exactly! Work, work and more work! And none of this, what do you call it, sighing on the park benches and strolling in the moonlight. As teachers we must fight for our sacred right to give fail marks. They are trying to bend us and we're not bending. If they push us, we must stand firm. So long live the two!'

'Two, bird-two, who invented you?' asked Markin [an untranslatable pun referring to the famous ending of Gogol's *Dead Souls*, Part I: 'troyka bird-troyka'], but received no supporting laughter.

Kravtsov was considering whether to rebuff Spivak's demagogy immediately or to bide his time. He decided to bide his time. At times he was a bit afraid of Semyon's stormy temperament.

'Who else wants to say something? Only keep strictly to the agenda and spare us the lyrical digressions. Perhaps you, Ella?'

Ella [the blonde] reluctantly began to speak.

'There are, of course, a lot of twos. The struggle for success is in principle a good thing. But one must think about the students as well. What sighing on the park benches? They don't even have time to sigh at their desks. It's all work; even copying up lecture notes takes time and there isn't any . . .'

Having only recently graduated herself, she still had not come round to the teachers' point of view and was always on the students' side. The class enmity of the oppressed towards the oppressor was not yet extinguished in her.

'They have all the conditions they need for work,' remarked Kravtsov, examining his nails.

'All the conditions they need! Have you been into student hostel number 2?'

'Not yet.'

'Well, you ought to. There's no conditions there; it's a nightmare. The pipes burst the other day; there's literally no washing water. They have to take kettles to the standpipe in the street. The lads don't mind, it's no skin off their noses, but it's difficult for the girls . . . They complained to me as their tutor. Women always understand each other. The exception being the hall warden. I went to see her. She was something out of the Dark Ages – only needed a burial mound built round her. She didn't want to do anything about it . . .'

'Naturally,' said Markin. 'A person whose welfare doesn't depend on the quantity and quality of his work never wants to do anything.'

'What about us, then?' shouted Spivak. 'Your welfare and ours depend on the quantity and quality of our work, only in reverse. The less you work, the better you live.'

'Another exaggeration,' remarked Kravtsov acidly. 'But let's get on with the departmental meeting. Who else wants to speak?'

Radiy Yuryev [a genial redhead] put his hand up. He stood up, smiling infectiously. Immediately everyone began to feel that everything was all right.

'Comrades,' said Radiy, 'we must try to find the inevitable compromise. A lot of people here are trying to turn things upside down and make radical changes. Given his head, what wouldn't any one of us do? But as university teachers we must not try to find solutions to national questions. Everybody has his speciality. And there are only two areas where everybody thinks he knows best: medicine and running the country. Forgive me, Nina, but your constructive suggestions are naïve. They are on a par with being one's own doctor or, worse still, going in for folk cures. For instance, I know a good mathematician who suddenly went off his head and took up acupuncture; possibly it's a very fine thing, but it should be left to the doctors, and mathematicians should stick to their subject – there's enough of it in our day and age.'

'I can only express my solidarity,' said Kravtsov approvingly.

Radiy thanked him with a bow and sat down. Nina Astashova threw an angry glance at him. Pasha Rubakin [a junior lecturer with long hair and tattered 'hippy-style' jeans] stood up and started to speak in a hollow, underground voice.

'The last speaker has reminded me of a joke. May I tell it?'

'Only if you keep to the time limit, two or three minutes,' said Kravtsov, looking at his watch.

'Don't worry. It'll only take a moment. This is a German joke, but I'll translate it. A man comes home from work and catches his friend with his wife, and she is very ugly. The husband says to his friend:

"Ich muss, aber du?" ("I have to, but why do you?") That's all. Did I keep to the time limit?'

'Yes,' said Kravtsov with displeasure, 'but your joke has no bearing on the matter in hand. I must ask other comrades to save their own and other people's time and not wander off the subject. Who still wants to speak?'

He yawned.

The lecturers rose one after another and announced their exam results. Those who had a higher than average percentage of twos were nervous and referred to objective reasons (most frequently the potato digging was mentioned [students are temporarily drafted into the countryside at harvest time]). It was Pasha Rubakin again who presented the exception: he announced that the only reason for the poor performance of his group was the poor quality of the teaching.

'Can I really be a lecturer? Someone like me can only get a job in an institute through a misunderstanding. I'm as developed as a frog. Even less, a tadpole. I promise I'll pull my socks up by the next exams and develop perhaps to the level of a chicken.'

Everyone had grown accustomed to Rubakin's paradoxes and paid insultingly scant attention to them. Kravtsov alone said: 'One can only welcome your self-criticism. But what sort of an example are you setting the students with your personal appearance? We're battling with long hair . . .'

At this moment the door opened and in came a tall, fair-haired girl with the stature of a basketball player; she was wearing a little suede skirt that ended halfway up her thigh. She stopped timidly, still holding the door handle. Her legs were so long, stately and tightly clad that the entire male contingent of the department (with the exception of NN, who was asleep), not without pleasure, fixed their eyes on them.

'What do you want, young lady?' asked Kravtsov, coming to his senses.

'I want to do my mathematical logic exam.'

'Why didn't you do it when the exam season was on?'

'I did. I failed . . .'

[From NN's diary.]

I keep thinking about higher education, about its fate and its prospects. More precisely, about higher technical education (that's the only field in which I'm relatively competent).

It seems to me that in chasing after mass production we have lost something here. Inflation in higher education has begun to make its appearance. We need a sort of currency reform in this area [a reference to the Stalin currency reform of 1947, by which the new rouble was worth ten old roubles].

It is difficult for me to judge without statistics, but it would appear that the economy does not need the number of specialists which the higher technical institutes all over the country turn out every year. The engineer's diploma has been devalued. A qualified worker earns more than an engineer; this is an alarming sign.

The fund of knowledge which we give the students is unnecessary for the majority of them, and for a minority of them it's too little. As a rule, an engineer gets by on the job without sophisticated science. He needs quite different knowledge and practices (those of an organiser, or provider). Our bad students often make decent engineers.

A minority of our graduates goes in for scientific work, and the volume of scientific knowledge thay have received in the institute is extremely inadequate for them.

We groom these and the others in exactly the same way, prepare them according to one programme for the same number of years. We don't teach either type to acquire knowledge from books on their own initiative, yet this is of the utmost importance these days, when any stock of ready-made knowledge will be made obsolete in five to ten years.

All this leads one to think (it has already been said somewhere before) that higher education ought to be two-tiered. Higher scientific training should be given only to those who have (and have been able to prove that they have) the ability, vocation and enthusiasm to take on scientific work. Such specialists must be turned out individually, not by the gross. To that end the number of students in each group must be sharply reduced, as must be the lecturer's teaching load. It is nonsense to talk of mass production with works of art. A highly qualified specialist is also a work of art.

Contact between teacher and student ought to be on a one-to-one basis and not impersonal. Nothing moulds the character of a student better than frequent discussions with his tutor unhampered by time. Both parties ought to have the time for this.

The process of instruction should be made an uninhibited pleasure. How does one attain this? It's not altogether clear. You sometimes notice traits of this freedom. A good lecture is always a holiday. The number of lectures ought to be cut down, thus giving the students the chance of reading up their subject independently.

The system of control we have today (exams), which makes Draconian demands on the student's memory, is terrible, above all because it crushes the natural curiosity of the young. Remember the

Pavlovian reflex 'What's this?' When a dog, especially a young one, comes across an unfamiliar object, it strives to smell it out, track it down. That reflex is suppressed in most of our students. They are not only not curious – they violently reject any information. Any teacher who gives them supplementary information becomes their personal enemy. And quite so, for he is increasing the volume of what they have to learn by heart and trot out in the exam. I consider the custom (accepted almost everywhere) of demanding that the examinee reproduce all the material from memory, without reference books or notes, quite wrong. Exams like that become an absurd procedure demeaning for both parties.

I find it particularly despicable the way some lecturers give their lectures without taking their eyes off their own notes and then require students in exams to do it all by heart. Thank God there's no such disgusting practice in our department. Our lecturers (a form of foppery!) go up to the blackboard with nothing at all in their hands, let alone lecture notes ('just belly and legs,' says Markin, in the words of Zoshchenko [Soviet satirist, 1895–1958]).

As regards exams, not everyone shares my liberal position.

In my opinion, the ideal would be for the candidate, using any textbooks he likes, to demonstrate his ability to apply a given science to the solution of a real problem. After all, that's just what life will demand of him!

People will retort: an exam like that will take too much time. They're probably right. But what does 'too much time' mean? Can one say that a writer has spent too much time on his novel? Or an artist too much time on his picture?

When I abandon all this free speculation and come down to actual reality, there are a lot of issues here which are not clear to me myself.

Is it perhaps impossible to accommodate both mass education and individuality? Our whole life is a series of attempts to unify the ununifiable, isn't it? We aren't completely successful, but we are partly. It's striking that even with our extremely imperfect system of education we still produce a quantity of top-flight specialists. Probably they are the same ones as we would segregate into groups in the top stream, if it existed. But then we would be able to give them more individual attention.

A few words about the entry procedure to the institutes of higher education: in its present form it is unsuitable and it does not perform its function of selecting the most worthy applicants. Neither the development nor the ability of the applicant is investigated, but (at best) his coachability for the exams. As a result we have a sham selection procedure and random entrance. Getting into an institute of higher education is difficult enough, but it is the final effort the student makes. Once he's accepted, the student as a rule graduates, irrespective of what his qualities (his talents, diligence, vocation) might be. From then on it's the gravy train, if you have connections [*blat*]. Parents will break their necks just to get their offspring accepted somewhere.

In our institute, as in the overwhelming majority of others, there's no bribery, no overt corruption, but 'string-pulling' is quite common. It is not the most deserving who get in (it's impossible to pick them out anyway) but those who have good connections.

Once again the unoriginal concept of 'deliberately overshooting the quota' comes up – the people who have been accepted are only regarded as probationary students and have then to prove themselves and win the right to study at a higher educational institute. There is obvious sense in this, but there's a traditional objection to it: it's expensive! But isn't it more expensive to make do with turning out second-rate specialists who have spent five years studying with the whip cracking over them and cultivating a profound aversion to any knowledge or hard work?

It might well be that I am quite wrong in all these musings. It's always easier to criticise than to do the job.

One thing is for certain: we must seek new forms of higher education, we must experiment and test. But it will all be done without me. I am old.

Irina Grekova, *The Department* [*Kafedra*], *Novy mir*, 1978, no. 9

Acknowledgements

We wish to thank the following for permission to use copyright material:

The Bodley Head and Random House for extracts from *The Yawning Heights* by Aleksandr Zinoviev.

W. W. Norton & Co. for the extract from *Metropol'* by Pyotr Kozhevnikov.

Jonathan Cape for the extract from *Pretender to the Throne* by Vladimir Voynovich.

Possev Verlag for the extract from *Letuchiy Gollandets* (*The Flying Dutchman*) by Viktor Sosnora.

Collier Macmillan for the extract from *Farewell to Matyora* by Valentin Rasputin.

Quartet Books for the extract from *Money for Maria* by Valentin Rasputin.

Hodder & Stoughton for the extract from *The White Steamship* by Chingiz Aytmatov.

The All-Union Copyright Agency (VAAP) in Moscow for permission to use the remaining materials in this book which were first published in the USSR after 1973.

Select Bibliography

(1) Literature

Brown, D., *Soviet Russian Literature since Stalin* (Cambridge, 1978).
Clark, K., *The Soviet Novel: History as Ritual* (Chicago, Ill., 1981).
Dunham, V., *In Stalin's Time: Middle Class Values in Soviet Fiction* (Cambridge, 1976).
Hingley, R., *Russian Writers and Society, 1917—1978* (London, 1979).
Hosking, G., *Beyond Socialist Realism* (London, 1980).
Schneidman, N., *Soviet Literature in the 1970s* (Toronto, 1979).

ANTHOLOGIES

The Ardis Anthology of Recent Russian Literature (Ann Arbor, Mich., 1975).
Hayward, M., and Blake, P. (eds), *Dissonant Voices in Russian Literature* (London, 1962).
Milner-Gulland, R., and Dewhirst, M. (eds), *Russian Writing Today* (Harmondsworth, 1977).

(2) Politics

Bialer, S., *Stalin's Successors* (London, 1980).
Breslauer, G., *Khrushchev and Brezhnev as Leaders* (London, 1982).
Brown, A., Fennell, J., Kaser, M., and Willetts, H. (eds), *The Cambridge Encyclopedia of Russia and the Soviet Union* (Oxford, 1982).
Brown, A., and Kaser, M. (eds), *The Soviet Union since the Fall of Khrushchev*, 2nd edn (London, 1978).
Cohen, S., Rabinowitch, A., and Sharlet, R. (eds), *The Soviet Union since Stalin* (London, 1980).
McAuley, M., *Politics and the Soviet Union* (Harmondsworth, 1977).

Index

* not officially published in the USSR.